T0356809

Get the eBook FREE!

(PDF, ePub, Kindle, and liveBook all included)

We believe that once you buy a book from us, you should be able to read it in any format we have available. To get electronic versions of this book at no additional cost to you, purchase and then register this book at the Manning website.

Go to https://www.manning.com/freebook and follow the instructions to complete your pBook registration.

That's it!
Thanks from Manning!

C# Concurrency

C# Concurrency

ASYNCHRONOUS AND
MULTITHREADED PROGRAMMING

NIR DOBOVIZKI

MANNING
SHELTER ISLAND

Manning Publications Co.
20 Baldwin Road
PO Box 761
Shelter Island, NY 11964

Development editor:	Doug Rudder
Technical editor:	Paul Grebenc
Review editor:	Dunja Nikitović
Production editor:	Kathy Rossland
Copy editor:	Lana Todorovic-Arndt
Proofreader:	Melody Dolab
Technical proofreader:	Tanya Wilke
Typesetter:	Tamara Švelić Sabljić
Cover designer:	Marija Tudor

ISBN 9781633438651
Printed in the United States of America

To my wonderful wife, Analia

brief contents

vii

contents

14 *Generating collections asynchronously/await foreach and IAsyncEnumerable   203*

preface

I've been a software developer for over 30 years now and have been developing high-performance servers using multithreading and asynchronous programming since the late 1990s. I've been using C# since 2003. For the last decade and a bit, I've worked as a consultant, coming into a project for a short period of time and helping solve a specific problem. Over that decade, I've had the privilege of visiting many companies, and I've gotten to see and help with a lot of projects.

While every project is obviously completely different, with each company inventing its own innovative, disruptive, and one-of-a-kind technology, after you encounter enough projects, you start to see some similarities. And one thing I've seen time and time again are problems arising from incorrect usage of multithreading and asynchronous programming.

Multithreading is a straightforward concept: it involves running multiple tasks simultaneously. It is notoriously difficult to get it right, but despite this difficulty, it has been widely used for a long time. Developers like you, who take the time to study multithreading through books, are able to use it effectively.

Asynchronous programming has existed since the invention of the microprocessor and has long been used in high-performance servers. However, it gained wider popularity among average developers when the `async`/`await` feature was introduced in C# in 2012. (It was introduced in JavaScript earlier, but in a limited way.) Based on my observations of various projects and my experience conducting job interviews, I've found that very few people understand how `async`/`await` works.

The problems arising from a lack of knowledge in multithreading and asynchronous programming are quite apparent. In just the month or so that I discussed publishing this book with Manning, I taught multithreading and `async`/`await` at three different companies.

And this is how this book was born. What followed was a little more than two years of very deep diving into multithreading and asynchronous programming in C#. During this time, I've learned a lot. There is truly no better way to learn something than teaching it, and I hope this book will be at least as beneficial to you as writing it was to me.

acknowledgments

I truly believe this is a very good book, but I didn't write it alone. Writing a book is a team effort, and it takes an enormous amount of work by many people. Without all those people, this book wouldn't be as good and, most likely, it wouldn't exist at all.

First, I want to thank my development editor at Manning, Doug Rudder, who had the patience to teach this first-time author how to write a technical book. Associate publisher Mike Stephens, who agreed to publish my idea of a book, helped with support and feedback. Using a food analogy in the first chapter was his idea. And technical editor Paul Grebenc was the first line of defense against technical mistakes. Paul is a Principal Software Developer at OpenText. He has over 25 years of professional experience in software development, working primarily with C# and Java. His primary interests are systems involving multithreading, asynchronous programming, and networking.

Next, I also want to thank all the reviewers who reviewed drafts of this book and everyone who commented while the book was in MEAP: your comments have been invaluable to improving the book. To all the reviewers—Aldo Biondo, Alexandre Santos Costa, Allan Tabilog, Amrah Umudlu, Andriy Stosyk, Barry Wallis, Chriss Barnard, David Paccoud, Dustin Metzgar, Geert Van Laethem, Jason Down, Jason Hales, Jean-Paul Malherbe, Jeff Shergalis, Jeremy Caney, Jim Welch, Jiří Činčura, Joe Cuevas, Jonathan Blair, Jort Rodenburg, Jose Antonio Martinez, Julien Pohie, Krishna Chaitanya Anipindi, Marek Petak, Mark Elston, Markus Wolff, Mikkel Arentoft, Milorad Imbra, Oliver Korten, Onofrei George, Sachin Handiekar, Simon Seyag, Stefan Turalski, Sumit Singh, and Vincent Delcoigne—your suggestions helped make this book better.

I also want to give my personal thanks to everyone who bought the book while in early access. Seeing that people are interested enough to spend their hard-earned money on a book I wrote is a wonderful feeling, and it was an important part of the motivation to complete the book.

And last, but most important, I want to thank my family, and especially my wife, who put up with all my nonsense in general and, in particular, with me spending a lot of our free time in my office writing.

about this book

This book is designed to help C# developers write safe and efficient multithreaded and asynchronous application code. It focuses on practical techniques and features you are likely to encounter in normal day-to-day software development.

It delves into all the details you need to know to write and debug multithreaded and asynchronous code. It leaves out the exotic, fun techniques that are only applicable if you need to build something like your own database server, but that are too complicated for normal application code and will probably get you into trouble if you try to use them in normal code, because normal multithreading is difficult enough as it is.

Who should read this book

This book is for any C# developer who wants to improve their knowledge of multithreading and asynchronous programming. The information in this book is applicable to any version of .NET, .NET Core, and .NET Framework released since 2012 and to both Windows and Linux (obviously only for .NET Core and .NET 5 and later, since earlier versions do not support Linux).

The book focuses more on backend development but also covers what you need to know to write UI applications.

How this book is organized: A road map

This book has two parts that include 14 chapters.

Part 1 covers the basics of multithreading and `async/await` in C#:

- Chapter 1 introduces the concepts and terminology of multithreading and asynchronous programming.

- Chapter 2 covers the techniques that the .NET compiler uses to implement advanced functionality.
- Chapter 3 is a deep dive into how `async`/`await` works.
- Chapter 4 explains multithreading.
- Chapter 5 ties chapters 3 and 4 together and shows how `async`/`await` interacts with multithreading.
- Chapter 6 talks about when you should use `async`/`await`—just because you can use it doesn't mean you should use it everywhere.
- Chapter 7 closes the first part with information about the common multithreading pitfalls, and more importantly, what you have to do to avoid them.

Part 2 is about how to use the information you learned about in part 1:

- Chapter 8 is about processing data in the background.
- Chapter 9 is about stopping background processing.
- Chapter 10 teaches how to build advanced asynchronous components that do more than just combine built-in asynchronous operations.
- Chapter 11 discusses advanced use cases of `async`/`await` and threading.
- Chapter 12 helps you debug a problem with exceptions in asynchronous code.
- Chapter 13 goes over thread-safe collections.
- Chapter 14 shows how you can build things that work like asynchronous collections yourself.

About the code

This book contains many examples of source code both in numbered listings and in line with normal text. In both cases, source code is formatted in a `fixed-width font` `like this` to separate it from ordinary text. Sometimes code is also **in bold** to highlight code that has changed from previous steps in the chapter, such as when a new feature adds to an existing line of code.

In many cases, the original source code has been reformatted; we've added line breaks and reworked indentation to accommodate the available page space in the book. In rare cases, even this was not enough, and listings include line-continuation markers (➥). Additionally, comments in the source code have often been removed from the listings when the code is described in the text. Code annotations accompany many of the listings, highlighting important concepts.

You can get executable snippets of code from the liveBook (online) version of this book at https://livebook.manning.com/book/csharp-concurrency.

Source code for the examples in this book is available for download from https://github.com/nirdobovizki/AsynchronousAndMultithreadedProgrammingInCSharp and the author web site at https://nirdobovizki.com. The complete code for the examples in the book is also available for download from the Manning website at https://www.manning.com/books/csharp-concurrency.

liveBook discussion forum

Purchase of *C# Concurrency* includes free access to liveBook, Manning's online reading platform. Using liveBook's exclusive discussion features, you can attach comments to the book globally or to specific sections or paragraphs. It's a snap to make notes for yourself, ask and answer technical questions, and receive help from the author and other users. To access the forum, go to https://livebook.manning.com/book/csharp-concurrency/discussion. You can also learn more about Manning's forums and the rules of conduct at https://livebook.manning.com/discussion.

Manning's commitment to our readers is to provide a venue where a meaningful dialogue between individual readers and between readers and the author can take place. It is not a commitment to any specific amount of participation on the part of the author, whose contribution to the forum remains voluntary (and unpaid). We suggest you try asking the author some challenging questions lest his interest stray! The forum and the archives of previous discussions will be accessible from the publisher's website as long as the book is in print.

about the author

NIR DOBOVIZKI is a software architect and a senior consultant. He's worked on concurrent and asynchronous systems, mostly high-performance servers, since the late 1990s. He's used both in native code and, since the introduction of .NET 1.1 in 2003, .NET and C#. He has worked with multiple companies in the medical, defense, and manufacturing industries to solve problems arising from incorrect usage of multithreading and asynchronous programming.

about the cover illustration

The figure on the cover of *C# Concurrency* is "Homme Tatar de Tobolsk" or "Tatar man from Tobolsk," taken from a collection by Jacques Grasset de Saint-Sauveur, published in 1788. Each illustration is finely drawn and colored by hand.

In those days, it was easy to identify where people lived and what their trade or station in life was just by their dress. Manning celebrates the inventiveness and initiative of the computer business with book covers based on the rich diversity of regional culture centuries ago, brought back to life by pictures from collections such as this one.

Part 1

Asynchronous programming and multithreading basics

The first part of this book covers asynchronous programming and multithreading in C#, explaining what they are and how to implement them. This part highlights common pitfalls and provides guidance on how to avoid them.

We start with the concepts and terminology of multithreading and asynchronous programming, as used in computer science generally and in C# specifically (chapter 1). Next, we'll dive right into how asynchronous programming with `async`/`await` works in C# (chapters 2 and 3). Then, we'll discuss multithreading in C# (chapter 4) and how multithreading and asynchronous programming work together (chapter 5). Finally, we'll talk about when to use `async`/`await` (chapter 6) and how to use multithreading properly (chapter 7).

By the end of part 1, you will learn how to write correct multithread code and use `async`/`await` properly.

Asynchronous programming and multithreading

This chapter covers

- Introduction to multithreading
- Introduction to asynchronous programming
- Asynchronous programming and multithreading used together

As software developers, we often strive to make our applications faster, more responsive, and more efficient. One way to achieve this is by enabling the computer to perform multiple tasks simultaneously, maximizing the use of existing CPU cores. Multithreading and asynchronous programming are two techniques commonly used for this task.

Multithreading allows a computer to appear as if it is executing several tasks at once, even when the number of tasks exceeds the number of CPU cores. In contrast, asynchronous programming focuses on optimizing CPU usage during operations that would typically make it wait, which ensures the CPU remains active and productive.

Enabling a computer to perform multiple tasks simultaneously is extremely useful. It helps keep native applications responsive while they work and is essential for building high-performance servers that can interact with many clients at the same time.

Both techniques can be employed to create responsive client applications or servers that handle a few clients. But when combined, they can greatly boost performance, allowing servers to handle thousands of clients at once.

This chapter will introduce you to multithreading and asynchronous programming and illustrate why they are important. In the rest of the book, we'll talk about how to use them correctly in .NET and C#, especially focusing on the C# async/await feature. You will learn how these technologies work, go over the common pitfalls, and see how to use them correctly.

1.1   What is multithreading?

Before we begin talking about async/await, we need to understand what multithreading and asynchronous programming are. To do so, we are going to talk a bit about web servers and pizza making. We'll start with the pizza (because it's tastier than a web server).

The high-level process of pizza making in a takeout place is typically as follows:

1 The cook receives an order.
2 The cook does stuff—takes preprepared dough, shapes it, and adds sauce, cheese, and toppings.
3 The cook places the pizza in the oven and waits for it to bake (this is the longest bit).
4 The cook then does more stuff—takes the pizza out of the oven, cuts it, and places it in a box.
5 The cook hands the pizza to the delivery person.

This is not a cookbook, so obviously, our pizza baking is a metaphor for one of the simplest server scenarios out there—a web server serving static files. The high-level process for a simple web server is as follows:

1 The server receives a web request.
2 The server performs some processing to figure out what needs to be done.
3 The server reads a file (this is the longest bit).
4 The server does some more processing (such as packaging the file content).
5 The server sends the file content back to the browser.

For most of the chapter, we are going to ignore the first and last steps because, in most backend web frameworks (including ASP.NET and ASP.NET Core), they are handled by the framework and not by our code. We will talk about them briefly near the end of this chapter. Figure 1.1 illustrates the web request process.

Now back to the pizza. In the simplest case, the cook will follow the steps in order, completely finishing one pizza before starting the next one. While the pizza is baking, the cook will just stand there staring at the oven and do nothing (this is a fully synchronous single-threaded version of the process).

In the world of web servers, the cook is the CPU. In this single-threaded web server, we have straightforward code that performs the operations required to complete the web request, and while the file is read from disk, the CPU is frozen doing nothing (in practice, the operating system will suspend our thread while this happens and hand over the CPU to another program, but from our program point of view, it looks like the CPU is frozen).

This version of the process has some advantages—it is simple and easy to understand. You can look at the current step and know exactly where we are in the process. As two things are never taking place at the same time, different jobs can't interfere with each other. Finally, this version requires the least amount of space and uses fewer resources at any one time because we only handle one web request (or pizza) at a time.

This single-threaded synchronous version of the process is apparently wasteful because the cook/CPU spends most of their time doing nothing while the pizza is baking in the oven (or the file is retrieved from disk), and if our pizzeria isn't going out of business, we are going to receive new orders faster than we can fulfill them.

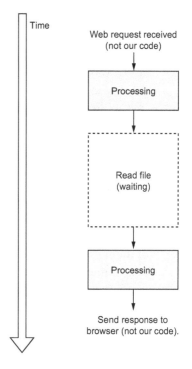

Figure 1.1 Single-threaded, single-request flow

For this reason, we want the cook to make more than one pizza at the same time. One approach might be to use a timer and have it beep every few seconds. Every time the timer beeps, the cook will stop whatever they are doing and make a note of what they did when they stopped. The cook will then start a new pizza or continue making the previous one (ignoring the unready pizzas in the oven) until the timer beeps again.

In this version, the cook is attempting to do multiple things at the same time, and each of those things is called a *thread*. Each thread represents a sequence of operations that can happen in parallel with other similar or different sequences.

This example may seem silly, as it is obviously inefficient, and our cook will spend too much time putting things away and picking up stuff. Yet this is exactly how multithreading works. Inside the CPU, there's a timer that signals when the CPU should switch to the next thread, and with every switch, the CPU needs to store whatever it was doing and load the other thread's status (this is called a *context switch*).

For example, when your code reads a file, the thread can't do anything until the file's data is retrieved from disk. During this time, we say the thread is *blocked*. Having the system allocate CPU time to a blocked thread would obviously be wasteful, so when a thread begins reading a file, it is switched to a blocked state by the operating system. When entering this state, the thread will immediately release the CPU to the next waiting thread (possibly from another program), and the operating system will not assign any CPU time to the thread while in this state. When the system finishes reading the file, the thread exits the blocked state and is again eligible for CPU time.

The operations that can cause the thread to become blocked are called *blocking operations*. All file and network access operations are blocking, as is anything else that communicates with anything outside the CPU and memory; moreover, all operations that wait for another thread can block.

Back in the pizzeria, in addition to the time we spend switching between pizzas, there's also all the information the cook needs to get back to exactly the same place they were before switching tasks. In our software, every thread, even if not running, consumes some memory, so while it's possible to create a large number of threads, each of them executing a blocking operation (so they are blocked most of the time and not consuming CPU time), this is wasteful of memory. It will slow the program down as we increase the number of threads because we must manage all the threads. At some point, we will either spend so much time managing threads that no useful work will get done or we will just run out of memory and crash.

Even with all this inefficiency, the multithreading cook, who jumps from one pizza to another like a crazy person, will make more pizzas in the same amount of time, unless they can't make progress or crash (I know, a cook can't crash; no metaphor is perfect). This mostly happens because the single-threaded cooks from before spent most of their time waiting while the pizza was in the oven.

As illustrated in figure 1.2, because we only have one CPU core (I know, everyone has multicore CPUs nowadays; we'll talk about them soon), we can't really do two things simultaneously. All the processing parts happen one after the other and are not truly in parallel; however, the CPU can wait as many times as you like in parallel. And that's why our multithread version managed to process three requests in significantly less time than it took the single-threaded version to process two.

If you look closely at figure 1.2, you can see that while the single-threaded version handled the first request faster, the multithreaded version completed all three before the single-threaded version managed to complete the second request. This shows us the big advantage of multithreading, which is a much better utilization of the CPU in scenarios that involve waiting. It also shows the price we pay—just a little bit of extra overhead every step of the way.

Until now, we've talked about single-core CPUs, but all modern CPUs are multicore. How does that change things?

1.2 Introducing multicore CPUs

Multicore CPUs are conceptually simple. They are just multiple single-core CPUs packed into the same physical chip.

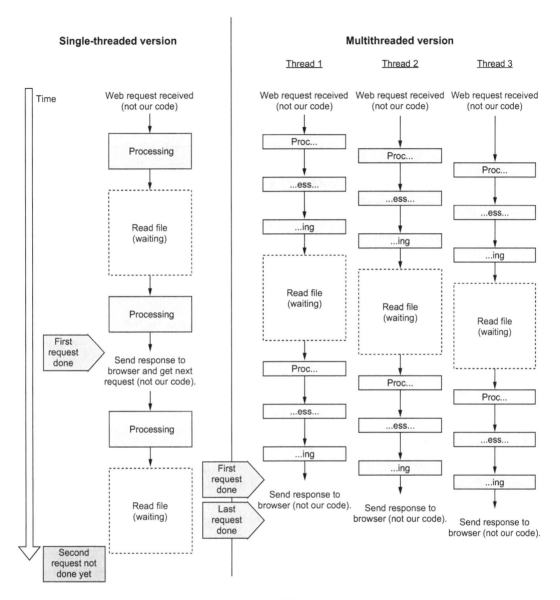

Figure 1.2 Single-threaded versus multithread with multiple requests

In our pizzeria, having an eight-core CPU is equivalent to having eight cooks carrying out the pizza-making tasks. In the previous example, we had one cook who could only do one thing at a time but pretended to do multiple things by switching between them quickly. Now we have eight cooks, each able to do one task at the same time (for a total of eight tasks at once), and each pretending to do multiple things by switching between tasks quickly.

In software terms, with multicore CPUs, you can really have multiple threads running simultaneously. When we had a single-core CPU, we sliced the work into tiny parts and interleaved them to make it seem like they were running at the same time (while, in fact, only one thing could run). Now, with our example eight-core CPU, we still slice the work into tiny parts and interleave them, but we can run eight of those parts at the same time.

Theoretically, eight cooks can make more pizzas than only one; however, multiple cooks may unintentionally interfere with each other's work. For example, they might bump into each other, try to put a pizza in the oven at the same time, or need to use the same pizza cutter—the more cooks we have, the greater the chance of this happening.

Figure 1.3 takes the same multithreaded work we had in figure 1.2 and shows how it would run on a dual-core CPU (just two cores because a diagram with enough work for an eight-core CPU would be too big to illustrate here).

Note that by default, there is no persistent relation between threads and cores. A thread can jump between cores at any time (you can set threads to run on specific cores, which is called "thread affinity," and except in really special circumstances, something you shouldn't do).

The dual-core CPU cut the time we spent processing by half compared to the single-core version but didn't affect the time we spent waiting. So while we did get a significant speedup, it did not cut the total time in half. Until now, we've gotten most of the performance improvement from doing other stuff while waiting for the hard drive to read the file, but we've paid for it with all the overhead and complexity of multithreading. Maybe we can reduce this overhead.

1.3 *Asynchronous programming*

Back in the pizzeria, there's a rational solution we ignored. The cook should make a single pizza without stopping and switching to other pizzas, but when the pizza is in the oven, they can start the next pizza instead of just sitting there. Later, whenever the cook finishes something, they can check whether the pizza in the oven is ready, and if it is, they can take it out, cut it, put it in a box, and hand it over to the delivery person.

This is an example of asynchronous programming. Whenever the CPU needs to do something that happens outside the CPU itself (for example, reading a file), it sends the job to the component that handles it (the disk controller) and asks this component to notify the CPU when it's done.

The asynchronous (also called nonblocking) version of the file function just queues the operation with the operating system (that will then queue it with the disk controller) and returns immediately, letting the same thread do other stuff instead of waiting (figure 1.4). Later, we can check whether the operation has been completed and access the resulting data.

If you compare all the diagrams in this chapter, you will see that this single-threaded asynchronous version is the fastest of all the options. It completes the first request almost as fast as the first single-threaded version while also completing the last request

Multithreaded dual core

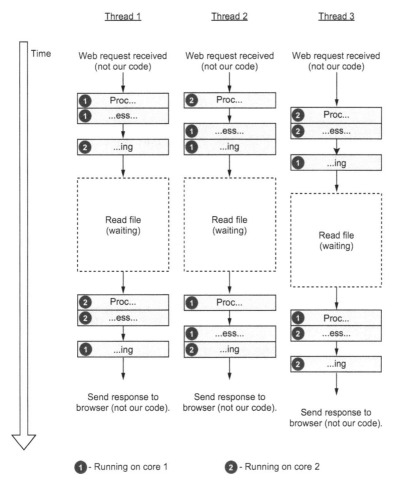

Figure 1.3 Three requests on a dual-core CPU

almost as fast as the dual-core multithreaded version (without even using a second core), which makes it the most performant version so far.

You can also clearly see that figure 1.4 is kind of a mess and is more difficult to read than the previous diagrams, and that is even without indicating in the diagram that the "second processing" steps depend on completing the read operations. The thing that makes the diagram more difficult to understand is that you can no longer see the entire process; the work done for every request is broken up into parts, and unlike the threading example, those parts are not connected to each other.

This is the reason that while multithreading is widely used, until the introduction of `async`/`await`, asynchronous programming has only been used by people building high-performance servers (or using environments where you have no other choice;

Asynchronous version

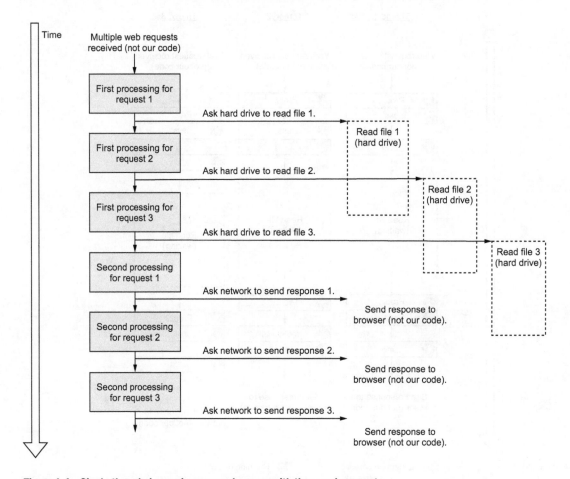

Figure 1.4   Single-threaded asynchronous web server with three web requests

for example, JavaScript). Like in figure 1.4, the code must be broken into parts that are written separately, which made the code difficult to write and even more difficult to understand—until C# introduced the `async`/`await` feature that lets one write asynchronous code as if it were normal synchronous code.

Also, in figure 1.4, I indicated that I use the same asynchronous techniques as for reading the file when sending the response back to the browser. That's because the first and last steps in our web request sequence, "get web request" and "send response to browser," are both performed mostly by the network card and not the CPU, just like reading the file is done by the hard drive, so the two can be performed asynchronously without making the CPU wait.

Even with multithreading only, without asynchronous programming, it's completely possible to write servers that can handle low and medium loads by opening a thread for every connection. However, if you need to build a server that can serve thousands of connections at the same time, the overhead of so many threads will slow the server down to the point of not being able to handle the load or will crash the server outright.

We talked about asynchronous programming as a way to avoid multithreading, but we can't take advantage of the power of multicore CPUs without multithreading. Let's see whether we can use multithreading and asynchronous programming jointly to get even more performance.

1.4 Using multithreading and asynchronous programming together

Let's jump back to the pizzeria one last time. We can improve our pizza making even more: instead of having the cook actively check the oven, just make the oven beep when the pizza is ready, and when the oven beeps, the cook can stop what they are doing, take the pizza out, put it in a box, hand it over to the delivery person, and then get back to what they were doing.

The software equivalent is, when starting the asynchronous operation, to ask the operating system to notify our program by calling a callback function we registered when starting the asynchronous operation. That callback function will need to run on a new thread (actually, a thread pool thread; we will talk about the thread pool later in the book) because the original calling thread is not waiting and is currently doing something else. That's why asynchronous programming and multithreading work well together.

1.5 Software efficiency and cloud computing

Today, we can just use our favorite cloud provider's "serverless" option and run 10,000 copies of our single-threaded code at the same time. So do we need to bother with all this multithreaded and asynchronous code?

Well, theoretically, we can just throw a lot of processing power at the problem. With the modern cloud offerings, you can basically get infinite compute power whenever you want, but you do have to pay for it. Because you pay exactly for what you use, every bit of efficiency you get saves you money.

Before cloud computing, you would buy a server, and as long as you didn't max out the server you bought, the efficiency of your code didn't really matter. Today, shaving off a part of a second of every request in a high-load site can save a significant amount of money.

In the past, CPUs got faster all the time. The rule of thumb was that CPU speed doubled every two years, which meant that you could fix slow software by waiting a bit and buying a new computer. Unfortunately, this is no longer the case because the modern CPU got so close to the maximum number of transistors that can be put in a specific area that it is basically not possible to make a single core much faster. Consequently, the single-thread performance of CPUs now rises rather slowly, and our only choice to improve performance is to use more CPU cores (there's a very influential paper called "The Free Lunch Is Over" by Herb Sutter covering this topic; see www .gotw.ca/publications/concurrency-ddj.htm).

Nonetheless, the modern CPU is still extremely fast, faster than other computer components, and obviously, much faster than any human. Therefore, a typical CPU spends most of its time waiting. Sometimes it's waiting for user input, and other times, it's waiting for the hard drive, but it's still waiting. Multithreading and asynchronous programming enable employing this waiting time to do useful work.

Summary

- Multithreading is switching between several things on the same CPU fast enough to make it feel like they are all running simultaneously.
- A thread is one of those things running simultaneously.
- A thread has significant overhead.
- Switching between threads is called *context switching*, and it also has overhead.
- When doing stuff that happens outside the CPU, such as reading a file or using a network, the thread must wait until the operation is complete to get the result and continue to operate on it, which is called a *blocking operation*.
- Asynchronous programming frees up the thread while operations are taking place by asking the system to send a notification when the operation ends instead of waiting, which is called a *nonblocking operation*. The program then needs to pick up processing later when the data is available, usually on a different thread.
- We need asynchronous and multithreading techniques because the complexity of our software grows faster than the single-thread performance of our CPUs.
- Because in cloud computing we pay for the exact resources we use, asynchronous and multithreading techniques that increase efficiency can save us some money.

The compiler rewrites your code

This chapter covers

- How the C# compiler supports features that do not exist in the .NET runtime
- The implementation of lambda functions by the compiler
- The implementation of `yield return` by the compiler

The compiler modifies your code, which means that the output is not a direct representation of the source code. This is done for two main reasons: to reduce the amount of typing required by boilerplate code generation and to add features not supported by the underlying platform. One such feature is `async/await`, which is primarily implemented by the C# compiler rather than the .NET runtime. To write correct asynchronous code, avoid the potential pitfalls, and especially to debug code, it's important to understand how the compiler transforms your code, that is, what happens when your code runs.

This chapter discusses how the C# compiler rewrites your code during compilation. However, because `async/await` is probably the most complicated code transformation in the current version of C#, we're going to start with lambda functions and `yield return`, which are implemented using the same techniques as `async`/`await`. By starting with simpler compiler features, we can learn the concepts behind `async`/`await` without having to deal with the complexities of asynchronous programming and multithreading. The next chapter will show how everything translates directly to `async`/`await`.

Now let's see how the C# compiler adds advanced features not supported by the underlying .NET runtime, starting with lambda functions (note that the C# lambda functions have nothing to do with the Amazon AWS Lambda service).

2.1 *Lambda functions*

Let's start with one of the simpler C# features implemented by the compiler—lambda functions. These functions are code blocks you can write inline, inside a larger method that can be used just like a standalone method. Lambda functions allow us to take code that, for technical reasons, needs to be a different method and write it in-line where it is used, making the code easier to read and understand. Lambda functions can also use local variables from the method that defined them.

However, the .NET runtime does not have in-line functions—all code in .NET must be in the form of methods that are part of classes. So how do lambda functions work? Let's take a very simple example: we will create a timer, set it to call us in 1 second, and then write the string `"Elapsed"` to the console.

Listing 2.1   Using lambda functions

```
public class LambdaDemo1
{
    private System.Timers.Timer? _timer;

    public void InitTimer()
    {
        _timer = new System.Timers.Timer(1000);
        _timer.Elapsed += (sender,args) => Console.WriteLine("Elapsed");
        _timer.Enabled = true;
    }
}
```

If we run this example, unsurprisingly, the program will print `"Elapsed"` after 1 second. The line I want you to focus on is the one that sets the `_timer.Elapsed` property. This line defines a lambda function and passes it the `Elapsed` property.

But I said that in .NET, all code must be in methods defined in classes, so how is this done? The answer is that the C# compiler rewrites your lambda function as a normal method. If you look at the compile output, it would be similar to

```
public class LambdaDemo2
{
    private System.Timers.Timer? _timer;
```

```
private void HiddenMethodForLambda(
    object? sender, System.Timers.ElapsedEventArgs args)    ◄───  The lambda
{                                                                 function
   Console.WriteLine("Elapsed");                                  becomes a
}                                                                 regular
                                                                  method.
public void InitTimer()
{
   _timer = new System.Timers.Timer(1000);
   _timer.Elapsed += HiddenMethodForLambda;
   _timer.Enabled = true;
}
}
```

The compiler rearranged our code and moved the body of the lambda function into a new method. That way, we can write the code inline, and the runtime can treat it as a normal method.

But the lambda function can also use local variables from the method that defined them. Let's add a variable defined in the `InitTimer` method and used inside the lambda function.

Listing 2.2 Lambda function that uses local variables

```
public class LambdaDemo3
{
   private System.Timers.Timer? _timer;

   public void InitTimer()
   {                                              The new variable
      int aVariable = 5;                    ◄───┘
      _timer = new System.Timers.Timer(1000);
      _timer.Elapsed += (sender,args) => Console.WriteLine(aVariable);
      _timer.Enabled = true;
   }
}
```

If we try to apply the same transformation on this code like in the previous example, we will get two methods that share a local variable. This is obviously not supported and doesn't even make sense. How can the compiler handle that? Well, it needs something that can hold data that can be accessed from two places, and we have such a thing in .NET: classes. So the compiler creates a class to hold our "local" variable:

```
public class LambdaDemo4
{
   private System.Timers.Timer? _timer;
                                               The compiler creates a class
   private class HiddenClassForLambda    ◄───┘ for our lambda function.
   {
                                               The local variable becomes
      public int aVariable;            ◄───┘   a field of the class.
```

```
        public void HiddenMethodForLambda(
                object? sender,
                System.Timers.ElapsedEventArgs args)
        {
            Console.WriteLine(aVariable);
        }
    }

    public void InitTimer()
    {
        var hiddenObject = new HiddenClassForLambda();
        hiddenObject.aVariable = 5;
        _timer = new System.Timers.Timer(1000);
        _timer.Elapsed += hiddenObject.HiddenMethodForLambda;
        _timer.Enabled = true;
    }
}
```

> The lambda function becomes a method inside that class.

Here, the compiler created a new method and an entirely new class. The local variable was moved to be a member of this class, and both the InitTimer method and the lambda function reference this new class member. This changes the way the local variable is accessed outside the lambda function—some operation that only used local variables can turn into access to class member fields when you introduce a lambda. If there are multiple lambda functions defined in the same method, they are placed in the same class so they can share local variables. The important point is that there is no magic here—everything the compiler adds to the .NET runtime is done by just writing code that we can write ourselves because we have basically the same access to the runtime's functionality as the compiler.

Now that we've seen the lambda function transformation, let's take a look at something a bit more complicated.

2.2   Yield return

The yield return feature uses the same tricks we've seen in the lambda function example to do even more advanced stuff. It's also somewhat similar to async/await, but without the complexities of multithreading and asynchronous code, so it's a good way to learn the fundamentals of async/await.

What is yield return? It basically lets you write functions that generate a sequence of values you can use in foreach loops directly without using a collection such as a list or an array. Each value can be used without waiting for the entire sequence to be generated. Let's write something extremely simple—a method that returns a collection with two items, the numbers 1 and 2. The following listing shows what it looks like without yield return.

> **Listing 2.3 Using a list**

```
private IEnumerable<int> NoYieldDemo()
{
    var result = new List<int>();
```

```
    result.Add(1);
    result.Add(2);
    return result;
}

public void UseNoYieldDemo()
{
    foreach(var current in NoYieldDemo())
    {
        Console.WriteLine($"Got {current}");
    }
}
```

Unsurprisingly, this code will output two lines, Got 1 and Got 2. The following listing shows the same functionality with yield return.

Listing 2.4 Using `yield return`

```
private IEnumerable<int> YieldDemo()
{
    yield return 1;
    yield return 2;
}

public void UseYieldDemo()
{
    foreach(var current in YieldDemo())
    {
        Console.WriteLine($"Got {current}");
    }
}
```

The code looks very similar, and the results are the same. So what is the big difference? In the first example, all the values were generated first and then used, while in the second example, each value was generated just when it was needed, as illustrated in figure 2.1.

In the non-yield return version, the code ran normally. The NoYieldDemo method started, did some stuff, and then returned. However, the YieldDemo method behaved differently—it suspended at startup, and then, every time a value was needed, it resumed, ran the minimal amount of code to provide the next value (until the next yield return), and suspended itself again. But .NET doesn't have a way to suspend and resume code. What kind of sorcery is that?

Obviously, there is no sorcery, as magic does not exist in computer science. Just like in the case of the lambda function examples we've seen before, the compiler just rewrote our code.

In computer science, code that can be suspended, resumed, and potentially return multiple values is called a *coroutine*. In C#, it is called *iterator methods* in relation to yield return and *async methods* in relation to async/await. This book uses the C# terminology. The IEnumerable<T> interface that I used as the return type for the YieldDemo method is the most basic interface for anything that can be treated as collections or sequences

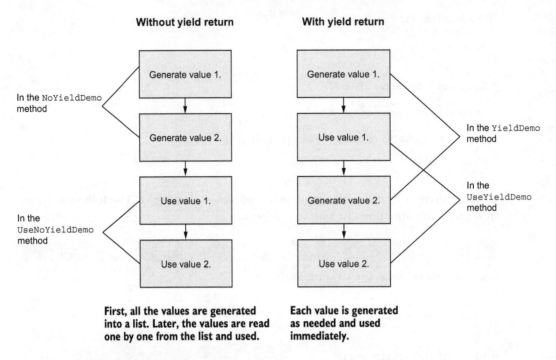

Without yield return

Generate value 1.

In the `NoYieldDemo` method

Generate value 2.

Use value 1.

In the `UseNoYieldDemo` method

Use value 2.

First, all the values are generated into a list. Later, the values are read one by one from the list and used.

With yield return

Generate value 1.

Use value 1.

In the `YieldDemo` method

Generate value 2.

In the `UseYieldDemo` method

Use value 2.

Each value is generated as needed and used immediately.

Figure 2.1   **Using a collection versus using** `yield return`

of items (including everything you can use `foreach` to iterate over). Every generic collection in .NET implements this interface (older collections classes, from before generics were introduced in .NET 2.0, use the nongeneric `IEnumerable` interface instead). This interface has just one method that returns an `IEnumerator<T>`, and this enumerator does all the work. An enumerator can do two things: return the current value and move to the next one.

The `IEnumerator<T>` interface is important because it lets us (and the compiler) write code that handles a sequence of items without knowing anything about that sequence. Every collection in .NET implements `IEnumerable<T>`, so constructs that deal with sequences (like the `foreach` loop) don't need to know how to work with every type of collection—they just need to know how to work with `IEnumerable<T>`. The inverse is also true—everything that implements `IEnumerable<T>` is automatically a sequence of items that can be used with `foreach` loops and all the other relevant parts of .NET and C#.

Just like in the lambda example, the compiler rewrote the `YieldDemo` method into a class, but this time, a class that implements `IEnumerator<int>`, so the `foreach` loop knows what to do with it. Let's rewrite the code ourselves to get the same result.

To begin, `YieldDemo` returned an `IEnumerable<int>`, so obviously, we have a class that implements this interface, so it can be returned from `YieldDemo`. Like I said before, the only thing the `IEnumerable<int>` does is provide an `IEnumerator<int>` (for historical reasons, to be compatible with code written before .NET 2.0, in addition to `IEnumerator<int>`, we also need to provide a nongeneric `IEnumerator`, and we will use the same class for both):

```
public class YieldDemo_Enumerable : IEnumerable<int>          ◄────  Our
{                                                                    IEnumerable<int>
    public IEnumerator<int> GetEnumerator()
    {
        return new YieldDemo_Enumerator();             ◄────  Returns an
    }                                                         IEnumerator<int>
    IEnumerator IEnumerable.GetEnumerator()
    {
        return new YieldDemo_Enumerator();             ◄────
    }
}
```

Now we need to write our `IEnumerator<int>` that will do all the work:

```
public class YieldDemo_Enumerator : IEnumerator<int>
{
```

We need a `Current` property to hold the current value:

```
    public int Current { get; private set; }
```

Now comes the important part. Here, we divide our original code into chunks, breaking it just after each `yield return`, and replace the `yield return` with `Current =`:

```
    private void Step0()
    {
        Current = 1;
    }
    private void Step1()
    {
        Current = 2;
    }
```

The next part is the `MoveNext` method. This method runs the correct chunk from the previous paragraph to update the `Current` property. It uses the `_step` field to remember which step to run, and when we run out of steps, it returns false to indicate we are done (if you have a computer science background, you may recognize this as a simple implementation of a finite state machine):

```
    private int _step = 0;                    ◄────  A variable to keep track
    public bool MoveNext()                           of where we are
    {
        switch(_step)
        {
            case 0:
                Step0();
```

```
        ++_step;
        break;
    case 1:
        Step1();
        ++_step;
        break;
    case 2:
        return false;          ◄───┐  We're done; return false.
    }
    return true;
}
```

Now there's some necessary technical stuff not relevant to this example:

```
object IEnumerator.Current => Current;
public void Dispose() { }
public void Reset() { }
}
```

And finally, wrap the classes we generated in a method so we can call it:

```
public IEnumerable<int> YieldDemo()
{
    return new YieldDemo_Enumerable();
}
```

The actual compiler-generated code is longer and more complicated, mostly because I completely ignored all the possible error conditions. However, conceptually, this is what the compiler does. The compiler rewrote our code into chunks and called each chunk in turn when needed, giving us an illusion of code that suspends and resumes.

For the yield return feature to work, we need

- The code transformation that divided our code into chunks and simulated a single method that can be suspended and resumed
- A standard representation for anything collection-like (`IEnumerable<T>`) so that everyone can use the results of this transformation

That brings us directly to `async`/`await` and the `Task` class in the next chapter.

Summary

- The C# compiler will rearrange and rewrite your code to add features that do not exist in .NET.
- For lambda functions, the compiler moves code into a new method and shared data into a new class.
- For `yield return`, the compiler also divides your code into chunks and wraps them in a class that runs the correct chunk at the correct time to simulate a function that can be suspended and resumed.

The async and await keywords

This chapter covers

- Using `Task` and `Task<T>` to check whether an operation has completed
- Using `Task` and `Task<T>` to notify your code when the operation has completed
- Using `Task` and `Task<T>` in synchronous code
- How `async`/`await` works

In the previous chapter, we saw how the compiler can transform our code to add language features. In this chapter, we'll learn how it applies to `async`/`await`.

`async`/`await` is a feature that lets us write asynchronous code as if it were normal synchronous code. With asynchronous programming, when we perform an operation that would normally make the CPU wait (usually for data to arrive from some device—for example, reading a file), instead of waiting, we just do something else. Making asynchronous code look like normal code is kind of a big deal because traditionally, you had to divide each sequence of operations into small parts (breaking at each asynchronous operation) and call the right part at the right time. Unsurprisingly, this makes the code confusing to write.

3.1   Asynchronous code complexity

To demonstrate this, I placed figures 1.1 and 1.4 side by side (figure 3.1).

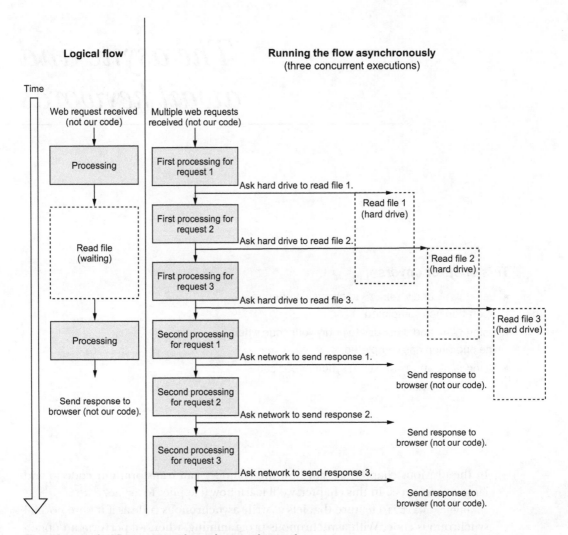

Figure 3.1   Logical flow versus code running asynchronously

Clearly, the left side describing the logical flow is simple, linear, and easy to understand, while the right side that describes how the asynchronous version is running is none of those things (it's also very difficult to debug).

Traditionally, asynchronous programming requires us to design and write our code for the right diagram, as well as divide our code into chunks that do not represent the logical flow of the code. Also, we need code to manage the whole mess and decide what to run when.

The `async`/`await` feature lets us write code that describes the logical flow, and the compiler will transform it to something that can run asynchronously automatically—it lets us write our code as shown on the left side of the diagram and have it run like the right side.

Let's illustrate this through a simple example—a method that reads the image width (in pixels) of a BMP image file. I've chosen BMP because unlike more modern image file formats, all the data in the BMP file is at a fixed location, which makes it easy to extract. We'll read the image width in two steps:

1. First, we check whether the file is a BMP image file at all. We do that by looking at the beginning of the file: BMP image files start with "BM."

2. We will then jump to the eighteenth byte in the file where the width is stored as a 32-bit (4 bytes) integer.

Our method will return the image width in pixels or throw an exception if the file is not a BMP image and if there are other errors. Because we haven't talked about how to write asynchronous code yet, the first version of this example will be simple, old-style, synchronous code.

Listing 3.1 Reading BMP width, non-asynchronous version

```
int GetBitmapWidth(string path)
{
    using (var file = new FileStream(path, FileMode.Open, FileAccess.Read))
    {
        var fileId = new byte[2];
        var read = file.Read(fileId, 0, 2);              The file should
        if (read != 2 || fileId[0] != 'B' || fileId[1] != 'M')   start with
            throw new Exception("Not a BMP file");        "BM."

        file.Seek(18, SeekOrigin.Begin);
        var widthBuffer = new byte[4];
        read = file.Read(widthBuffer, 0, 4);             Reads the width
        if(read != 4) throw new Exception("Not a BMP file");   from byte 18
        return BitConverter.ToInt32(widthBuffer, 0);
    }
}
```

As you can see, the code is straightforward. We read the first two bytes and check whether their value is "BM." Next, we skip to the eighteenth byte and read the image width.

3.2 *Introducing Task and Task<T>*

Now let's make this code asynchronous. We have two excellent reasons for doing so:

- The first and most important reason is that this is a book about asynchronous programming.

- The second reason is that the main thing our code does is read a file, and reading a file is a blocking operation that will make our thread wait for data to arrive from the hard disk. That means we can improve efficiency by using our thread to do other stuff while waiting instead of making the operating system switch to another thread (or another process entirely).

The main thing our method does is read a file using the `Stream.Read` method, and luckily, there's an asynchronous version of the `Stream.Read` method called `Stream.ReadAsync`. Let's take a look at the difference in the method signature between those two methods:

```
public int Read(byte[] buffer, int offset, int count);

public Task<int> ReadAsync(byte[] buffer, int offset, int count,
    CancellationToken cancellationToken);
```

We can see the following two differences in the method signature:

- While `Read` returns an `int`, `ReadAsync` returns `Task<int>`. The `Task` and `Task<T>` classes are an important part of modern asynchronous programming in C#, and we will explore their usage here.
- `ReadAsync` also accepts a `CancellationToken`, but we're going to ignore it for now because there's an entire chapter about it later in this book.

Earlier in this chapter, I wrote that for asynchronous code, we need to divide our code into parts, and we also need a system to manage the execution of those parts. `Task` is the class that we use to interact with that system. A `Task` does multiple things: it represents an ongoing asynchronous operation, lets us schedule code to run when an asynchronous operation ends (we'll talk about these two in this chapter), and lets us create and compose asynchronous operations (we'll talk about those later in this book).

Chapter 2 introduced us to `IEnumerable<T>` and how it enables `yield return`. The `Task` and `Task<T>` classes are the `IEnumerable<T>` of async programming. They are a standard way to represent the `async` stuff, so everyone knows how to work with it.

The name of the `Task` class is confusing; the word "task" implies there's an operation, something that runs, but this is not the only meaning of `Task`. A `Task` represents an event that may happen in the future, while `Task<T>` represents a value that may be available in the future. Those events and values may or may not be the results of something we will describe using the English word task. In computer science, those concepts are often called *future*, *promise*, or *deferred value*, but in this book, we'll refer to them using the .NET/C# term `Task`.

It's important to note that while it is common to create a `Task` or a `Task<T>` for code we run in the background (as we'll see in the next chapter), some classes and methods in .NET use the word task to refer to this code or to manage context information related to it. The `Task` or `Task<T>` objects themselves do not let you manage the background operation and do not carry context related to it. A `Task` just lets you know when that background operation finishes running (the `Task` object represents the event of the background operation ending), and `Task<T>` adds the ability to get the result of the background operation (`Task<T>` represents the value produced by the background operation). A `Task` is not a thread or a background operation, but it is sometimes used to convey the results of a background operation.

In .NET/C# terminology, we say that the task is completed when the event represented by a `Task` happens or the value represented by a `Task<T>` is available. The `Task` is also considered completed if it is marked as canceled or faulted.

For example, when we call `Task.Delay(1000)`, we get an object that represents an event that will happen in 1 second but has no corresponding thread or activity. In the same way, if we call `File.ReadAllBytesAsync`, and, for example, there is no thread reading in the background, the system asks the disk controller (a different hardware device than the CPU) to load data and calls us when it's done, so we get back a `Task<byte[]>` object that represents the data that will be received from the disk in the future.

The `Read` method we used in our example fills the buffer we gave it and returns the number of bytes that were successfully read. For compatibility and performance reasons, the `ReadAsync` method works in the same way, except it returns a `Task<int>` instead of an `int`. The returned `Task<int>` represents the number of bytes successfully read that will be available after the operation completes. Note that we should not touch the buffer we passed `ReadAsync` until the operation is complete.

So a `Task` or `Task<T>` object represents an event or a value that may be available in the future. When we want to know whether this event happened or the value is available yet, there are two asynchronous approaches supported by `Task` and `Task<T>`—to use a travel metaphor, there are the "Are we there yet" model and the "Wake me up when we arrive" model. Furthermore, there is also the synchronous approach if you can't or don't want to use asynchronous programming.

3.2.1 Are we there yet?

In the "Are we there yet" model, you are responsible for asking the `Task` whether it has completed yet, usually in a loop that does other things between those checks (this is called *polling*), which is done by reading the `IsCompleted` property. Note that `IsCompleted` is `true` even if the task has errored out or was canceled.

`Task` also has a `Status` property we can use. The task has completed if `Status` is `RanToCompletion`, `Canceled`, or `Faulted`. Using the `IsCompleted` property is better than using the `Status` property because checking one condition as opposed to three is more concise and less error-prone (we will talk about canceled and faulted tasks later in this book).

You should not check `IsCompleted` or `Status` in a loop unless you are doing other work between the checks. If most of what you do is just waiting for the task to complete, you are not only using up a thread for waiting, completely negating the advantages of asynchronous techniques, but you are also wasting CPU cycles, thus wasting resources that other code on the computer (including the work you are waiting for) could utilize for useful stuff.

This is just like asking "Are we there yet?" in a car. If you do it too often, you are interfering with what everyone else in the car is doing and might even arrive later if you annoy the driver.

Here's an example of using `IsCompleted` in a loop to check whether the task has completed:

```
var readCompleted = File.ReadAllBytesAsync("example.bin");
while(!readCompleted.IsCompleted)
{
    UpdateCounter();
}
var bytes = readCompleted.Result;
// do something with bytes
```

In this example, the program needs to continuously update a counter while waiting for the data to arrive from the disk. So it updates the counter and checks whether the read has completed in a loop. When the data is available, it exits the loop to process the data it just received.

Most of the time, we don't have anything useful to do while waiting for `IsCompleted` to become true, so this model is rarely used. In most cases (and most of this book), we will let the .NET runtime schedule and run our tasks and will not use the "Are we there yet" model. This is only beneficial when we have something to do while waiting and don't want to return and release the thread for some reason (we will see an example with UI threads later in this book).

3.2.2 *Wake me up when we get there*

In the "Wake me up when we get there" model, you pass a callback method to the task, and it will call you when it's complete (or errored out or canceled). This is done by passing the callback to the `ContinueWith` method.

The task is passed as a parameter to the callback, so you can use it to check whether the operation completed successfully and, in the case of `Task<T>`, read the result value:

```
var readCompleted = File.ReadAllBytesAsync("example.bin");
readCompleted.ContinueWith( t =>
    {
        if(t.IsCompletedSuccessfully)
        {
            byte[] bytes = t.Result;
            // do something with bytes
        }
    });
```

Unlike the previous model, this fits the needs of our example code very well. If we take a look at just the code immediately around the first `Read` call, it changes from

```
var fileId = new byte[2];
var read = file.Read(fileId, 0, 2);
```

```
if (read != 2 || fileId[0] != 'B' || fileId[1] != 'M')
...
```

to

```
var fileId = new byte[2];
var read = file.ReadAsync(fileId, 0, 2, CancellationToken.None).
   ContinueWith(t=>
   {
      if (t.Result != 2 || fileId[0] != 'B' || fileId[1] != 'M')
...
```

In this case, we only replaced `Read` with `ReadAsync` and passed all the code that was after the `Read` call into `ContinueWith` as a lambda function (doing some more required changes if we use `using` or `throw`, but fortunately, it doesn't affect the three lines of code in this snippet—we'll talk about it later in this chapter).

Technically speaking, you can make multiple asynchronous calls by chaining `ContinueWith` calls with lambdas, as shown in the example, although this tends to be unreadable and creates extremely long lines of code. For example, reading 3 bytes from a file 1 byte at a time will look like this:

```
f.ReadAsync(buffer, 0, 1, CancellationToken.None).
   ContinueWith( t1 =>
   {
      f.ReadAsync(buffer, 1, 1, CancellationToken.None).
         ContinueWith( t1 =>
         {
            f.ReadAsync(buffer, 2, 1, CancellationToken.None).
               ContinueWith( t1 =>
               {
                  // finished readin 3 bytes!
               });
         });
   });
```

The code isn't very readable, and each `ContinueWith` pushes our code farther to the right. If I wanted to change this example to read 4 or more bytes in the same way, it wouldn't fit within the width of the book's page. (Spoiler: Later in this chapter, we'll see how `async`/`await` solves this problem.)

3.2.3 *The synchronous option*

There is also the possibility that you will want to wait for a task in a non-asynchronous way. For example, if you write old fashion synchronous code that uses an API that only has a `Task`-based asynchronous method, the best way is to call the `Task.Wait` method or read the `Task<T>.Result` property. The `Wait` method and `Result` property will block the current thread until the task is complete and will throw an exception if the task is canceled or errored out, making it behave like synchronous code. Note that using the `Wait` method or the `Result` property to wait for a task to complete is inefficient and negates the advantages of using asynchronous programming in the first place. It also might cause deadlocks in some scenarios (deadlocks make your program become stuck, and we will talk about them extensively later in the book):

```
var readCompleted = File.ReadAllBytesAsync("example.bin");
var bytes = readCompleted.Result;          ◄——————┐ This will wait until the
// do something with bytes                          read has completed.
```

Generally, you would only use this approach when you had no other choice (mostly when integrating asynchronous and non-asynchronous code).

3.2.4   *After the task has completed*

After the task is completed, you need to check whether it completed successfully or not; both `Task` and `Task<T>` have the `IsFaulted`, `IsCanceled`, and `IsCompleted-Successfully` properties that do exactly what their name suggests. They can be used after the task is complete to check the status of the task. (It's okay to call them before the task completes; in that case, they just return `false`.) If `IsFaulted` is true, you can read the `Exception` property to see what went wrong.

In case the task is faulted, the easiest way to throw the error stored in a task so you can handle it with a normal try-catch block is to call `Wait`. Calling `Wait` after the task has completed is safe and will not block the thread (because the event it is waiting for has already happened). It will just return immediately if the task completed successfully or throw an exception if the task was canceled or has errored out. Because of this behavior, you don't even have to check that the task is in a faulted or canceled state (it will throw an exception if the task was completed unsuccessfully).

So if you want to check whether the task has errored out and check the exception object without throwing, you would use

```
if(task.IsFaulted)
    HandleError(task.Exception);
```

However, if you want to check whether the task has errored out and throw the exception *only after the task has completed,* you could just use

```
task.Wait();
```

This works because, like we said, calling `Task.Wait` when the task has already completed will either do nothing and return immediately or throw an exception. Note that the last two code snippets behave differently if the task was canceled (there is an entire chapter about cancellation later in the book).

The exception in the `Task.Exception` property (or the exception thrown by the `Wait` method or `Result` property if the task is in a faulted state) will be an `Aggregate-Exception`. The `AggregateException` will contain the original exception in its `Inner-Exceptions` (plural) property, which should not be confused with the `InnerException` (singular) property that is inherited from `Exception` and is not used in this case.

AggregateException is used here to support situations where the task represents the combination of several operations.

If you know there is just one exception, and you want to access it and not the AggregateException, you use something like

```
If(task.IsFaulted)
    HandleError(task.Exception.InnerExceptions[0]);
```

Task<T> (but not Task) also has a Result property that is used to get the value stored in the task. Typically, we will only read the Result property after the task has completed (IsCompleted is true or ContinueWith is called). If we try to read the Result property before the task is completed, the Result property will block and wait until the task is completed. This is equivalent to calling Wait and has all the same inefficiencies and dangers we talked about. If the task is in an error or canceled state, then reading Result will throw an exception.

To summarize, when using tasks without async/await, you can use the IsCompleted or Status properties to ask "Are we there yet?" And just like in a car, you don't want to ask too often. You can use ContinueWith to make the task call you when it completes ("Wake me up when we arrive"). Finally, you can call Wait or Result to make the task synchronous, but that's inefficient and dangerous because it will block the thread until the task is complete (calling Wait or Result after the task has completed is perfectly efficient and safe because the result is already available, and there's no need for blocking).

Now that we understand how Task and Task<T> work, let's see how async/await makes it easier to use.

3.3 How does async/await work?

We've already seen that Task and Task<T> are all we need to write asynchronous code, but writing any nontrivial code using ContinueWith and lambdas (like in the "Wake me up when we get there" example) gets tedious and unreadable pretty quickly. Let's copy just the part that reads the file from our "get BMP width" example and convert it to use ReadAsync and ContinueWith.

We will do the simplest mechanical conversion possible. Every time there is a call to Read, we will replace it with a call to ReadAsync and just pass the rest of the code as a lambda function to ContinueWith:

```
file.ReadAsync(fileId, 0, 2,CancellationToken.None).
    ContinueWith(firstReadTask =>
    {
        int read = firstReadTask.Result;
        if (read != 2 || fileId[0] != 'B' || fileId[1] != 'M')
        {
            // get error to caller somehow
        }
        file.Seek(18, SeekOrigin.Begin);
        var widthBuffer = new byte[4];
        file.ReadAsync(widthBuffer, 0, 4, CancellationToken.None).
```

```
        ContinueWith(secondReadTask =>
        {
            read = secondReadTask.Result;
            if(read != 4) throw new Exception("Not a BMP file");
            var result = BitConverter.ToInt32(widthBuffer, 0);
            // get result back to our caller somehow
        });
    });
```

What a mess! What was a simple and readable method looks awful now. It is less readable because the code is divided by the `async` calls and no longer follows the logic of our algorithm. And worst of all, our conversion isn't even correct! The original code had a using statement that disposed of the file on completion and on exception, so to get the same behavior, we have to wrap everything in try-catch blocks and do it ourselves (I didn't add those to the code because it's difficult to read even without it). We also need to get the exception and results to the caller, and because the lambdas are running asynchronously, we can no longer use `return` and `throw` to communicate with the caller of the method. Fortunately, we have `async/await` that takes care of this for us.

To rewrite our example with `async/await` and `ReadAsync`, we need to make the following changes:

- First, we start by marking our method with the `async` keyword, and as we'll see a bit later, this by itself does nothing.
- We can no longer return an `int` because as an asynchronous method, our method will return immediately and complete its work later. It's not possible to return an `int` because we don't know the correct value at the time the method returns! Fortunately, we do have a way to return "an `int` that will be available in the future"—`Task<int>`.
- And finally, insert the `await` keyword before every `ReadAsync` call. The `await` keyword tells the compiler that the code needs to be suspended at this point and resumed when whatever `async` operation you are waiting for completes.

The following listing shows our method with `async/await`. Changes from the original non-async version are in bold.

Listing 3.2   Reading the BMP width (`async version`)

```
public async Task<int> GetBitmapWidth(string path)
{
    using (var file = new FileStream(path, FileMode.Open, FileAccess.Read))
    {
        var fileId = new byte[2];
        var read = await file.ReadAsync(fileId, 0, 2);
        if (read != 2 || fileId[0] != 'B' || fileId[1] != 'M')
            throw new Exception("Not a BMP file");

        file.Seek(18, SeekOrigin.Begin);
        var widthBuffer = new byte[4];
        read = await file.ReadAsync(widthBuffer, 0, 4);
```

```
        if(read != 4) throw new Exception("Not a BMP file");
        return BitConverter.ToInt32(widthBuffer, 0);
    }
}
```

It looks basically the same as the original non-async version, only with the `async` and `await` keywords added, but it's actually very different. Let's see what the code really does.

Note that the code in listing 3.3 describes what the compiler does conceptually. The actual code generated by the compiler is very different and much more complex. I'm using this simplified version because it is easier to understand while giving a good mental model of what the compiler does. At the end of this section, I'll talk about the major differences between my version and the actual compiler code.

asynch/await uses the "Wake me up when we arrive" model. It breaks the code into chunks (like the `yield return` feature from the previous chapter) and uses the task's `ContinueWith` method to run the chunks at the correct time.

Let's see how the compiler rewrites our code. But before exploring what the compiler does, we'll make just one tiny change: in the `async/await` example, we returned `Task<int>`, but we didn't talk about how you can create a `Task` yet (don't worry, there is a whole chapter about it later). Instead, we're going to pass two callbacks to our method: `setResult`, which will be called when our code completes successfully, and `setException`, which will be called in case we get an exception.

What the compiler does is separate the code after an `await` into a different method (like we did with `yield return` in the previous chapter) and pass it to the Task's `ContinueWith` method. To be able to share variables between the methods, we will move the local variables into a class like we did with lambda functions.

Listing 3.3 Reading the BMP width (async with `ContinueWith` only)

```
public void GetBitmapWidth(string path,
        Action<int> setResult, Action<Exception> setException)
{
    var data = new ClassForGetBitmapWidth();
    data.setResult = setResult;                                 Code from listing 3.2
    data.setException = setException;
    data.file = new FileStream(path, FileMode.Open, FileAccess.Read);  ◄───┐
    try                                                                     │
    {                                                                       │
        data.fileId = new byte[2];                                  ◄───    │
        var read = data.file.ReadAsync(data.fileId, 0, 2).         ◄───     │
            ContinueWith(data.GetBitmapWidthStep2);               ◄───  ────┘
    }
    catch(Exception ex)
    {
        data.file.Dispose();                          Code added to simulate
        setException(ex);                             the using statement
    }
}
```

This took care of the code before the first `await`. Note that our changes didn't make this part run asynchronously at all. Everything before the first `await` runs like normal non-async code. And if you have a method marked with the `async` keyword without an `await`, then the entire method will run as if it weren't an `async` method (except that the return value will be wrapped in a `Task`).

We had to replace the using statement with try-catch to make sure the file is disposed properly on exception (not try-finally because, if this part of the code succeeds, we need to keep the file open until the next part finishes).

Now for the class that we need to store the "local" variables, we use

```
private class ClassForGetBitmapWidth
{
    public Stream file;
    public byte[] fileId;
    public byte[] widthBuffer;
    public Action<int> setResult;
    public Action<Exception> setException;
```

In this class, the code between the first and second `await` is

```
public void GetBitmapWidthStep2(Task<int> task)
{
    try
    {
        var read = task.Result;
        if (read != 2 || fileId[0] != 'B' || fileId[1] != 'M')
            throw new Exception("Not a BMP file");

        file.Seek(18, SeekOrigin.Begin);
        widthBuffer = new byte[4];
        file.ReadAsync(widthBuffer, 0, 4).
            ContinueWith(GetBitmapWidthStep3);
    }
    catch(Exception ex)
    {
        file.Dispose();
        setException(ex);
    }
}
```

Code from listing 3.2

Code added to simulate the using statement

It looks like we didn't check the result of the previous operation. We didn't read the `Task IsCompletedSuccessfully` property or the `Task.Status` property. Thus, we don't know if there was an error. However, reading `Task.Result` will throw an exception if the task was completed unsuccessfully, so writing code to explicitly check for errors is not required. Also note that because this was called from `ContinueWith`, we know the task has already completed, and we are guaranteed the task is completed and reading `Result` is a nice, safe, and fast nonblocking operation.

Now for the part after the last `await`, we have

```
public void GetBitmapWidthStep3(Task<int> task)
{
    try
    {
        var read = task.Result;
        if(read != 4) throw new Exception("Not a BMP file");
        file.Dispose();
        var result = BitConverter.ToInt32(widthBuffer, 0);
        setResult(result);
    }
    catch(Exception ex)
    {
        file.Dispose();
        setException(ex);
    }
}
```

Code from listing 3.2

Instead of a return statement

Code added to simulate the using statement

Just like we've seen with `yield return` in chapter 2, the compiler divided our function into chunks and added code to call them at the correct time. We've also seen that the correct time for the first chunk, before the first `await`, is when the method was called. Marking the method as `async` does not make it asynchronous. It's just a compiler flag to tell the compiler to look for `await` keywords and divide the method into chunks. In the same way, `await` does not wait—it actually ends the current chunk and returns control to the caller.

As promised, here are the major differences between the code we just talked about and the code the compiler really generates:

- The compiler does not divide your code into different methods. It builds a single state machine method that keeps track of the current position using a variable and uses a big switch statement to run the correct piece of code.

- The compiler does not use `ContinueWith`; instead, it uses an internal object called an *awaiter*. I've chosen to use `ContinueWith` because it's conceptually similar, and unless you are writing a compiler or a replacement of the .NET asynchronous framework, you don't need to know about it.

- `await` actually does much more than `ContinueWith`. `ContinueWith` just makes the callback run when the `Task` is complete, while the former has other useful features that we will talk about later in this book.

3.4   *async void methods*

Let's say we are writing a WinForms app, and we want to add a feature that copies all the text from one file into another file when the user clicks a button. Let's also say we know those are small files, so we can just load the entire contents into memory. The code for that feature will look something like the one in the following listing.

Listing 3.4   `async` event handler

```
private async void Button1_Click(object sender, EventArgs ea)
{
    var text = await File.ReadAllTextAsync("source.txt");
    await File.WriteAllTextAsync("dest.txt", text);
}
```

This code just asynchronously loads all the content of a file into a variable and then asynchronously writes the contents of the variable into another file. Now let's use what we've learned in this chapter and transform it like we transformed the `GetBitmapWidth` method in listing 3.3, except that this time, we must keep the event handler signature. We can't add the `setResult` and `setException` parameters (this is analogous to how in the `async` version we had to return `void` and couldn't return `Task`).

Listing 3.5   Compiler transformation for `async` event handler

```
private void Button1_Click(object sender, EventArgs ea)
{
    var data = new ClassForButton1_Click();
    File.ReadAllTextAsync("source.txt").
        ContinueWith(data.Button1_ClickStep2);
}

private class ClassForButton1_Click
{
    public void Button1_ClickStep2(Task<string> task)
    {
        try
        {
            var text = task.Result;
            File.WriteAllTextAsync("dest.txt", text).
                ContinueWith(Button1_ClickStep3);
        }
        catch
        {
            // ?                    ◀——  We have no way to notify
        }                                that we had an exception.
    }

    public void Button1_ClickStep3(Task task)
    {
        if(task.IsFaulted)
        {
            // ?                    ◀——  We have no way to notify that
        }                                we had an exception (again).
        else
        {
            // ?                    ◀——  We have no way to notify
        }                                that we are done.
    }

}
```

Because this method is simple, the transformation was also simple (but maybe just a bit tedious). We didn't even have to move any local variables into the class. However, we do have a problem: after we finish copying the data, we don't have any way to notify the rest of the program that we are done. Even worse, if there is any error, we also have no way to notify anyone. We have the three question mark comments in the code, and we don't know what to write there.

This is exactly what happens with `async` methods with a `void` return type. Because there is no `Task`, the caller of the method has no way of knowing when the method finished running (all the ways we talked about—`await`, `Wait`, `IsCompleted`, and even `ContinueWith`—require a `Task` object). This is not a problem in this case because event handlers are usually "fire-and-forget" operations where the caller doesn't care what the handler does or when it finishes (as long as it returns control to the caller quickly, which our code does).

There is also no way to report the exception to the caller (like in the success case, there's no access to the `Task.Exception` property or any other way to get to the exception because there is no `Task`), but unlike the success case, this is a real problem. Some code is going to get an exception it didn't expect and most likely crash. We'll talk about all the details in the chapter about exceptions, but the solution is just to not let `async void` methods throw exceptions—if you write an `async void` method, you need to catch all exceptions and handle them yourself.

So if this feature is so problematic, why do we have `async void` methods to begin with? The reason for `async void` is event handlers. By convention, just like in our example, event handlers always have a `void` return type, so if `async` methods didn't support `void`, we couldn't use `async/await` in event handlers.

This brings us to the official guidance about `async void` methods: you should only use `async void` for event handlers and avoid throwing exceptions from `async void` methods. So the correct way to write the event handler from listing 3.4 is as follows.

> **Listing 3.6 `async` event handler with error handling**

```
private async void Button1_Click(object sender, EventArgs ea)
{
    try
    {
        var text = await File.ReadAllTextAsync("source.txt");
        await File.WriteAllTextAsync("dest.txt", text);
    }
    catch(Exception ex)
    {
        // Do something with the exception
    }
}
```

3.5   *ValueTask and ValueTask<T>*

Certain methods are sometimes (but not always) asynchronous. For example, let's say we have a method that performs an asynchronous operation but only if it can't satisfy the request from a cache:

```
public async Task<int> GetValue(string request)
{
    if(_cache.TryGetValue(request, out var fromCache))
    {
        return fromCache;
    }
    int newValue = await GetValueFromServer(request);
    return newValue;
}
```

Returns value from cache if possible

Otherwise performs async operation

Note that _cache is not a Dictionary. Dictionary is not thread safe and is unsuitable to be used with async methods. We'll talk about thread-safe data structures that can be used to build a thread-safe cache in chapter 13.

The GetValue method first checks whether the requested value is in the cache. If so, it will return the value before the first time it uses await. As we've seen in this chapter, the code before the first await runs non-asynchronously, so if the value is in the cache, it will be returned immediately, making the Task<int> returned by the method just a very complicated wrapper for an int.

Allocating the entire Task<int> object when it's not required is obviously wasteful, and it would have been better if we could return an int if the value could be returned immediately and only return the full Task when we need to perform an asynchronous operation. This is what ValueTask<T> is. ValueTask<T> is a struct that contains the value directly if the value is available immediately and a reference to a Task<T> otherwise. The nongeneric ValueTask is the same, except it only contains a flag saying the operation has completed and not the value.

You can await a ValueTask or a ValueTask<T>, just like Task and Task<T>. They also have most of the properties of Task and Task<T>. If you want to use a feature of Task that is not available in ValueTask (for example, Wait), you can use the ValueTask .AsTask() method to get the Task stored inside a ValueTask.

ValueTask and ValueTask<T> are slightly less efficient than Task and Task<T> if there is an asynchronous operation, but much more efficient if the result was available immediately. It is recommended to return a ValueTask in methods that usually return a value without performing an asynchronous operation, especially if those methods are called often.

3.6   *What about multithreading?*

In chapter 1, I said that asynchronous programming and multithreading work very well together. Yet in this entire chapter, we didn't talk about multithreading at all. Also, I said the callback you pass to ContinueWith will run later, but we completely ignored how and where the callback will run. This leads us to the next chapter, which covers multithreading.

Summary

- Task represents an event that may happen in the future.
- Task<T> represents a value that may be available in the future.

- When the event happens or the value is available, we say that the `Task` or `Task<T>` has completed.

- The `IsCompleted` or `Status` properties can be used to test whether the task has completed.

- Use `ContinueWith` to make the task call you when it completes.

- You can call `Wait` or `Result` to make the task synchronous, but that's inefficient and dangerous.

- Calling `Wait` or `Result` after the task has completed is perfectly efficient and safe.

- `async` is just a compiler flag. It tells the compiler that the method needs to be broken into chunks whenever there's an `await` keyword.

- The `async` keyword does not make the code run in the background. Without `await`, it does nothing (except make the compiler generate an awful lot of boilerplate code).

- The compiler breaks the method after each `await` and passes the next chunk to `ContinueWith` (conceptually).

- `await` does not wait but ends the current chunk and returns to the caller.

- `async` methods can be `void`, but then there's no way to know when the method has finished, and you should catch and handle all exceptions inside the method.

- If an `async` method often returns a result immediately without doing anything asynchronous, you can improve the efficiency by returning `ValueTask` or `Value-Task<T>` instead of `Task` or `Task<T>`.

Multithreading basics

4

Chapter 1 discussed how a system can run multiple pieces of code simultaneously—much more than the number of CPU cores—by quickly switching between them. This functionality is made possible by a hardware timer inside the CPU. Each time the timer ticks, the operating system can pause the currently running code and switch to another piece of code. If the switching is fast enough, it creates the illusion that all threads are running simultaneously.

This chapter explores how to use threads for parallel execution and discusses key aspects of concurrent programming. In the next chapter, we will connect these topics to the `async`/`await` feature.

When a process starts, it begins with one thread that runs the `Main` method (along with a few other system-controlled threads, which we will set aside for now). This initial thread is referred to as the main thread. We will now look at how to utilize additional threads to allow multiple pieces of code to run simultaneously.

4.1 Different ways to run in another thread

Now that we've decided we want to run code in parallel, we need to talk about how to do it. This section covers the three most common ways to run code in another thread in C#. We will start with the oldest and most flexible option—creating your own thread.

4.1.1 Thread.Start

In .NET, a thread is represented by the appropriately named `System.Threading` `.Thread` class. This class lets you inspect and control existing threads, as well as create new ones.

To create a new thread, you first create a new `Thread` object, passing a callback with the code you want to run in the new thread to the constructor. After that, you have a chance to configure the thread before it starts running. Finally, you call `Thread` `.Start` to start the thread. In the following listing, we are going to create and configure a thread.

> **Listing 4.1 Creating a thread**

```
public void RunInBackground()
{
    var newThread = new Thread(CodeToRunInBackgroundThread);   ← Creates thread object
    newThread.IsBackground = true;   ← Configures thread
    newThread.Start();   ← Starts running
}

private void CodeToRunInBackgroundThread()   ← Code to run in new thread
{
    Console.WriteLine("Do stuff");
}
```

As you can see, this code example follows exactly the described steps:

1 We created a thread, passing the method we want to run in that thread to the constructor.

2 We configured the thread, in this case by making it a background thread (we'll talk about background threads later in the book). This step is optional.

3 We started the thread by calling `Thread.Start`.

The `Thread` class constructor has two versions that each accept a different delegate. There's the simple version we used in this example that accepts a `void` method with no parameters, and there is also a parameterized version that accepts a `void` method that takes one parameter of type `object`.

The `Thread.Start` method also has two corresponding versions: one that has no parameters and one that accepts a parameter of type `object`. If you use the second version of both, you can pass whatever object you want to your thread code by passing it to Thread.Start.

This option lets you write a single method for threads doing slightly different things and pass a different parameter value to each thread to differentiate between them. For example, let's create 100 threads and pass a different number to each.

Listing 4.2   Creating a thread with a parameter

```
public void RunLotsOfThreads()
{
    var threads = new Thread[100];
    for(int i=0;i<100;++i)
    {
        threads[i] = new Thread(MyThread);        ◄─── Passes a value
        threads[i].Start(i);                            per thread
    }
}
private void MyThread(object? parameter)
{
    Console.WriteLine($"Hello from thread {parameter}");  ◄─── Uses that value
}
```

In this listing, we just passed our loop index to Thread.Start, and it was conveniently provided to our MyThread method when it started running in the new thread.

Mixing it up by passing a non-parameterized method to the Thread constructor and then using the parameterized version of Thread.Start, or vice versa, doesn't make much sense but is fully supported. If you use the parameterized delegate and the non-parametrized Thread.Start, your method parameter value will be null. If you use the non-parametrized delegate and the parameterized Thread.Start, the value will be ignored.

The Thread class also contains a method that will wait until the thread completes its work, called Join. *Join* is the standard computer science term for waiting for a thread. I've found conflicting stories about the origin of this term, all of them using metaphors that I don't want to repeat here because they don't work that well. We'll just have to accept that in this context, *join* means *wait*.

The Join method is very useful when we want to run several threads in parallel and then, after they all finish, do something like combining the results from multiple threads. Thread.Join will return immediately if the thread has already finished. In the following listing, we run three threads and wait for them all to finish before notifying the user we are done.

Listing 4.3   Waiting for threads to finish

```
public void RunAndWait()
{
    var threads = new Thread[3];
    for(int i=0;i<3;++i)                ◄─── Runs all threads
```

```
    {
        threads[i] = new Thread(DoWork);
        threads[i].Start();
    }
    foreach(var current in threads)
    {
        current.Join();
    }
    Console.WriteLine("Finished");
}

private void DoWork()
{
    Console.WriteLine("Doing work");
}
```

Waits for threads to finish

Here we start three threads in one loop and then wait for them in a second loop. It's important that those are two separate loops because we want to start all threads and only then wait for all of them. We don't want to start and wait repeatedly, as that would cause sequential execution, just with threading overhead (this problem is called *synchronization*, and we will discuss it in chapter 7).

The second loop looks like it depends on the order of the threads in the list, but it doesn't. It doesn't matter in what order we wait for the threads. If the longest-running thread is the first, we will wait for it to complete, and then the Join calls for the other already finished threads will return immediately. If the longest-running thread is the last, the loop will wait for the first thread, and when it finishes, it will wait for the next one until it gets to the last one. In both cases, the loop will wait until the longest running of the threads finishes.

The Thread class also has other methods that let us control threads: Suspend, Resume, and Abort. Those may seem handy at first, but they are in fact extremely dangerous, and you should never use them. You will discover why later in the chapter.

Using the Thread class and Thread.Start is the only way to get a thread that is completely under your control, and you can do whatever you want with it without interfering with other code running in your app.

Creating and destroying threads is relatively resource intensive, and if you create a lot of threads where each thread does just a little bit of work, your app might spend more time managing threads than doing actual useful work.

This affects asynchronous code because even if it takes a long time to complete, it is usually composed of many short parts. For example, the following method performs two asynchronous operations:

```
private async Task SoSomethingComplicated()
{
    await DoFirstPart();
    await DoSecondPart();
}
```

When this method starts, it will get to the `DoFirstPart` call and then return control to its caller as soon as `DoFirstPart` does something asynchronous (and the caller is likely to be using `await` and do the same until there are no more callers and the thread is released). When the asynchronous operation is complete, the method will resume, requiring a thread run for just long enough to get to the `DoSecondPart` call and release the thread again. Later, when `DoSecondPart` completes, the method will resume, requiring a thread again. If this involved creating and destroying threads, there would have been two thread destructions and two thread creations involved.

Short tasks have the same problem. If we spin up a thread to run just a quick, tiny calculation, we can easily find ourselves wasting a significant amount of time creating and destroying the thread relative to actually doing useful work. And that brings us to our next topic—the thread pool.

When to use Thread.Start

Use `Thread.Start` for

- Long-running code.
- If you need to change the thread properties such as language and locale information, background status, COM apartment, etc. (We'll talk about all the thread settings near the end of this chapter.)

Do not use `Thread.Start` for

- Asynchronous code
- Short tasks

4.1.2   *The thread pool*

The thread pool is the solution for the thread creation and destruction overhead we talked about. With the thread pool, the system keeps a small number of threads waiting in the background, and whenever you have something to run, you can use one of those pre-existing threads to run it. The system automatically manages those threads and creates new ones when needed (between a minimum and maximum number of threads you control).

The thread pool is optimized for short-running tasks where the same thread can pick up multiple tasks one after the other. If you use the thread pool for a long-running task, you are taking a thread out of rotation for a long time, and when all the threads in the pool are busy, new work must wait until one of the threads frees up.

Also, because you are "borrowing" a thread, you should not change any of its properties, since any change will affect future code that runs in that same thread (just like you wouldn't rearrange someone's furniture if you're just visiting). If you need to change the thread properties, you must create the thread with the `Thread` class.

The thread pool is controlled by the appropriately named `System.Threading` `.ThreadPool` class. To run something on the thread pool, you will use the less-appropriately named `QueueUserWorkItem` method.

```
Listing 4.4   Running in the thread pool

public void RunInBackground()
{
    ThreadPool.QueueUserWorkItem(RunInPool);        ◄──┐  Queues code to run
}                                                        │  in thread pool

private void RunInPool(object? state)            ◄──┐  Code to run
{
    Console.WriteLine("Do stuff");
}
```

The code is similar to that in listing 4.1, but we can't change the thread configuration (because we are borrowing an existing thread) and don't have to manually start the thread (because the thread is already running).

Like `Thread.Start`, `QueueUserWorkItem` also has a parametrized and a non-parametrized version. But unlike the `Thread` class, the method that runs on the thread pool always accepts an object parameter; if you use the non-parameterized `QueueUserWorkItem`, the parameter will be `null`. Let's rewrite the code from listing 4.2 to use the thread pool.

```
Listing 4.5   Running in the thread pool with a parameter

public void RunInBackground()
{
    for(int i=0;i<10;++i)
    {
        ThreadPool.QueueUserWorkItem(RunInPool,i);   ◄──┐  Passes a value
    }                                                     │  to the thread
}

private void RunInPool(object? parameter)        ◄──┐  The value is received in
{                                                     │  the parameter.
    Console.WriteLine($"Hello from thread {parameter}");
}
```

The code in this example is unsurprising—it's exactly like code from listing 4.2, except we don't have to start the thread manually.

Unlike the `Thread` class with its `Join` method, the thread pool does not give us a built-in way to wait until the code we run on it ends. We will see later in this chapter how we can build our own way to wait until the background code completes.

This chapter talks about the thread pool. There is one thread pool created for you by the framework, and all the examples here use it. However, you can easily create your own thread pools, but you probably shouldn't.

The thread pool interface is old and clunky (for example, you use a method named `QueueUserWorkItem`) and doesn't work well with `Tasks` and `async-await` (because it predates them by a decade), which is why we have `Task.Run`.

When to use ThreadPool.QueueUesrWorkItem

Use `ThreadPool.QueueUesrWorkItem` for

- Short-running tasks

Do not use `ThreadPool.QueueUesrWorkItem`

- For long-running tasks
- When you need to change the thread properties
- With `Task`-based asynchronous operations
- With `async/await`

4.1.3   *Task.Run*

We've seen that the thread pool is optimized to run many short-running tasks, and we know that asynchronous tasks are actually a sequence of short tasks, so the thread pool is ideal for running asynchronous code, except that the `QueueUserWorkItem` method doesn't use the `Task` class (because it predates `async/await` and `Task` by about a decade). This is why we have `Task.Run`.

The `Task.Run` method runs code on the thread pool, just like `ThreadPool.Queue-UserWorkItem`, but it has a nicer interface that works well with `async/await`. For the simple scenario, it works basically the same as in the previous example.

Listing 4.6   Running in the thread pool with `Task.Run`

```
public void RunInBackground()
{
    Task.Run(RunInPool);                ◀── Queue code to run
}                                           in thread pool

private void RunInPool()                ◀── Code to run
{
    Console.WriteLine("Do stuff");
}
```

The code is the same as the thread pool example in listing 4.4, except `ThreadPool.QueueUserWorkItem` was replaced with `Task.Run`. But unlike with the `ThreadPool` class, `Task.Run` works very well with `async/await` (and other methods that return a `Task`).

Listing 4.7   Running `async` code with `Task.Run`

```
public void RunInBackground()
{
    Task.Run(RunInPool);                ◀── Queues code to run
}                                           in thread pool

private async Task RunInPool()          ◀── Code to run
{
    await Task.Delay(500);
```

```
    Console.WriteLine("Did async stuff");
}
```

As you can see from the code, it just works. We didn't have to do anything special to run an `async` method with `Task.Run`.

Also, `Task.Run` returns a `Task` itself, and we can use it to know when the code we run on the thread pool is finished—a feature the `ThreadPool` class does not have. Here's an adaptation of the example from listing 4.3 that creates multiple threads with the `Thread` class and waits for all of them to finish.

> **Listing 4.8 Waiting for tasks to finish with `Task.Run`**

```
public async Task RunInBackground()
{
    var tasks = new Task[10];
    for(int i=0;i<10;++i)
    {
        tasks[i] = Task.Run(RunInPool);          ◄──┘ Queues tasks to run
    }                                                  on thread pool
    await Task.WhenAll(tasks);                    ◄──┘ Waits for tasks to complete
    Console.WriteLine("All finished");
}

private void RunInPool()
{
    Console.WriteLine("Do stuff");
}
```

Here we can wait with the `Task.WhenAll` method that is much more elegant than the `Thread.Join` loop. Not only does it not require a loop, but it also waits asynchronously.

Note that when you use `Task.Run` without waiting for it, the compiler will generate a warning, but adding an `await` is almost never the right thing to do. If you `await Task.Run`, you are telling your compiler to wait for the task to complete before moving to the next line of code, essentially making it run sequentially, which defeats the purpose of using `Task.Run`. If you `await Task.Run`, you're taking on the overhead of managing different tasks without getting any benefits; it's more efficient to just run the code without `Task.Run`. The exception to this rule is the UI thread, and we will talk about it near the end of this chapter.

To get rid of the warning, you can assign the `Task` returned by `Task.Run` to a discard variable:

```
Task.Run(MethodToRunInBackground);          ◄──┘ Might generate
                                                  a warning
_ = Task.Run(MethodToRunInBackground);      ◄──┐ No warning
```

`Task.Run` doesn't have a parameterized version like `Thread.Start` and `ThreadPool.QueueUserWorkItem`, but we can easily use lambdas to simulate it and pass data to the code we run.

Listing 4.9   Using lambdas to create a parametrized `Task.Run`

```
public void RunInBackground()
{
    for(int i=0;i<10;++i)
    {
      var icopy = i;
      Task.Run(()=>
          {
              Console.WriteLine($"Hello from thread {icopy}");
          });
    }
}
```

Here we used the lambda's feature of capturing local variables to pass a unique value to each task. Note that we had to use the `icopy` variable that is scoped inside the loop because otherwise, all threads would have shared the same `i` variable as the `for` loop, and because it takes time for the task to start, by the time tasks run, the loop will have finished, so all tasks will have only the final value of `i` (10 in this case).

> **When to use Task.Run**
>
> Use `Task.Run` for
>
> - Code that uses async-await
> - Short running tasks
>
> Do not use `Task.Run` for
>
> - Non-asynchronous long running tasks

In this case, we could create a different copy of `i` for each thread, but in many cases, we have shared data that multiple threads need to access, and that brings us to accessing the same variables from multiple threads.

4.2   Accessing the same variables from multiple threads

Now that we know how to run code in parallel, we must deal with the consequences. Most programs manipulate data in memory, and the problem with manipulating data in a multithreaded program is that data access is often not a single uninterruptable operation, even when it's just one line of code or even one operator.

Let's take the simplest data manipulation operation I can think of—incrementing an integer:

```
int n=0;
++n;
```

The ++n line sure looks like it does a single thing. It's just one variable and one operator, and it's just three characters long. How many distinct operations can we do in just three characters? Well, it's actually three distinct operations:

1 Read the value from the memory location allocated for the `n` variable into the CPU.

2 Increment the value inside the CPU.

3 Save the new value from the CPU back into the memory location allocated for the n variable.

In a single-threaded program, this looks like a single operation because I can never accidentally break this sequence or sneak some code that runs in the middle of the sequence; however, in a multithreaded program, I can.

Operations that can't be interrupted in a multithreaded application, usually because they are a single operation at the hardware level, are called atomic operations. Figure 4.1 compares incrementing a variable twice in a single-threaded application, where everything is sane and works as expected; in a multithreaded application on a single-core CPU, where the way the system simulates multithreading can and will suspend threads at the wrong time; and finally, multithreaded on multicore CPUs, where things really happen in parallel.

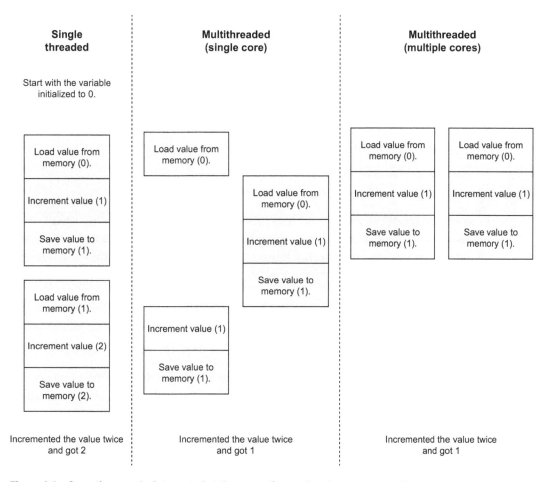

Figure 4.1 Operations can be interrupted at the wrong time and produce wrong results.

As figure 4.1 illustrates, only in single-threaded applications, or applications that don't share data between threads, does our simple operation act like an operation that can't be interrupted. In all other configurations, anything can happen.

Let's write code that demonstrates that point. In this example, we will create two threads and increment the same variable from both. We will increment the variable five million times in each thread.

Listing 4.10   Incorrect value when accessing shared data without locking

```
public void GetIncorrectValue()
{
    int theValue = 0;

    var threads = new Thread[2];
    for(int i=0;i<2;++i)
    {
        threads[i] = new Thread(()=>
        {
            for(int j=0;j<5000000;++j)
                ++theValue;
        });
        threads[i].Start();
    }

    foreach(var current in threads)
    {
        current.Join();
    }
    Console.WriteLine(theValue);
}
```

If we run this code, we may expect it to print 10000000, but after reading what I wrote before the code sample, you already know that won't be the case. In fact, the result will change every time we run code, but it but will be around 6000000 most of the time.

So how do we solve this problem?

4.2.1   *No shared data*

The simplest solution is to never share any data between threads. If each thread has its own set of variables that can only be accessed by that thread, we never get a chance to read or write the variable from another thread, and we are safe.

This is possible some of the time. For example, if we are writing a server that accepts data from the client, calculates something based solely on that data, and then returns results, each thread can operate without ever touching any value accessible to other threads. However, this isn't possible most of the time because our app is usually all about manipulating shared data.

But what if we bypass the problem another way, for example, by not modifying the shared data?

4.2.2 Immutable shared data

If our problem is that it is not safe for one thread to access data while another is modifying it, we can eliminate the problem completely if we just never modify any shared data. A common example is a web server serving static files; because those files never change, you can read them as many times as you like in parallel without causing any problems.

For most applications, it isn't as easy as that, but this is the standard solution in functional languages and can be done in C#. However, this is not how we usually write C#.

Making all the shared data immutable, which might seem impractical to developers who aren't used to functional programming, is actually not only possible but technically an extremely good solution. The only problem is that it requires us to write our code completely differently than we usually do in C#. I'm going to ignore it here because I could fill an entire book on the subject (and Manning has actually published a book on this topic; see *Concurrency in .NET* by Riccardo Terrell), and you would still not use this approach because it would feel alien to the way we usually write C#. However, .NET does have some built-in immutable data structures, which we'll discuss in chapter 13.

And that brings us to the standard solution—locks and mutexes.

4.2.3 Locks and mutexes

What we are left with is synchronizing access to the shared state—whenever a thread needs to access the shared state, it "locks" it, and when it is finished with the data, it "releases" the lock. If another thread tries to lock the data while it is already locked, it must wait until the data is released by the current user.

In computer science, this is called a *mutex* (short for *mutual exclusion*). In C#, we have the `Mutex` class that represents the operating system's mutex implementation and the `lock` statement that uses an internal .NET implementation. The `lock` statement is easier to use and faster (because it doesn't require a system call), so we will prefer to use it. Let's rewrite our program from before using a lock.

Listing 4.11   Adding locks to avoid simultaneous access problems

```
public void GetCorrectValue()
{
   int theValue = 0;
   object theLock = new Object();

   var threads = new Thread[2];
   for(int i=0;i<2;++i)
   {
      threads[i] = new Thread(()=>
      {
         for(int j=0;j<5000000;++j)
         {
            lock(theLock)
            {
               ++theValue;
            }
```

Locks for the duration
of the modification

```
        }
    });
    threads[i].Start();
}

foreach(var current in threads)
{
    current.Join();
}
Console.WriteLine(theValue);
}
```

We can see that the `lock` statement is followed by a code block, and the lock is released when we exit the block, so we can't accidentally forget to release the lock. (The lock will also be released if we exit the code block because of an exception, which is nice.)

We can also see that the `lock` statement accepts an object. We can use any .NET object; however, the best practice is to utilize an internal object that is used just for the lock and is accessible only to the code that needs it. Usually, it will be a private class member of your code.

Why use lock with an object

In .NET 8 and earlier, the best practice is to use an object of type `Object` (that can also be used with the keyword `object`) because we're not going to use this object for anything else, and an object of type `Object` has the lowest overhead of all reference type objects.

In .NET 9 and later, it's better to use an object of type `System.Threading.Lock`. Using a `lock` statement with the new `Lock` class is clearer (because it's obviously a lock) and may be faster in newer versions.

Using the `lock` statement with an `Object` is still supported, safe, and correct in .NET 9 and later. In this book, all the examples will use an `Object` and not a `Lock` for backward compatibility.

Using `lock` in this example was required to make our program produce the correct result, and synchronization objects such as `lock` and `Mutex` are needed for multi-threaded programming. Those same objects also introduce a number of new failure modes, the biggest of them being the deadlock.

4.2.4   *Deadlocks*

A deadlock is the situation where a thread or multiple threads are stuck waiting for something that will never happen. The simplest example is where one thread locked mutex A and is waiting for mutex B, while a second thread locked mutex B and is waiting for mutex A. Thus, thread A is waiting for thread B to complete, which is waiting for thread A to complete, that we already established is waiting for thread B, which we said is waiting for thread A, and so on—forever(figure 4.2).

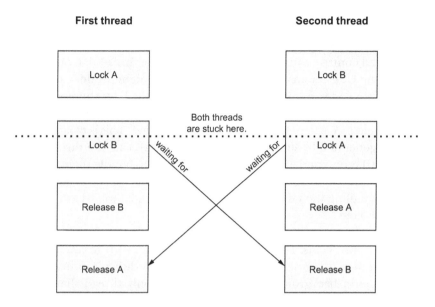

Figure 4.2 Deadlock that occurs when one thread has locked mutex A and is waiting for mutex B, while another thread has locked mutex B and is waiting for mutex A. This creates a situation where thread A is dependent on thread B to finish, but thread B is also dependent on thread A, which leads to an endless cycle of waiting.

Now you can see why the best practice for the `lock` statement is to use a private object that is only accessible by the code that needs it. It's because external code could, otherwise, accidentally or intentionally lock the same object we've locked at a time we don't expect and cause a deadlock. If we use a private object, we can still cause a deadlock, but with both sides under our control, there are techniques we can use to prevent deadlocks. There is an entire chapter on deadlocks and other typical multithreading problems in this book, including on how to prevent them.

This is also why I said earlier that `Thread.Suspend`, `Thread.Resume`, and `Thread.Abort` are so dangerous. Let's say you wrote a very clever system to manage your program's work that uses `Suspend` and `Resume` to control threads. From the thread's point of view, your calls to `Suspend` can happen at any time (for example, when the thread is in the middle of allocating memory and is holding a lock inside the memory manager). Normally this lock would be completely safe because it is released quickly, and the code never waits for anything while holding the lock, but now you've made the memory manager's code wait until you call `Resume`. In the meantime, no one can allocate memory, including the thread that is supposed to call `Resume`. If this thread tries to allocate memory (a very common operation), you've just created a deadlock.

A deadlock can even happen without using locks or mutexes when two threads share other resources; in some cases, this resource might even be the thread itself. This is especially common with special-purpose threads, and the most common special-purpose thread is the UI thread in native applications.

4.3   *Special considerations for native UI apps*

In all Windows desktop application technologies (WinForms, WPF, UWP, and WinAPI), UI windows and controls can only be accessed from the thread that created them. Trying to access the UI elements from a different thread might produce potentially incorrect results, error codes, or exceptions, depending on the UI technology you are using.

When the program starts, you set up the main window and then call `Dispatcher .Run` or `Application.Run` (depending on UI technology). This is typically done in boilerplate code generated by Visual Studio. When you call `Run`, the thread enters a loop that waits for UI events and, if needed, calls your code to handle them. If you block the thread or perform any long activity in your UI event handlers, you are preventing the thread from handling the UI events, and the program's UI will freeze until your event handler is complete.

You can take advantage of the fact that the UI thread is waiting and handing events and inject your own events. This lets other threads ask for code to run on the UI thread, which is useful because otherwise, it would have been difficult to update the UI due to activity done in background threads (since the only thread that can access the UI directly is the UI thread). You can do this by using the `Control.BeginInvoke` or `Control.Invoke` method in WinForms and `Dispatcher.BeginInvoke` or `Dispatcher .Invoke` methods in WPF or the generic `SynchronizationContext` interface.

In a typical workflow, in an event handler you write that is called in response to a UI event such as a button click, the event handler uses the `Thread` class or the thread pool to run code in the background, and when it finishes doing its work, this background code calls `BeginInvoke` to make the UI thread update the UI with the results.

You must be extra careful with code that is running on the UI thread because you can get into a situation where code is blocked or busy waiting for something that happens in response to an `Invoke`/`BeginInvoke` call (or in some cases, and as we will see in the next chapter, `await`). But because the thread is blocked or busy, the code passed to `Invoke /BeginInvoke` never runs, which creates a deadlock situation and a frozen UI.

4.4   *Waiting for another thread*

Sometimes, one thread must wait for another thread to do something. If we are waiting for a thread we created to complete its work and terminate, we can use `Thread.Join` (as discussed earlier in this chapter). But if the thread we are waiting for needs to continue running after notifying us, we can't use `Thread.Join`, and we need some mechanism for one thread to send a signal to another thread and for that other thread to wait until such a signal arrives. This mechanism is called `ManualResetEventSlim` and is a newer, faster, and simpler implementation of `ManualResetEvent`. Like all the classes that end with `Slim`, it forgoes some functionality, mostly cross-process capabilities and compatibility with native code, in exchange for better performance.

`ManualResetEventSlim` works like a gate. When the event is in the unset state, the gate is closed, and any thread calling its `Wait` method will wait. When the event is in the set stage, the gate is open, and the `Wait` method will return immediately for any thread currently waiting and for all future calls (until the event is reset to the unset state).

The `ManualResetEventSlim` constructor has a single parameter that can be `false` to create the event in the unset state (gate closed) or `true` to create the event in the set state (gate open). The `Set` method switches to the set state and opens the gate, while the `Reset` method switches to the unset state and closes the gate. Let's write code with one thread waiting for another using `ManualResetEventSlim`.

Listing 4.12 Waiting for another thread

```
var myEvent = new ManualResetEventSlim(false);              Creates a "gate
var threadWeWaitFor = new Thread(()=>                       closed" event
    {
        Console.WriteLine("Doing something");
        Thread.Sleep(5000);
        Console.WriteLine("Finished");
        myEvent.Set();                          Opens gate
    });
var waitingThread = new Thread(()=>
    {
        Console.WriteLine("Waiting for other thread to do something");
        myEvent.Wait();
        Console.WriteLine("Other thread finished, we can continue");
    });
threadWeWaitFor.Start();                              Waits for gate
waitingThread.Start();                               to open
```

In this example, we create two threads. The first simulates running a long operation by waiting, and after completing the operation, it sets an event. The second thread uses the event to wait for the first thread to complete.

4.5 *Other synchronization methods*

In addition to the two multithreading synchronization methods discussed in this chapter—the `lock` statement and `ManualRestEventSlim`—.NET contains a vast collection of other multithreading primitives. Each of those was written for a reason and is extremely useful in some circumstances. All of them have something in common: in most cases, you should avoid using them.

The `lock` statement is the simplest and safest thread synchronization construct in .NET, and even it may have the deadlock problem we talked about earlier and a whole lot of other pitfalls we'll examine in chapter 7. For this reason, I recommend staying with the `lock` statement and using the more advanced, and more dangerous, mechanisms only if you have to—that is, only after you've profiled the code and discovered that there is a real bottleneck in your code that can be solved by switching to another thread synchronization technique.

For example, let's take everyone's favorite thread synchronization tool—the `Interlocked` class—which provides operations that are both thread safe and do not require locking. Seemingly, this is a magical class that solves all our problems; however, it, too, has its pitfalls, the most common being

- It supports only a limited set of operations, namely `Increment`, `Decrement`, and `Add`, as well as bitwise `And` and `Or` for some integer types (`int`, `uint`, `long`, and `ulong`).

- All other operations can be implemented by the `Exchange` and `CompareExchange` methods, and these methods must be used in a very specific way (you'll see some examples in chapter 13).

- It protects the operation, not the variable. If anyone accesses the variable "protected" by an interlocked operation by anything other than members of the `Interlocked` class, all bets are off, and your code is no longer thread safe, even the parts of the code that do use the `Interlocked` class. If you just want to read the variable without modifying it, you must use `Interlocked.Read` and not use the variable directly.

- While the value you get from the interlocked methods is guaranteed to be correct when the interlocked method runs, by the time you use it, even if it's in the same line of code, it might already be outdated.

- Only a single interlocked method call is thread safe. If you call `Interlocked .Increment` twice for two variables, for example, it is possible for another thread (even one also using the `Interlocked` class) to read or modify any of the variables between those two operations. This is a special case of the "composing thread-safe operations rarely results in a thread-safe operation" problem we'll discuss in chapter 7.

- While the `Interlocked` class members are faster than using a `lock`, they might be significantly slower than using the normal operations (using the `+=`, `++`, `--`, `&`, and `|` operators).

With all those pitfalls (and more), it's easier and safer to use the `lock` statement and only use the `Interlocked` class (carefully) in code that is very performance sensitive. The same goes for all the other multithreading primitives we didn't discuss—avoid using them unless you absolutely have to because they are complicated and not as safe and easy to use as the `lock` statement.

4.6   *Thread settings*

When talking about the `Thread` class, I said that you should only change the settings of threads you create yourself using the `Thread` class (or the main thread if you are writing the application and not a library) and never change the settings of a thread pool or a thread created by another component. The reason is that the component that created the thread probably relies on the thread settings, and changing them would interfere with the operation of the component.

Note that none of those settings works well with asynchronous code because any time you use `await` (or `ContinueWith`), execution can continue on another thread that has different settings. Here are the settings you can change using the `Thread` class in the order of usefulness.

4.6.1 Thread background status

This is the most commonly used of all the thread settings. It is set by using the `Thread` `.IsBackground` property, and it controls when your application exits. An application exits when all the non-background threads exit. That means that if you start a thread using the `Thread` class (and don't set its `IsBackground` property), and your `Main` method ends, the application will keep running until the thread exits. If you don't want the thread you created to keep the application running, you can just set the `IsBackgroud` property to `true`.

This property must be set before calling `Thread.Start`. It has no effect when the application is deliberately terminated (for example, by using `Environment.Exit` or `Environment.FailFast`) or if the application exits due to an unhandled exception.

4.6.2 Language and locale

You can change the thread language and locale using the `Thread.CurrentCulture` property, which affects how values, mostly numbers and dates, are formatted (if you don't pass a `CultureInfo` object to the specific formatting method). It also affects the selection of UI resources in GUI applications. The default is the language and formatting used on the user's computer.

You should only use this property if your application has a way for the user to change the language. Otherwise, you should respect the user's computer settings.

4.6.3 COM Apartment

You can use the `Thread.SetApartmentState` and `Thread.TrySetApartmentState` methods to control the thread's COM apartment type. This is only relevant to applications utilizing COM components in threads you create using the `Thread` class (for the main thread, you should probably use the `STAThread` or `MTAThread` attributes on your `Main` method).

COM is a huge topic and outside the scope of this book. The short explanation for readers who are lucky and don't use COM is that COM has a concept of *apartment type*, and most COM objects can only run as a specific apartment type. Reading or setting the COM apartment is only supported on Windows because other operating systems don't use COM.

4.6.4 Current user

This property is mostly (but not officially) obsolete. You can use the static `Thread` `.CurrentPrincipal` property to attach identity and permissions to the thread, which does not change the thread's permissions at the operating system level. It's just a place for you (or a library you are using) to store user information for your own permission system.

In ASP.NET classic (.NET Framework 4.x and earlier), if you used the built-in authentication system, the current web user information was stored in the `CurrentPrincipal` property. This is no longer the case in ASP.NET Core (.NET Core and .NET 5 and later); in the newer version, the current user is in HttpContext.User only.

4.6.5   *Thread priority*

Setting the thread priority is dangerous, and you shouldn't do it. Unless you are extremely careful, setting the thread priority is likely to cause performance degradation and/or deadlocks.

The problem is that it's too easy to get into some variation of a high-priority thread that is waiting for a resource held by a lower-priority thread, but that lower-priority thread can't release the resource because the higher-priority thread is taking all the CPU time.

Controlling the thread's priority is required for some kinds of system programming, but you should never set thread priorities in normal applications. The priority is controlled by the Thread.Priority property. The system is allowed to ignore the priority you set.

Summary

- You can run multiple things in parallel. Each one of these things is called a thread.
- The program starts with one thread running the Main method. This thread is called the main thread.
- You can create dedicated threads that are completely under your control with the Thread class by creating a Thread object, optionally reconfiguring it, and calling the Thread.Start method to start running it.
- The thread pool is a collection of threads managed by the system and is available for use when you have code to run. It is optimized for short-running tasks and can create new threads as needed.
- Traditionally, you run code in the thread pool by using the ThreadPool.Queue-UserWorkItem method.
- A simpler and more async/await friendly way to run code in the thread pool is using Task.Run.
- The main thread and threads you create with the Thread class are the only threads that are completely under your control and that you can reconfigure any way you want. However, you should never reconfigure threads created by other components, especially threads managed by the thread pool.
- When you access data shared by more than one thread, you have to use a lock; otherwise, different threads may overwrite data written by other threads, leading to incorrect results.
- The same also applies to reading shared data. If you don't use locks to synchronize reads as well as writes, you may get stale data and even the results of incomplete writes.

- In native UI applications, the thread running the UI is called the UI thread. It is typically the main thread, but it can be a different thread if needed. The UI thread is the only thread that may access windows and other UI controls.
- You should avoid blocking the UI thread because this makes the UI freeze.

5

async/await and multithreading

Asynchronous programming is about doing stuff (such as reading a file or waiting for data to arrive over the network) that doesn't require the CPU in the background while using the CPU to do something else. Multithreading is about doing stuff that may or may not require the CPU in the background while using the CPU to do something else. Those two things are obviously similar, and we use the same tools to interact with them.

In chapter 3, we talked about `async/await` but didn't mention threads; we especially ignored where the callback passed to `ContinueWith` runs. In chapter 4, we talked about multithreading and almost didn't mention `async/await` at all. In this chapter, we'll connect these two together.

5.1   Asynchronous programming and multithreading

To demonstrate the interaction between asynchronous programming and multithreading, we'll start with a method that reads 10 files in parallel using asynchronous operations and then waits for all the read operations to complete. And just for the fun of it, we won't make the method itself `async` but just use asynchronous operations.

Listing 5.1   Reading 10 files

```
public void Read10Files()
{
    var tasks = new Task[10];
    for(int i=0;i<10;++i)
    {
        tasks[i] = File.ReadAllBytesAsync($"{i}.txt");
    }
    Task.WaitAll(tasks);
}
```

This is obviously asynchronous programming. Reading a file is a textbook example of work done mostly outside the CPU (and yes, I completely ignored the data we loaded from the file—this is just a demonstration of the mechanics of `Task` and asynchronous operations). But what would it look like if instead we wrote code to compute 10 values (or, for simplicity's sake, let's print text claiming we are calculating) in parallel and wait for the results? We'll use `Task.Run`, which runs our code in a thread pool thread (see chapter 4).

Listing 5.2   Calculating 10 values

```
public void Compute10Values()
{
    var tasks = new Task[10];
    for(int i=0;i<10;++i)
    {
        tasks[i] = Task.Run(()=>Console.WriteLine("Calculating"));
    }
    Task.WaitAll(tasks);
}
```

I literally changed just one line and didn't even change the entire text of the line. This demonstrates that the same tools used for asynchronous operations work in the exact same way for multithreading. Let's take it one step further and use multithreading to read the files in parallel.

Listing 5.3   Reading 10 files using multithreading

```
public void Read10Files()
{
    var tasks = new Task[10];
```

```
    for(int i=0;i<10;++i)
    {
       var icopy = i;
       tasks[i] = Task.Run(()=>File.ReadAllBytes($"{icopy}.txt"));
    }
    Task.WaitAll(tasks);
}
```

We needed to create a local variable inside the loop. Otherwise, all the threads would have shared the same i variable, and by the time the threads ran, the loop would have finished already, so i would have had its final value of 10. That would have made all the threads try to read 10.txt and fail because our files are 0.txt–9.txt.

Other than that, the code looks almost the same as the one in listing 5.1, and it does exactly the same thing. However, it does it in a much more wasteful way because this example uses up to 10 separate threads (depending on how quickly the system can read the files). Furthermore, each and every one of them is stuck waiting for the file to arrive from the hard drive, while listing 5.1 uses just one thread waiting for all the files.

But a real program wouldn't read files and ignore the data. A real program would read the file and then do something with the file's content. Let's fix the latest example to also do something (or just write to the console that we are doing something).

Listing 5.4   Reading 10 files and doing something with the data

```
public void Process10Files()
{
    var tasks = new Task[10];
    for(int i=0;i<10;++i)
    {
       var icopy = i;
       tasks[i] = Task.Run(()=>
       {
           File.ReadAllBytes($"{icopy}.txt");
           Console.WriteLine("Doing something with the file's content");
       );
    }
    Task.WaitAll(tasks);
}
```

This will use up to 10 threads from the thread pool (because remember, Task.Run uses the thread pool), possibly creating new threads if there weren't enough threads already in the thread pool and then immediately putting all those threads in a blocked state where they would be doing nothing except waiting for the hard drive. Let's see what would happen if we wrote the exact same thing using asynchronous operations only.

Listing 5.5   Reading 10 files asynchronously and processing the data

```
public void Process10Files()
{
    var tasks = new Task[10];
```

```
    for(int i=0;i<10;++i)
    {
        var icopy = i;
        tasks[i] = Task.Run(async ()=>
        {
            await File.ReadAllBytesAsync($"{icopy}.txt");
            Console.WriteLine("Doing something with the file's content");
        });
    }
    Task.WaitAll(tasks);
}
```

The code looks exactly the same, except we switched from `File.ReadAllBytes` to `File.ReadAllBytesAsync` and added the `async` and `await` keywords; however, what happens at runtime is very different. Instead of using 10 threads for the whole time, this will pick up a thread from the thread pool, use it to start the read operation, and then free the thread and use the callback mechanism we talked about in chapter 3. That means the program will use a small number of threads to start the read operations (maybe even one; it depends on the current load on the computer and the state of the thread pool), and then use no threads at all while waiting. Only after the data arrives will it start using 10 threads (that is, only when there is work for them to do).

In fact, this is even better because as we are reading all the files from the same hard drive, we are likely to get the files' contents one after the other and not all at once (because there's just one hard drive with one data connection to the motherboard), and each task will only pick up a thread after its data is available. That means it's likely we'll never actually use 10 threads simultaneously (but we can't tell in advance because multithreaded programming is inherently unpredictable).

There was one small lie two paragraphs ago: I said we don't use any threads while waiting for the files, but we are actually using one thread—the thread that called `Process10Files` and is waiting for all the processing to complete. We can fix this; if we just make `Process10Files` itself `async`, we will get the following.

> **Listing 5.6   Making the caller `async` too**

```
public async Task Process10Files()          ◀─────┐  Makes the
{                                                  │  method async
    var tasks = new Task[10];
    for(int i=0;i<10;++i)
    {
        var icopy = i;
        tasks[i] = Task.Run(async ()=>
        {
            await File.ReadAllBytesAsync($"{icopy}.txt");
            Console.WriteLine("Doing something with the file's content");
        });
    }                                        ┌─  Changes WaitAll
    await Task.WhenAll(tasks);          ◀────┘   to WhenAll
}
```

This will free the thread that called `Process10Files` itself and will truly use no threads at all until we finish reading some files.

If we free up all the threads while waiting for the data to arrive, when the data finally arrives, we need to continue running, but we can't because we freed up the thread. So where does our code run after the `await` call?

5.2   *Where does code run after await?*

If you remember from chapter 2, I said that using the `await` keyword is equivalent to calling `Task.ContinueWith`, so the code

```
var buffer = await File.ReadAllBytesAsync("somefile.bin");
Console.WriteLine(buffer[0]);
```

is translated by the compiler to

```
File.ReadAllBytesAsync("somefile.bin").ContinueWith(task=>
{
    var buffer = task.Result;
    Console.WriteLine(buffer[0]);
});
```

I also mentioned that this is a simplification and that `await` is a bit more complicated. Now it's time to see exactly what `await` does differently.

`ContinueWith` runs the callback in the thread pool, just like `Task.Run`. Technically, `ContinueWith` has a version that accepts parameters specifying how to run the callback passed to it, but I won't go into that because `await` takes care of it for us, and `ContinueWith` is very rarely used directly in application code.

`await` tries to run the code after it in a thread of the same type, so in most cases, you don't have to think about the possibility of a thread change. If `await` can't use a thread of the same type, it will use the thread pool instead. The specific rules are

- If you are using `await` on the UI thread of a WinForms, WPF, or UWP app, the code after the `await` will run on the same thread.
- If you are using `await` while processing a request in an ASP.NET Classic application (.NET framework 4.8 and earlier), the code after the `await` will run on the same thread.
- If your code or a framework you are using changes the current thread's `SynchronizationContext` or `TaskFactory` (we'll talk about them later in the book), then `await` will use those. This is how the frameworks in the previous bullet points control the behavior of `await`; except for UI frameworks, this is extremely rare.
- In all other cases, the code after `await` will run on the thread pool. Here are some common examples:
  - If the code calling `await` is running in the thread pool, the code after the `await` will also run in the thread pool. However, it might run on a different thread.

- This also applies to code processing a request in an ASP.NET Core application (.NET Core or .NET 5.0 and later) because ASP.NET Core uses the thread pool for all processing.
- If you use `await` in the main thread of a non-UI app, the code after the `await` will also run in the thread pool and not in the main thread. The system will keep the main thread (and the entire application) alive until the `Task` you are awaiting completes.
- If you use `await` in a thread you created with the `Thread` class, inside the method you passed to the `Thread` constructor, the thread will terminate, and the code after the `await` will run on the thread pool.

Those rules only apply if `await` has to actually wait. If the operation you are awaiting has already completed by the time `await` runs, in almost all cases, the code will just continue normally without switching threads. The most common situation in which this happens is if you are awaiting a method that doesn't do anything asynchronous. For example, the following method calls a remote server to retrieve a result, and it uses a very simple cache to avoid repeating those costly network calls if it already got the result.

Listing 5.7   Getting a value from a server with caching; not thread safe

```
// This method is not thread safe, keep reading for the correct version
private Dictionary<string,string> _cache = new();

public async Task<string> GetResult(string query)
{
    if(_cache.TryGetValue(query, out var cacheResult)        If the result is in the
        return cacheResult;                                  cache, return it.
    var http = new HttpClient();
    var result = await http.GetStringAsync(        Calls server to
       "https://example.com?"+query);              get the result
    _cache[query] = result;
    return result;                         Saves the result in the cache
}
```

This method first checks whether the query string is in the cache; if the value is already there, it returns it without doing asynchronous work. If not, the code performs an asynchronous HTTP call to get the result from the server. After the code gets the result from the server, it stores it in the cache.

The first time you call this method for a given query, it will return a `Task` that needs awaiting, but on subsequent calls for the same query, it will return a `Task` that has already completed because no asynchronous operation has happened. To demonstrate this, let's write some code that calls this method from a thread created using the `Thread` class.

Listing 5.8   Calling `GetResult` from a thread created by the `Thread` class

```
var thread = new Thread(()=>
{
    var result = await GetResult("my query");
```

```
    DoSomething(result);
});                                          On which thread
thread.Name = "Query thread";                will this run?
thread.Start();
```

We create a thread that calls the `GetResult` method from listing 5.7 and then does something with the result. One of the reasons for using the `Thread` class is the ability to change the thread properties. In this case, I changed the thread name. The thread name is just a string attached to the thread. We can view it in the threads window in Visual Studio to quickly identify the thread and understand its purpose. It has no effect on how the thread runs.

If this code happens to be the first time, we call `GetResult("my query")`. The thread will terminate because, if you remember from chapter 3, `await` registers code to run later and then returns control to the caller like a `return` statement, and later, when `DoSomething` runs, it will run on the thread pool and not in our named thread. In contrast, if the result for "my query" is already in the cache, the code will continue in our named thread as if the `await` wasn't there.

Now let's see how to make the `GetResult` method from listing 5.7 thread safe.

5.3   *Locks and async/await*

The problem with the `GetResult` from listing 5.7 is that it will most likely run in a multithread environment (by virtue of having an `await` statement), but it is not thread safe. It is not safe to access a `Dictionary<TKey,TValue>` (either to modify it or to read from it) while it is being modified by another thread. The code in listing 5.7 modifies the dictionary without protecting it from concurrent access. Fortunately, we learned about the `lock` statement in the previous chapter. Unfortunately, if we just add a lock around the entire method body, it won't compile.

Listing 5.9   Getting a value from a server with caching protected by a lock

```
private Dictionary<string,string> _cache = new();
private object _cacheLock = new();
public async Task<string> GetResult(string query)
{
    lock(_cacheLock)
    {
        if(_cache.TryGetValue(query, out var cacheResult)
          return cacheResult;
        var http = new HttpClient();
        var result =
          await http.GetStringAsync(                         Compiler error
          "https://example.com?"+query);
        _cache[query] = result;
    }
    return result;
}
```

This doesn't compile because we are not allowed to use `await` inside the code block of the `lock` statement. There are two reasons for this—one conceptual and one practical:

- The conceptual problem is that calling `await` frees up the thread and potentially runs other code, so we don't even know what code will run. This is a problem because, as we talked about in the previous chapter, running code you don't control while holding a lock can cause deadlocks.

- The practical problem is that the code after the `await` can run on a different thread, and the system used internally by the `lock` statement only works if you release the lock from the same thread that locked it.

How can we solve the problem? It's easy. Rearrange the code so that the `await` is outside the lock. We don't need to hold the lock while doing the HTTP call. We just need to protect the cache access before and after the call.

Listing 5.10 Releasing the lock while awaiting

```
private Dictionary<string,string> _cache = new();
private object _cacheLock = new();
public async Task<string> GetResult(string query)
{                                                          Lock while checking
    lock(_cacheLock)                          ◄───────┘   the cache
    {
        if(_cache.TryGetValue(query, out var cacheResult)
            return cacheResult;
    }
    var http = new HttpClient();
    var result = await http.GetStringAsync(        The async HTTP call
        "https://example.com?"+query);
    lock(_cacheLock)                          ◄──────┐
    {
        _cache[query] = result;               Lock while updating
    }                                         the cache
    return result;
}
```

In this code, we solved our compilation problem by moving the lock to protect only the cache access and not the whole method, but at the cost of releasing the lock in the middle of the method. In the hypothetical method that was completely protected by a lock, trying to run the method twice simultaneously would result in the sequence shown in figure 5.1.

One of the concurrent calls gets to run first. It tests the cache, does not find a cached result, makes the HTTP call, and updates the cache, all while inside the lock block. The other call will run second after the cache is updated and will return the cached value. But in the version of the method that actually compiles, we get the sequence as shown in figure 5.2.

One of the concurrent calls gets to run first, tests the cache, and does not find a cached result inside the first lock block. It will then release the lock. At this point, the

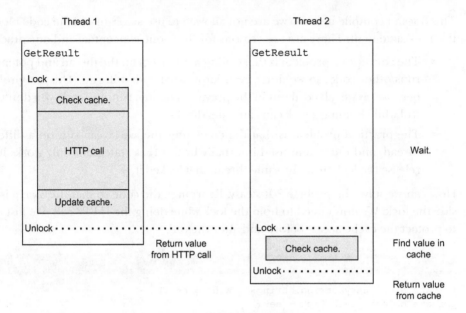

Figure 5.1 Sequence when locking the entire body of the method

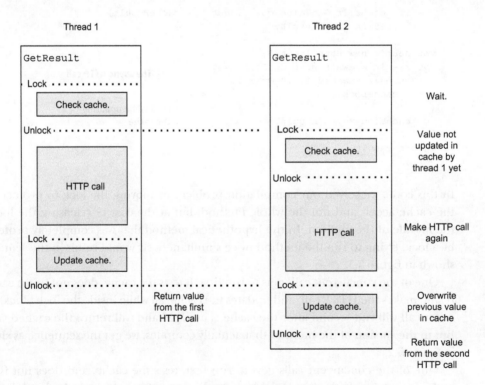

Figure 5.2 Sequences when locking only the parts that touch the dictionary

other call will get to run and also test the cache, also not finding a cached result because the first HTTP call hasn't finished yet. At some point, the first HTTP call will complete, and the first thread will update the cache. A bit later, the second HTTP call will complete, and the second thread will overwrite the value in the cache (that is why we use the operator [] and not Add to update the cache—Add would have thrown an exception).

This is a simple form of caching that works very well for any long process (both asynchronous and non-asynchronous) if that process always returns the same value for the same inputs, we are willing to accept the potential performance hit of running the long process multiple times before the first run completes, and the cache is populated. If we are not willing to run the long process multiple times, this way of writing the cache won't work.

5.4 UI threads

The rules for which thread runs the code after the await have a special case for the UI thread of native apps. Let's see why. To demonstrate the problem this solves, let's write an event handler for a WinForms button click that does some long calculation and updates the UI with the result (don't worry, you don't need to know WinForms to understand the code).

Listing 5.11   Long calculation that freezes the UI

```
private void MyButtonClick(object sender, EventArgs ea)
{
    int result = 0;
    result = LongCalculation();          ◀——| Freezes the UI
    MyLabel.Text = result.ToString();
}
```

In response to a button click, this code calls LongCalculation and then displays its result in a label control. However, we have a problem: the thread will be busy while running LongCalculation, so the application's UI will be frozen until the calculation is done. But we can fix it with multithreading.

Listing 5.12   Calculation that doesn't freeze the UI but throws an exception

```
private void MyButtonClick(object sender, EventArgs ea)
{
    Task.Run(()=>
    {
        int result = 0;
        result = LongCalculation();
        MyLabel.Text = result.ToString();    ◀——| Exception
    }
}
```

We just used Task.Run to move all the calculations to a background thread so the UI thread will be free to handle UI events, and the UI will not freeze. We solved the previous problem, but we created another one. Now when we try to display the result, we are doing it from the wrong thread, and this will throw an exception and crash the program instead of showing the result. We need a way to return to the UI thread after the background process completes. Luckily, `Task.Run` returns a `Task` we can use. Specifically, we can use it to know when the result is ready.

Listing 5.13   Running in the background from the UI code correctly

```
private async void MyButtonClick(object sender, EventArgs ea)
{
    int result = 0;
    await Task.Run(()=>
    {
        result = LongCalculation();          Runs in background;
                                             UI not frozen
    });
    MyLabel.Text = result.ToString();        Back in the UI thread
}
```

Here we used `Task.Run` to run the long calculation in the background and `await` to free up the UI thread until the calculation is complete. Because we called `await` in the UI thread, when the calculation is complete, our code runs in the UI thread again and so can safely set the text of the label.

Now you can see why `await Task.Run` is valuable when used to run a background process from the UI thread, unlike almost every other case where it is just wasteful (see the previous chapter).

Summary

- The tools for using asynchronous operations are also good for using multi-threaded operations.
- The high-performance code that benefits from multithreading is also likely to benefit from using asynchronous operations.
- In UI apps, when using `await` in the UI thread, the code after the `await` will also run in the UI thread.
- In all other cases, the code after `await` will run in the thread pool (except if someone used `SynchronizationContext` or `TaskFactory` to override this behavior).
- If the code calling `await` is running in the thread pool, the code after the `await` might run in a different thread in the thread pool.
- You can't use `await` inside the code block of a `lock` statement. The best solution is to rearrange your code and move the `await` outside of the `lock` block.

When to use
async/await

You probably won't find it surprising that I, the author of a book about multithreading and asynchronous programming, think that they are important, useful, and something that every software developer should know. However, it's important to acknowledge that they are not suitable for every situation, and if used inappropriately, they will make your software more complicated and create some bugs that are really difficult to find.

This chapter talks about the performance gains of multithreading and asynchronous programming, as well as how asynchronous programming can backfire sometimes and make our life miserable. For the rest of this chapter, I'm going to talk about the concept of asynchronous programming and the C# feature of `async/await` as if they were interchangeable—while they are different, `async/await` is by far the easiest way to do asynchronous programming in C#. If you want to use asynchronous programming in C#, you should use async/await, and conversely, if you don't use asynchronous programming, you will find async/await mostly useless.

First, let's quickly go over the scenarios where async/await truly shines.

6.1   Asynchronous benefits on servers

No one builds non-asynchronous single-threaded servers. Such a server would only be able to handle one client at a time, and the maximum load would be one, or maybe the number of connections we configure this server to have in a pending state before our software starts handling them, depending on how you measure load.

Single-threaded asynchronous servers are quite common, but almost exclusively in languages that don't support multithreading, such as node.js and Python. Well-written asynchronous servers can be quite efficient, especially if they are mostly IO bound and do very little processing (for example, serving static files or making database queries). But if you have to do any nontrivial processing, it is advantageous to be able to use that expensive multicore CPU inside the server.

To demonstrate the performance advantage of adding asynchronous techniques to a multithreaded server, we will build two nearly identical servers, a classic one-thread-per-request server you will find in network programming tutorials and an asynchronous server. Those will be simple servers serving a static file. They will wait for a network connection, and when a client connects, they will read a file from disk and send it to the client.

But before we can test our servers, we need a load-testing client. We'll make our client asynchronous too because it's more efficient (as we'll see from running the tests later in this chapter), and we want to minimize the effect of the client on performance so we can better measure the performance of the servers. Also, the client is a nice example of an asynchronous program.

In this program, we start by getting the number of connections from the command line, as this will let us easily run tests with different loads. We will then call Run-Test, which actually connects to the server. We will measure how long it takes until all instances of RunTest complete using the System.Diagnostics.Stopwatch class. We will also count the number of times we failed to connect because that will give us a clue about the maximum number of connections the server can handle.

Listing 6.1   Asynchronous load-testing client

```
using System.Diagnostics;
using System.Net;
using System.Net.Sockets;

int count = int.Parse(args[0]);
Console.WriteLine($"Running with {count} connections");

var tasks = new Task[count];
int failCount = 0;
var faileCountLock = new object();
```

```
Stopwatch sw = Stopwatch.StartNew();        ◄────┐ Starts stopwatch

for (int i = 0; i < count; ++i)
{
    tasks[i] = RunTest(i);          ◄──────┘ Runs individual test
}
Task.WaitAll(tasks);             ◄──────┘ Waits for all tests to complete
sw.Stop();                    ◄──────┐ Stops stopwatch

lock(faileCountLock)
    if (failCount > 0) Console.WriteLine($"{failCount} failures");
Console.WriteLine($"time: {sw.ElapsedMilliseconds}ms");

Task RunTest(int currentTask)
{
    return Task.Run(() =>       ◄──────┘ Runs tests in parallel
    {
        var rng = new Random(currentTask);
        await Task.Delay(rng.Next(2*count));
        using var clientSocket =
            new Socket(SocketType.Stream, ProtocolType.Tcp);
        try
        {
            await clientSocket.ConnectAsync(                ◄──── Connects to server
                new IPEndPoint(IPAddress.Loopback, 7777));
            var buffer = new byte[1024 * 1024];
            while (clientSocket.Connected)
            {
                int read = await clientSocket.ReceiveAsync(
                    buffer, SocketFlags.None);              ◄──── Reads data
                if (read == 0) break;
            }
        }
        catch
        {
            lock (faileCountLock)
                ++failCount;                 ◄──── Counts failures
        }
    });
}
```

Note that in the loop, when we called the RunTest method that actually connects to the server, we did not await it because we want all instances to run in parallel. If you remember from chapter 3, calling an async method does not run it in the background—the method runs normally until the first await.

Inside the RunTest method, we made sure everything ran in the background using Task.Run. Because RunTest only called Task.Run, we can just return the Task we got from Task.Run instead of making RunTest async and using await. This improves efficiency because the compiler doesn't have to do the async transformation and doesn't have to create and manage a Task for RunTest that would only mirror the Task returned from Task.Run.

Inside the test code, we add a small random delay before connecting, because in real-world scenarios, we don't have all clients trying to connect at exactly the same time, and then we connect to the server and read all the information the server sends. We use sockets because this is the lowest overhead network access technology we have access to.

Socket communication

We used socket communication in the load testing client and server. Because this isn't a book about networking, I won't go into details, but here's a very short explanation of the networking calls we used.

On the server, we first must use `Bind` to take control of a network port, and then we call `Listen` to signal we are waiting for connections from clients. `Accept` will actually wait for the next connection. When a client connects to the server, `Accept` will return a new socket representing the new connection. `AcceptAsync` is the asynchronous version of `Accept` that, instead of waiting, returns a `Task<Socket>` that will complete when a client connects.

On the client, we then call `ConnectAsync` to connect to the server. We use `IPAddress.Loopback` as the server address, that is, a special address that always contacts the current computer. It is better known as `localhost` in most networking tools.

`Send` sends data, and it returns after the data is handed over to the network stack inside the sending computer (not after the data is sent and not after the data is received by the other side; you can't know when those happen). `Send` returns the number of bytes that were actually accepted by the network stack on a modern computer, which will almost always be the entire buffer you are trying to send. `SendAsync` is the asynchronous version. It returns immediately and returns a `Task<int>` that will complete when `Send` would have returned.

`ReceiveAsync` reads data into an array we give it and returns a `Task<int>` with the number of bytes received. If that `Task`'s result is 0, it means no more data is available, and we assume the server closed the connection.

And finally, `Shutdown` shuts down the connection gracefully, including sending a message to the other side notifying it that the connection is now closed. It also clears all the resources held by the connection.

That was all the code for the test client. Now we need a server. Our first server will be the classic textbook one-thread-per-request server.

Listing 6.2   One-thread-per-request server

```
using System.Net;
using System.Net.Sockets;
var listenSocket = new Socket(SocketType.Stream, ProtocolType.Tcp);
listenSocket.Bind(new IPEndPoint(IPAddress.Any, 7777));
listenSocket.Listen(50);
```

```
while (true)
{
    var connection = listenSocket.Accept();          Handles connection
    var thread = new Thread(() =>                     in a new thread
    {
        using var file = new FileStream(@"somefile.bin",
            FileMode.Open, FileAccess.Read);
        var buffer = new byte[1024 * 1024];
        while (true)
        {
            int read = file.Read(buffer, 0, buffer.Length);
            if ((read) != 0)
            {                                          Sends file content
                connection.Send(                       to client
                  new ArraySegment<byte>(buffer, 0, read),
                  SocketFlags.None);
            }
            else
            {
                connection.Shutdown(SocketShutdown.Both);
                connection.Dispose();
                return;
            }
        }
    });
    thread.Start();                Don't forget to
}                                  start the thread.
```

That is our classic multithreaded non-asynchronous server. Now it's time to test it.

I've run the server and then the client with 50 connections. The test completed successfully in just under 8 seconds. I looked at the number of threads that the server spun up, and the server used 56 threads. Of those, 50 threads are the threads we created to handle the requests. Apart from this, there's also the main thread and five more background threads created by the .NET runtime.

I repeated the test with 100 connections. The test also completed successfully, this time in about 16 seconds. Looking at the threads of the server process, I've seen 106 threads: 100 worker threads instead of the 50 in the previous test, and the same number of overhead threads.

After that success, I doubled the number of connections to 200. This time, the test failed with 61 of the connections not being able to complete receiving the file (the time the test took to complete is irrelevant because it didn't do all the work). The failure is caused by the program being too slow to get to new connections because it is too busy handling the earlier connections. This will overwhelm the pending connection queue and make the network stack refuse to accept any more connections.

Now that we've seen the limits of the first server, let's write an asynchronous one. To keep everything as fair as possible, we will only change all the blocking and thread-management calls to their asynchronous version.

Listing 6.3   Asynchronous server

```
using System.Net;
using System.Net.Sockets;

var listenSocket = new Socket(SocketType.Stream, ProtocolType.Tcp);
listenSocket.Bind(new IPEndPoint(IPAddress.Any, 7777));
listenSocket.Listen(100);

while(true)
{
    var connection = await listenSocket.AcceptAsync();        ◄──  AcceptAsync instead
    Task.Run(async () =>                                        ◄──  of Accept
    {
        using var file = new FileStream("somefile.bin",              Task.Run instead
            FileMode.Open, FileAccess.Read);                         of new Thread
        var buffer = new byte[1024*1024];
        while (true)
        {
            int read = await file.ReadAsync(buffer,
                0, buffer.Length));
            if (read != 0)                                     ◄──  File.ReadAsync
            {                                                       instead of Read
                await connection.SendAsync(
                    new ArraySegment<byte>(buffer, 0, read),
                    SocketFlags.None);                         ◄──  SendAsync instead
            }                                                       of Send
            else
            {
                connection.Shutdown(SocketShutdown.Both);
                connection.Dispose();
                return;
            }
        }
    });
}
```

This code is identical to that in listing 6.2, except we changed `Accept` to `AcceptAsync`, `Send` to `SendAsync`, `new Thread` to `Task.Run`, and of course, we've added the `async` and `await` keywords where needed.

The difference between servers in run time is that `AcceptAsync`, `SendAsync`, and `ReadAsync` will all release the thread instead of blocking it. This means we need just a small number of threads to handle the same number of connections in parallel. Instead of creating a new thread for each connection, we can use the thread pool (that we use with `Task.Run`).

Now we can finally compare the performance of the asynchronous and non-asynchronous versions (see table 6.1). Like with the first server, I've first run the test with 50 connections. The test completed successfully in just under 8 seconds—the same as the non-asynchronous version. However, when looking at the number of threads, this version used only 27 threads instead of the 56 used by the non-asynchronous version (those are 20 thread pool threads doing all the work, the main thread, and six threads created by the framework or operating system—one more overhead thread compared to the non-asynchronous version).

After the first successful test, I doubled the number of connections to 100, and the test completed successfully in about 16 seconds—again the same as the non-asynchronous version. Looking at the threads, we see only 27 threads—the same number of threads as in the 50-connection run (compared to 106 for the non-asynchronous version).

I doubled the number of connections again to 200 (if you remember, at this point, the non-asynchronous version started failing), but the asynchronous version completed successfully again. Looking at the threads, we can again see only 27 threads.

I'll spare you all the boring details of the rest of the tests. On the poor laptop I'm writing this on, the non-asynchronous version managed to handle around 130 connections, while the asynchronous version got to just above 300.

Table 6.1 Differences between non-asynchronous and asynchronous connection handling

Number of connections	Non-asynchronous			Asynchronous		
	Failures	Time	No. of threads	Failures	Time	No. of threads
50	0	8389 ms	56	0	8534 ms	27
100	0	16538 ms	106	0	16310 ms	27
200	61	N/R	N/R	0	32132 ms	27
300	168	N/R	N/R	0	48229 ms	27
400	265	N/R	N/R	72	N/R	N/R

Those numbers might not look impressive, but it's unlikely that a real-world server will have to handle this number of connections in such a short time (an average of a connection every 2 ms) while also running Word and Visual Studio. In addition, it's important to note those numbers are very "noisy"; the exact number of connections will vary depending on your hardware, details of your application, what is running at the time, usage patterns, .NET version, operating system version, and more. But you should see that the asynchronous version consistently uses fewer resources and can handle greater loads. Basically, what we see here is that the asynchronous server could easily handle a double load of the non-asynchronous version while using a fraction of the resources.

These days, I expect most C# development to be done on the server, but there are also native and desktop applications.

6.2 Asynchronous benefits on native client applications

Asynchronous programming is also very useful in desktop applications. While desktop applications typically don't do tens of thousands of things simultaneously (due to the hardware limits of the person in front of the computer), they do need to keep the thread managing the UI available at all times so the UI does not become frozen.

For example, if we have a long calculation that is making our UI nonresponsive, the code making the UI nonresponsive is likely to look like this:

```
public void button1_Click(object sender, EventArgs args)
{
    LongCalculation();
    UpdateUIWithCalculationResults();
}
```

We need to move `LongCalculation` to a background thread, but we must keep `Update-UiWithCalculationResults` in the UI thread. Thus, we need to do something like

```
public void button1_Click(object sender, EventArgs args)
{
    Task.Run(()=>
    {
        LongCalculation();
        BeginInvoke(()=>
        {
            UpdateUIWithCalculationResults();
        });
    });
}
```

We used `Task.Run` to run code on a background thread and then `BeginInvoke` to run code back on the UI thread. With `async/await`, we can rely on `await` to get us back to the correct thread, and then we only need to write

```
public async void button1_Click(object sender, EventArgs args)
{
    await Task.Run(()=>
    {
        LongCalculation();
    });
    UpdateUIWithCalculationResults();
}
```

Those three advantages of `async/wait` (that asynchronous code can handle higher loads, that it uses less resources even at lower loads, and that it makes it easy to use multithreading in conjunction with code that has to run on a specific thread) are pretty significant and can easily outweigh all the downsides. But the downsides are there, and you should learn about them.

6.3   *The downside of async/await*

Up until now, we talked extensively about the benefits of asynchronous programming and why `async/await` makes it easy. But, like just about everything, asynchronous programming also has some significant downsides.

6.3.1 Asynchronous programming is contagious

Any code that calls asynchronous code must be asynchronous itself. If you are calling asynchronous code, you must use `await` or callbacks to get the results. This is often referred to as "asynchronous all the way down."

To illustrate this, we'll start with a program that takes a picture using the camera attached to the computer. The following code snippet is representative of what you need to do to use a camera using Windows' UWP API. To simplify the example, I removed all the parameters and the code that searches for a camera, but the structure of the code is correct:

```
public void TakeSinglePicture()
{
    cameraApi.AquireCamera();
    cameraApi.TakePicture();
    cameraApi.ReleaseCamera();
}
```

The code first acquires the camera, then uses it to take a picture, and finally frees the camera and any associated resources. Now let's say that in the newest version of our imaginary camera, API made the `TakePicture` method asynchronous. If we just switch to the new asynchronous version, we get

```
public void TakeSinglePicture()
{
    cameraApi.AquireCamera();
    cameraApi.TakePictureAsync();          ◄──── Error: Releases camera before
    cameraApi.ReleaseCamera();                   TakePictureAsync is complete
}
```

However, this is a logic error: taking the picture is asynchronous, so it will complete in the background, but in this example, we don't wait for it to complete, so we release the camera while it's still taking the picture. What we need to do is to somehow wait for the `TakePictureAsync` to complete before continuing. Luckily for us, `async/await` makes it easy, but it does require changing the `TakeSinglePicture` method to be `async` too:

```
public async Task TakeSinglePicture()     ◄──── Changes from void
{                                                to async Task
    cameraApi.AquireCamera();
    await cameraApi.TakePictureAsync();
    cameraApi.ReleaseCamera();
}
```

It looks like it was an easy fix, but now we need to do the same to the code that calls `TakeSinglePicture`, and the code that calls that, and the code that calls that, all the way back to the entry point of our code.

You may think that we can use `Task.Wait()` and `Task.Result` to bypass the problem by turning the asynchronous code into blocking code, but unless the asynchronous code was specifically designed to support this use case, this might cause weird bugs and deadlocks. Some APIs (like the UWP camera API this example is inspired by) will outright fail and throw an exception. And even if it does work, by turning the asynchronous call into a blocking call, we are eliminating any benefits of having an asynchronous method to begin with.

6.3.2   *Asynchronous programming has more edge cases*

Another problem is that by making your code asynchronous, you add new edge cases and failure modes that just don't exist in nonasynchronous single-threaded code. Let's take some straightforward WinForms code. We have a program that manages sources that provide values, and this specific code chooses a random source and displays the source name and the provided value (for extra realism, this code also uses the Win-Forms editor's autogenerated names):

```
private void button1_Click(object sender, EventArgs args)
{
    var source = GetRandomSource();
    label1.Text = source.Name;
    label2.Text = source.GetValue();
}
```

This code is pretty straightforward, and except for failures in the source itself, there's basically nothing that can go wrong. But if GetValue takes a long time to run, it will make the UI unresponsive. We can solve this problem by making GetValue and this method async. The changes to this method are minimal, and our UI will no longer become unresponsive:

```
private async void button1_Click(object sender, EventArgs args)
{
    var source = GetRandomSource();
    label1.Text = source.Name;
    label2.Text = await source.GetValue();
}
```

This may look like an easy fix, but we introduced a bug. Now that the UI is not frozen while GetValue is running, the user can click the button again, and if we are unlucky with timing, it's easy to encounter a situation where the code displays that the source value is from the first click, while the source name is from the second, showing the user incorrect information. To fix the problem, we need to at least disable the specific button while the code is running:

```
private async void button1_Click(object sender, EventArgs args)
{
    button1.Enabled=false;
    var source = GetRandomSource();
    label1.Text = source.Name;
```

```
        label2.Text = await source.GetValue();
        button1.Enabled=true;
}
```

Sometimes we might even have to disable all the UI controls in the application, depending on the details of the app and the dependencies between different UI elements.

6.3.3 *Multithreading has even more edge cases*

The reason that the previous demo is using WinForms is that WinForms makes it easy to write code that is asynchronous and not multithreaded. But nowadays, we mostly don't write desktop applications, and that innocent-looking `await` you added to the code might have made your code multithreaded without even knowing it.

Multithreading has many pitfalls, so many that there's an entire chapter about it later in the book.

6.3.4 *async/await is expensive*

`async`/`await` is expensive compared to single-threaded code. It adds a lot of compiler-generated code and mechanisms required to make the code asynchronous. It's important to remember that this is compared to single-threaded code, and in most cases, asynchronous code is more efficient than non-asynchronous multithreading, even with all the overhead.

For example, let's take this complete but useless C# program:

```
Thread.Sleep(1000);
```

What is the actual code that was generated for this program? To answer this question, we'll use IlSpy—a free program that can take a .NET-compiled program and reverse-engineer it back to source code form. Because IlSpy looks at the compiled code, it sees all the generated code we talked about in the previous chapters.

When we decompile our program, we get eight lines of code. One line is our original line of code, and seven lines wrap our code in a `Main` method and a class (because while the C# compiler lets you just write code, the runtime only supports code inside classes and methods), and that's it. If we take the equivalent asynchronous program

```
await Task.Delay(1000);
```

we get a whopping 63 lines of code. The compiler did what we talked about in chapter 3: it turned this line into a class implementing a state machine with two states (before and after the `await`) with all the associated code to manage it.

So after discussing all those advantages and drawbacks, when should we use `async`/`await`, and when should we avoid it?

6.4 *When to use async/await*

Here are some simple guidelines that can help you decide when to use `async`/`await` and when to opt for non-asynchronous blocking operations:

- If your code needs to manage a large number of connections simultaneously, use `async/await` whenever you can.

- If you are using an `async`-only API, use `async/await` whenever you use that API.

- If you are writing a native UI application, and you have a problem with the UI freezing, use `async/await` in the specific long-running code that makes the UI freeze.

- If your code creates a thread per request/item, and a significant part of the run time is I/O (for example, network or file access), consider using `async/await`.

- If you add code to a codebase that already uses `async/await` extensively, use `async/await` where it makes sense to you.

- If you add code to a codebase that does not use `async/await`, avoid `async/await` in the code as much as possible. If you decide to use `async/await` in the new code, consider refactoring at least the code that calls the new code to also use `async/await`.

- If you write code that only does one thing simultaneously, don't use `async/await`.

- And in all other cases, absolutely and without a doubt, consider the trade-offs and make your own judgement.

The list is sorted by importance, from the most important consideration to the least important one. If your project fits the conditions of more than one of the listed guidelines, give more weight to the earlier entry in the list. But in any such case, or if the best fit is that annoying last bullet, you really do need to weigh the trade-offs and decide for yourself. I wish I could give you straightforward rules that cover every possibility, but the truth is that software design is complicated, and there is no alternative to making difficult choices based on the specific details of your specific project—after all, if software development was that easy, you wouldn't have to read books about it.

Summary

- Asynchronous code can handle a much higher load than non-asynchronous code, while using significantly fewer resources.

- In cases where it's important to run code on a specific thread (like in native UI applications), `async/await` makes it easy to use multithreading and asynchronous calls.

- However, asynchronous code also has some disadvantages:
  - Code that calls asynchronous methods must be made asynchronous itself.
  - Asynchronous code has more failure modes than non-asynchronous single threaded code.
  - Multithreaded code has more failure modes than single-threaded code.
  - Asynchronous techniques require more code than non-asynchronous code (but it's still faster and more efficient than non-asynchronous multithreaded code).

- You should consider the trade-offs when you choose whether to use `async/await`.

Classic multithreading pitfalls and how to avoid them

7

This chapter covers

- Classic multithreading pitfalls: partial updates, deadlocks, race conditions, synchronization, and starvation
- Memory access reordering and the C# memory model
- Following simple rules to avoid the classic multithreading pitfalls

When transitioning from single-thread to multithreaded programming, it's important to recognize that multithreading introduces certain types of bugs that don't occur in single-threaded applications. Fortunately, by understanding these common bug categories, we can avoid them. This chapter contains straightforward guidelines you can follow to significantly reduce the likelihood of encountering such problems.

We'll start by examining the most fundamental multithreading side effect. In a single-threaded environment, each piece of code must complete its task before the next one can begin. However, when two pieces of code run simultaneously, one can access the data the other is still processing, leading to potential problems with incomplete work.

7.1 Partial updates

Partial updates happen when one thread updates some data, and then, in the middle of that update, another thread reads the data and sees a mix of the old and new values.

Sometimes, this problem is obvious, such as in

```
x = 5;
y = 7;
```

The first line sets x, and the second line sets y. There is a short time between those lines when x has already been set to 5, but y is still not 7. However, often, the problem is not so obvious. For example, the following method has only one assignment and still has a potential partial updates problem:

```
void SetGuid(Guid src)
{
    _myGuid = src;
}
```

In this case, Guid is a struct, and while C# lets us copy a struct with a single assignment operator, internally, the compiler will generate code to copy the members of the struct one by one, thereby making this equivalent to the first code snippet.

But things can get worse. In the following code, we assign a decimal variable. decimal is a basic type in .NET and not a struct. So how can this go wrong?

```
void SetPrice(decimal newPrice)
{
    _price = newPrice;
}
```

The problem here is that decimal is 128 bits long, and in 64-bit CPUs, memory access is done in 64-bit–long blocks. So assigning a decimal variable is split into two distinct memory operations, basically making it exactly as problematic as the other two examples.

However, decimal is kind of a weird basic type. It is a basic type in .NET, but it is not natively supported in any CPU architecture I know of, so let's talk about a basic type: long. The long type is a 64-bit integer and is the most natively supported type in 64-bit CPUs. We even said that memory access is done in 64-bit blocks, so assigning a single long value should be safe, right?

```
void SetIndex(long newIndex)
{
    _index = newIndex;
}
```

This assignment will most likely be atomic in 64-bit systems, but .NET still supports 32 bits, and if your code runs on a 32-bit computer (or a 32-bit operating system on a 64-bit CPU, or a 32-bit process running in a 64-bit OS—you get the point), then memory access is done in 32-bit blocks, and we're facing the exact same problem.

The solution to all those problems is using a locking mechanism of some sort, and the easiest locking mechanism in C# is the `lock` statement. For example, in the following listing, we use `lock` statements in every access to a member variable (both reads and writes), so we are completely safe from partial updates.

> **Listing 7.1 Using the `lock` statement**

```
private int _x;
private int _y;
private object _lock = new object();

public void SetXY(int newX, int newY)
{
    lock(_lock)                          ◄─── lock statement
    {                                         around writes
        _x = newX;
        _y = newY;
    }
}

public (int x, int y) GetXY()
{
    lock(_lock)                          ◄─── Another lock statement
    {                                         around reads
        return (_x,_y);
    }
}
```

`lock` statements prevent more than one thread from running code that is inside the lock's code block simultaneously. If a thread reaches the lock statement, and another thread is already running code in the code block of a `lock` statement, the first thread will stop and wait until the other thread exits the block.

The `lock` statement accepts a parameter that lets us have different locks for different variables. When reaching the `lock` statement, a thread will only wait if there is another thread inside a `lock` statement with the same parameter. In the following listing, we have two values named A and B. If you call both `GetA` and `GetB` at the same time from different threads, one of them will run immediately, and the other will wait until the first one exits the `lock` code block.

> **Listing 7.2 Single lock for two variables**

```
private object _lock = new object();
private int _a;
private int _b;
```

```
public int GetA()
{
    lock(_lock)
    {
        return _a;
    }
}

public int GetB()
{
    lock(_lock)
    {
        return _b;
    }
}
```

However, in the following example, because `GetA` uses `_lockA` and `GetB` uses `_lockB`, they can run simultaneously and will only wait if called at the same time as another piece of code that uses the `lock` statement with `_lockA` or `_lockB`, respectively.

Listing 7.3   Two locks for two variables

```
private object _lockA = new object();
private object _lockB = new object();
private int _a;
private int _b;

public int GetA()
{
    lock(_lockA)
    {
        return _a;
    }
}

public int GetB()
{
    lock(_lockB)
    {
        return _b;
    }
}
```

It is best practice to use a private member of type `object` (in .NET 9 and later, you can also use an object of type `Lock`) that is only used for the `lock` statement and not exposed anywhere outside your class. The reason for not exposing it outside your class is that you don't want to risk external code using the `lock` statement with the same object because it can mess up your locking strategy and cause deadlocks (as we will see later in this chapter). The reason for using an object of type `object` is that any other class that actually does something might use `lock(this)` (this is common in older code from before using a private `object` became a best practice), thereby messing with your locking strategy and causing a deadlock.

You may think that you can prevent partial updates by being careful about the order of assignments, but this doesn't work due to memory access reordering.

7.2 *Memory access reordering*

In modern hardware architectures, accessing memory is painstakingly slow relative to processing data inside the CPU, and different memory access patterns can have a significant effect on performance. To help with better utilization of the hardware, the compiler will change the order of operations in your code to reduce the number of memory access operations and make memory access faster.

The computer I'm using right now for writing this book has 2.666Mhz DDR4 memory. This type of memory has a latency of about 14.5 nanoseconds (that is, 0.0000000145 seconds), but the computer has 12 virtual cores running at 2.66Ghz, which means each clock cycle takes just 0.37 nanoseconds (to put this in perspective, by the time light travels from the screen to your eye, each CPU core has already finished around seven operations). A simple division tells us that each CPU core can perform roughly 40 operations in the time it takes to retrieve one value from memory, or considering the number of cores, the CPU can do up to 480 operations in the time it takes to get just one value from memory (the real world is, of course, more complicated, and the amount of work the CPU can do in a clock cycle can vary based on what exactly your code does; this is the maximum value). To put this in human terms, if the CPU could do one operation per second, then loading a single value from memory would take 8 minutes.

Let's see a simple example of how the compiler can improve performance by moving and eliminating memory access. Let's take a simple loop that increments a variable 100 times:

```
int counter=0;
for(int i;i<100;++i)
{
    ++counter;
}
```

Now let's translate this C# code into pseudo-machine code. In machine code, each statement or expression is divided into instructions. Instructions that do calculations can work only on internal variables inside the CPU itself. Those variables are called *registers*, and there are a limited number of them. Loading a value from memory into a register or storing the value of a register in memory are separate instructions. To keep the results short and readable, we're not going to translate the loop itself:

```
Set register to 0 (fast)
Store register to memory location "counter"(slow)
for(int i;i<100;++i)
{
    Load from memory location "counter" into register (slow)
```

```
        Increment value of register (fast)
        Store register to memory location "counter"(slow)
}
```

When this pseudo-code runs, it will execute 101 fast and 201 slow operations (ignoring the overhead of the for loop itself). Now let's move the memory access outside the loop:

```
Set register to 0 (fast)
Store register to memory location "counter" (slow)
Load from memory location "counter" into register (slow)
for(int i;i<100;++i)
{
    Increment value of register (fast)
}
Store register to memory location "counter" (slow)
```

This new pseudo-code will generate the exact same result but with only 4 slow operations compared to 201 in the direct translation. But we can do even better. At the beginning, we are storing a variable and then immediately loading it. We can skip those two operations and get

```
Set register to 0 (fast)
for(int i;i<100;++i)
{
    Increment value of register (fast)
}
Store register to memory location "counter" (slow)
```

And we're at 101 fast operations and only 1 slow operation, down from 101 fast and 201 slow operations in the direct translation. If we say that each fast operation takes 1 time unit and each slow operation takes 10 units, the direct translation would run in 2,111 time units, and the optimized version would only need 121 time units to do the same work, which is a 20-fold improvement!

The general rule is that the compiler is allowed to make any changes that do not alter the observed results of the code *in a single-threaded environment*; in our example, the only result is the value of the counter variable at the end of the loop. In a single-threaded environment, all our transformations did not change any observable results because there is no other thread that can observe the value of counter in the middle of our code. In a multithreading environment, the situation is different. In the original code, another thread could have seen counter gradually increasing, while in the optimized version, counter jumps directly to the final value.

Now let's take the same logic and apply it to another piece of code. We will try to prevent two threads from running the same block of code by using a flag that we set before starting and resetting after we finish. Before entering the code, we will check the value of this flag and stop if the flag is set:

```
if(_doingSomething) return;
_doingSomething = true;
// do something
_doingSomething = false;
```

But when we exit this code, the _doingSomething flag will always be false, which means that in a single-threaded environment, no one can ever observe the flag as true, so this code is equivalent to

```
if(_doingSomething) return;
// do something
_doingSomething = false;
```

The compiler is free to move or remove the code that sets the flag, thereby completely eliminating our homemade thread synchronization. And we can see that optimizing the code by making alterations that don't change the results of the code in a single-threaded environment might lead to results that are obviously nonsensical in a multithreaded environment.

Things are even worse than that because access to the computer's memory is so slow. CPUs have smaller and faster (but still slower than the CPU's processing) blocks of memory built into the CPU. This is called *cache memory*. The CPU tries to load data from the main memory into the cache before it is needed (in the background, while doing other things), so when the instruction to load a value from memory is executed, the value is already in the cache. Different cores may have their own cache memories.

All this together means code like

```
public void Init()
{
    _value = 7;
    _initialized = true;
}
```

does not guarantee that if _initialized is true, _value is set. The compiler is allowed to swap the order of those assignments, and even if it doesn't, your code might see an outdated uninitialized version of _value simply because it was already in the cache.

If you read just the first paragraph of the C# volatile keyword, you may get the (wrong) impression that it can solve this problem. However, the C# volatile semantics are so complicated that it doesn't guarantee access to the latest value and might cause even more problems. Basically, don't use volatile—it doesn't do what you think it does.

Obviously, it's impossible to write correct multithreaded code when any memory access can be moved or eliminated. That's why we have tools to limit the way the system moves memory access. There are operations that tell the system, "Don't move reads earlier than this." This is called *acquire semantics*, and all the operations that acquire a lock have this property. There are operations that tell the system "Don't move writes later than this point." This is called *release semantics*, and all the operations that release a lock have this property. Figure 7.1 shows how acquire and release semantics affect the system's ability to move memory operations.

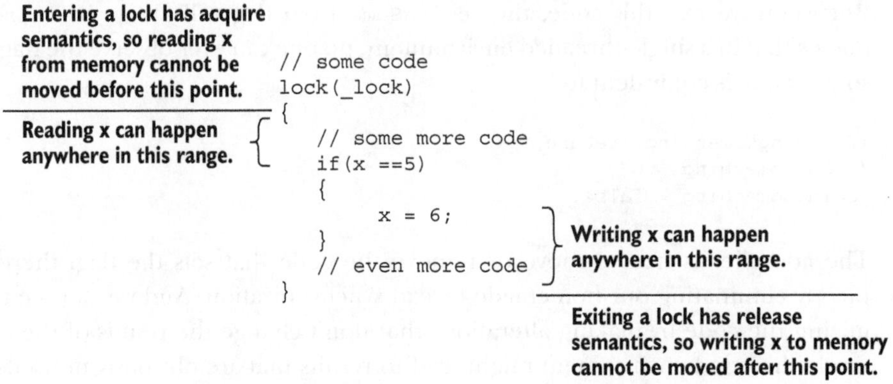

Entering a lock has acquire semantics, so reading x from memory cannot be moved before this point.

Reading x can happen anywhere in this range.

```
// some code
lock(_lock)
{
    // some more code
    if(x ==5)
    {
        x = 6;
    }
    // even more code
}
```

Writing x can happen anywhere in this range.

Exiting a lock has release semantics, so writing x to memory cannot be moved after this point.

Figure 7.1   Acquire and release semantics

There are also operations that prevent the compiler from moving both reads and writes across them in any direction. Those are called *memory barriers*. The set of rules of exactly how the compiler and CPU are allowed to move memory access, in addition to what operations have to acquire or release, or memory barrier semantics, is called the *memory model*.

The important fact about memory reordering and the C# memory model is that if you always use locks when accessing any data that is shared between threads, everything just works. Acquiring a lock has acquire semantics and will give you the most up-to-date values from memory. Releasing a lock has release semantics that will write all changes back to memory, so they are available for the next thread that enters the lock. This also brings us to the first rule for simple multithreading: always use a lock when accessing shared data.

And now that we know we absolutely must use locks, we can talk about the most common problem with locks—deadlocks.

7.3   *Deadlocks*

A deadlock, as we mentioned back in chapter 4, is a situation where a thread is stuck waiting for a resource that will never become available because of something that the same thread did. In the classic deadlock, one thread is holding resource A while waiting for resource B at the same time that another thread is holding resource B while waiting for resource A. At this point, both threads are stuck, each waiting for the other one to complete. And that will never happen because the other one is also stuck, as illustrated in figure 7.2.

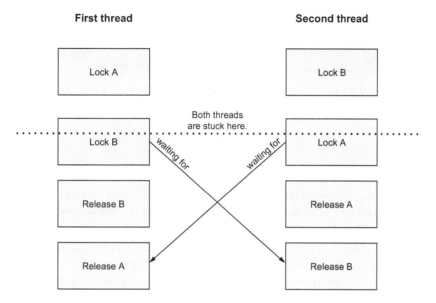

Figure 7.2 Simple deadlock between two threads

While this is the classic and most common deadlock, deadlocks can be and often are more complicated. There can be any number of threads in a ring (thread 1 holding A waiting for B, thread 2 holding B waiting for C, and thread 3 holding C waiting for A) or even a single thread waiting for itself, which can happen when a thread is holding a resource while trying to acquire that same resource again.

Some types of resources, like the lock statement or the Mutex class, will let the same thread acquire them more than once (and you must release them the same number of times as you acquired them). Those are called *recursive locks*. Other resources, like the Semaphore class or files in exclusive access mode, will consider each attempt to acquire them—even by the same thread—as a separate attempt and will block (causing a deadlock) or fail, depending on the actual resource.

Sometimes you can see the problem by just reading the code. For example, in the following code, there are two methods, and one acquires locks in the reverse order of the other one.

Listing 7.4 Code with a simple deadlock bug

```
public int Multiply()
{
    lock(_leftOperandLock)                      ◀──── lock left then right
    {
        lock(_rightOperandLock)
        {
            return _leftOperand * _rightOperand;
        }
```

```
        }
    }
    public int Add()
    {
        lock(_rightOperandLock)                    ◄──┘ lock right then left
        {
            lock(_leftOperandLock)
            {
                return _leftOperand * _rightOperand;
            }
        }
    }
```

In this example, the person who wrote the Multiply method locked the left operand first because you read math from left to right, and the person who wrote the Add method locked the right operand first because they are right-handed. In each of the methods, the order does not matter, but if you run the two methods simultaneously and get unlucky with your timing, you get a deadlock.

This brings us to the second rule for easy multithreading: always acquire the locks in the same order. The order itself doesn't matter. You can painstakingly analyze the code to deduce the optimal order, or you can always lock in alphabetical order—it doesn't matter. The point is to always lock in the same order. This is called *lock hierarchy.*

The following listing fixes the bug in the previous listing by defining a lock hierarchy—locks are acquired in math-reading order, so _leftOperandLock is always acquired before _rightOperandLock.

Listing 7.5   Solving the deadlock with lock hierarchy

```
public int Multiply()
{
    lock(_leftOperandLock)                         ◄──┘ lock left and then right
    {
        lock(_rightOperandLock)
        {
            return _leftOperand * _rightOperand;
        }
    }
}
public int Add()
{
    lock(_leftOperandLock)                         ◄──┘ Also lock left and then right
    {
        lock(_leftOperandLock)
        {
            return _leftOperand * _rightOperand;
        }
    }
}
```

It's important to always keep the same lock order, even if we think we have a good reason to change it. For example, let's add a Divide method, and because division by zero is not allowed in math, this method will check that the right operand is not zero before dividing the numbers (if the second number is zero, it will invoke the `DivideByZero` event). We might be tempted to lock and check the right operand before locking the left operand because if the right operand is zero, we don't need to access the left operand at all.

Listing 7.6 Causing a deadlock by trying to avoid unnecessary locking

```
public int Divide()
{
    lock(_rightOperandLock)              ◀━━━━┐ Locks right operand first (bug)
    {
        if(_rightOperand==0)
        {
            DivideByZeroEvent?.Invoke(this,EventArgs.Empty);
            return 0
        }
        lock(_leftOperandLock)           ◀━━━┐ Only locks left
        {                                     │ operand if needed
            return _leftOperand/_rightOperand;
        }
    }
}
```

In this code, while trying to avoid unnecessary locking, we broke the lock order by locking the right operand before the left operand, thereby introducing a potential deadlock. We must always keep the lock ordering, as in the following listing.

Listing 7.7 Correct lock order but with unnecessary locking

```
public int Divide()
{
    lock(_leftOperandLock)               ◀━━━┐ Locks left operand first,
    {                                         │ even if we don't need it
        lock(_rightOperandLock)
        {
            if(_rightOperand==0)
            {
                DivideByZeroEvent?.Invoke(this,EventArgs.Empty);
                return 0
            }
            return _leftOperand/_rightOperand;
        }
    }
}
```

In this listing, we kept the lock ordering, but if the right operand is zero, we acquire the left operand lock without using it. This is bad because we could delay another operation that needs the left operand. If we do not want to hold a lock we don't need (like in listing 7.7) and also do not want to risk getting into a deadlock (listing 7.6), then whenever we need to acquire a lock out of order, we have to release and reacquire locks as needed to keep the order intact—and deal with the possibility that things have changed because we released the lock. The correct way to write the previous listing while avoiding unnecessary locking is as follows.

Listing 7.8   Correct lock order without unnecessary locking

```
public int Divide()
{
    lock(_rightOperandLock)          ◄───┐ Locks only the
    {                                     │ right operand
        if(_rightOperand==0)
        {                                             If the right operand
            DivideByZeroEvent?.Invoke(this,EventArgs.Empty);   is zero, the method
            return 0                         ◄───┐    ends here.
        }
    }
    lock(_leftOperandLock)                Releases lock and reacquires
    {                                     in the correct order
        lock(_rightOperandLock)
        {
            if(_rightOperand==0)                     Rechecks
            {                                        condition because
                DivideByZeroEvent?.Invoke(this,EventArgs.Empty);   it could have
                return 0                             changed while the
            }                                        lock was released
            return _leftOperand/_rightOperand;
        }
    }
}
```

In this code, we acquired the right operand lock and handled the case where the right operand is zero. We then released the lock to acquire both locks in the correct order. Next, we had to handle the case where the right operand is zero again because it could have changed in that tiny period between when we released the right operand lock and when we acquired it again. And only then could we finally do the calculation and return the result.

But those were the easy cases. Sometimes, the deadlock is more difficult to find. The previous two listings, the ones with the correct locking order, still have a potential deadlock bug. Let's take a look at this code again (we'll use the shorter and simpler code from listing 7.7).

Listing 7.9   Correct lock ordering but still a potential deadlock

```
public int Divide()
{
    lock(_leftOperandLock)
    {
        lock(_rightOperandLock)
        {
```

```
        if(_rightOperand==0)
        {
            DivideByZero?.Invoke(this,EventArgs.Empty);
            return 0
        }
        return _leftOperand/_rightOperand;
    }
  }
}
```

This code acquires both locks in the correct order, and then, if the second operand is zero, it invokes the DivideByZero event; otherwise, it divides the first operand by the second and returns the result. The problem is in the call to the DivideByZero event handler. The code in that event is outside our control. It could be written by someone from a different organization and could do different things in different applications. This code could, for example, have locks of its own.

Listing 7.10   Code that triggers the deadlock bug in listing 7.9

```
public void SomeMethod()
{
    lock(_outputLock)
    {
        Console.WriteLine(_numbers.Add());
    }
}

Private void Numbers_DivideByZeroEvent(object sender, EventArgs ea)
{
    lock(_outputLock)
    {
        Console.WriteLine("Divide by zero");
    }
}
```

This code acquires a lock to call the Add method from listing 7.5 and acquires the same lock if it is called by the Divide method from listing 7.9. By itself, this code looks correct, just like our Divide method that also by itself looks correct.

But if one thread calls SomeMethod while another thread tries to use Divide to divide by zero, we might get a deadlock. The first thread acquires a lock on _output-Lock (in SomeMethod) first and then tries to acquire _leftOperandLock and _right-OperandLock (inside Add), while the second thread acquires _leftOperandLock and _rightOperandLock (inside Divide) and then tries to acquire _outputLock (in Numbers_DivideByZeroEvent).

The first thread is holding _outputLock while waiting for _leftOperandLock and _rightOperandLock, while the second thread is holding _leftOperandLock and _rightOperandLock while waiting for _outputLock. This is the exact same problem we've seen before, only now it's spread out over multiple files and is more difficult to debug.

This brings us to the third rule: never call code that is not under your control while holding a lock. When you need to call any code that is not under your control, you must call it after releasing the locks. For example, the current way to write the code from listing 7.9 is as follows.

Listing 7.11 Solving the event deadlock bug

```
public int Divide()
{
    lock(_leftOperandLock)
    {
        lock(_rightOperandLock)
        {
            if(_rightOperand!=0)               Reverses the condition
            {
                return _leftOperand/_rightOperand;   If the right operand is not
            }                                        zero, the method ends here.
        }
    }
    DivideByZero?.Invoke(this,EventArgs.Empty);   Calls the event
    return 0                                       outside the lock
}
```

With this version, instead of checking whether the right operand is zero and invoking the event, we check whether the right operand is not zero and perform the calculation. This means that if we get to the code at the end of the method, after we release all the locks, the operand is zero, and at this point, it's safe to invoke events.

You might think we can solve the problem by never holding more than one lock at the same time, but that can lead to race conditions.

7.4 Race conditions

A *race condition* is a situation where the result of the code is dependent on uncontrollable timing events. For example, let's say someone "fixed" the Add method from earlier to only hold one lock at a time, and that same developer also added a SetOperands method to set the two operands using the same locking strategy.

Listing 7.12 Holding just one lock at a time

```
public int Add()
{
    int leftCopy,rightCopy;
    lock(_leftOperandLock)
    {
        leftCopy = _leftOperand;
    }
    lock(_rightOperandLock)
    {
        rightCopy = _rightOperand;
    }
```

```
        return rightCopy + leftCopy;
}

public int SetOperands(int left, int right)
{
    lock(_leftOperandLock)
    {
        _leftOperand = left;
    }
    lock(_rightOperandLock)
    {
        _rightOperand = right;
    }
}
```

In the `Add` method, this code acquires a lock for both operands one at a time, copies the value to a local variable, and then immediately releases the lock. Likewise, in the `SetOperands` method, the code acquires one lock, sets the values, and then releases the lock before repeating this for the second operand. Because the code never tries to acquire a lock while holding another, it is completely deadlock proof. However, together, those two methods present a new problem. If those two methods are called at exactly the same time, we can't be sure in what order the four lock statements will execute. If we are lucky, the two blocks from the same thread will execute together—let's call those situations the "good options" (figure 7.3).

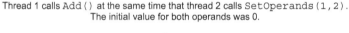

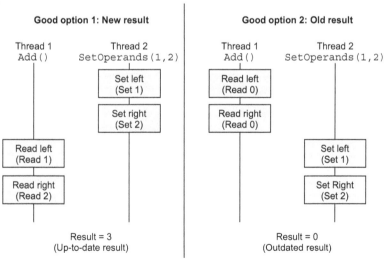

Figure 7.3   Locking operations ordering with correct results

In option 1, we get the correct result; we set the new values and then immediately use them. In option 2, we get an outdated result, but it's only outdated by less than a millisecond, so I'm going to call this a correct result too. Usually, it is okay to produce a result that is just a little bit outdated (the acceptable value of "a little bit" varies greatly between projects), and it's exceptionally difficult to guarantee that the results are never outdated because of physics. If you look out the window and see that there is light outside, it only tells you that the sun existed 8 minutes ago (it takes the light from the sun about 8 minutes to get to the earth). It's possible (but, very fortunately for us, extremely unlikely) that during the last 8 minutes, the sun exploded, and we just don't know it yet.

Because we can get different results based on tiny thread scheduling differences, this is already a race condition. But it gets worse because the operation from the two threads can interleave in any way. It's also possible the two operations from one thread will run between the operations from the other thread. Then we get the situation shown in figure 7.4.

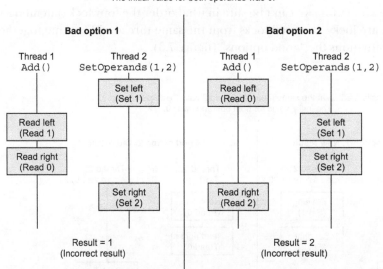

Figure 7.4 **Locking operations ordering with incorrect results**

In those two options, we clearly get incorrect results. What happened is that because we used separate short locks, we managed to get the results of a partial update despite using locks. This is due to the unfortunate fact that composing several thread-safe operations together does not necessarily result in a thread-safe operation—each of the two locks is individually thread safe, but two locks in succession are likely to introduce race conditions.

And this brings us to the fourth rule: you must hold locks for the entire operation. In case you are now screaming, "No, you must hold locks only for the absolute minimal duration!" you are right and should keep reading because holding a lock for too long is likely to cause synchronization.

7.5   *Synchronization*

Synchronization is the situation when operations happen sequentially and not in parallel. To demonstrate, let's revisit listing 4.11 for a quick recap of our adventure in chapter 4. We wrote a program that counts from 0 to 10 million. To count faster, we created two threads, each counting to five million. But then we didn't get the correct result because of the partial update problem that we talked about in chapter 4 and in more detail at the beginning of this chapter. After we fixed the problem by adding locks, we got the following.

Listing 7. 13   Multithreaded counting to 10 million

```
public void GetCorrectValue()
{
    int theValue = 0;
    object theLock = new Object();

    var threads = new Thread[2];
    for(int i=0;i<2;++i)
    {
        threads[i] = new Thread(()=>
        {
            for(int j=0;j<5000000;++j)
            {
                lock(theLock)
                {
                    ++theValue;
                }
            }
        });
        threads[i].Start();
    }

    foreach(var current in threads)
    {
        current.Join();
    }
    Console.WriteLine(theValue);
}
```

This code creates two threads, and each increments a value five million times. To avoid the partial updates problem we talked about at the beginning of this chapter, the code uses a lock while incrementing the value. But there is still a problem with this code. We use two threads so we can increase performance, but because of the locks around the actual incrementing operations, the incrementing itself happens sequentially and not in parallel. Figure 7.5 is a diagram showing how the code runs.

The first bar shows what would happen if we just built this code as a single-threaded program: we would have a single thread that starts, counts to 10 million, and then exits. The second two bars look like what we wanted to happen: two threads each doing half the work—finishing the same work in about half the time. The last two columns are what actually happened: we did divide the work between two threads, but whenever one of the threads is doing useful work, the other has to wait, resulting in no real parallelism and slower speed than the single-threaded case (because of thread synchronization overhead).

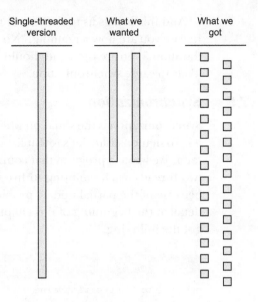

Figure 7.5   Not getting performance gains from multithreading due to synchronization

This brings us to the fifth rule for easy multithreading: to avoid synchronization, we need to hold locks for the shortest time possible, preferably just for the time it takes to access the shared resource, and not for the duration of the entire operation. You may think that this rule conflicts with the previous one, that "hold locks for the minimum duration, and not for an entire operation" somehow contradicts "hold locks for the entire operation." And if that is what you think, you are absolutely right. If our locks are too short, we risk race conditions, and if our locks are too long, we get synchronization.

We should try to aim for the happy middle ground where the locks are long enough to prevent race conditions but short enough to avoid synchronization. But this happy middle ground doesn't always exist. There are situations where reducing the lock's duration to anything that doesn't cause synchronization will cause race conditions. In those cases, you should remember that synchronization may hurt performance, but race conditions will produce incorrect and unexpected results. So prefer synchronization to race conditions.

Synchronization is bad if we intend to do things in parallel and synchronize them unintentionally, but it is actually desirable in some other cases. For example, in banking, it's generally frowned upon if money is transferred twice just because two wire transfer instructions arrived simultaneously. To avoid this situation, the international banking system (which is a highly decentralized digital distributed system run by thousands of different independent organizations around the world) synchronizes access to your bank account. Whenever you look at your bank account or credit card transaction history, you will see a sequence of transactions where each transaction ends before the next one begins.

Even if two credit card transactions started at the exact same time at two shops in different countries, and each shop used a different payment processor and a different bank (much more parallel than different threads in the same computer can ever be), the system will still synchronize them into an ordered sequence and act like one of them started after the other completed.

When you want to synchronize operations, you can use locks like in the counting example we've just seen, or you can use one of the other more advanced strategies we will discuss in the next chapter. In cases when synchronization is not desired, when parallel operations become sequential unintentionally and reduce the performance of the system, two or more threads need exclusive access to the same shared resource (usually a lock) to do their work, so the threads alternate between themselves. Each thread acquires the resource, does a little bit of work, and releases it. However, sometimes the one thread might hold that resource for a very long time, preventing another thread from working at all. This is called starvation.

7.6 *Starvation*

Starvation is the situation when one thread or a group of threads monopolizes access to some resource, never letting another thread or group of threads do any work. For example, the following program will create two threads, with each thread acquiring a lock and writing a character in the console (the first thread is a minus sign and the second thread is an x) in an infinite loop.

Listing 7.14 Starvation due to locking

```
using System.Diagnostics;

var theLock = new object();
var thread1 = new Thread(() =>
{
    lock(theLock)
    {
        while (true)
        {
          Console.Write("-");
          }
    }
});
thread1.Start();

var thread2 = new Thread(() =>
{
    while (true)
    {
        lock (theLock)
        {
            Console.Write("x");
        }
    }
});
thread2.Start();
```

The first thread acquires the lock before entering the loop and releases it after the loop (because it's an infinite loop, that means never), while the second thread acquires and releases the lock for each character written to the console. If we run this program, we will see it writes only minus signs because the first thread holds the lock for the duration of the program, and the second thread never gets a chance to acquire the lock.

This brings us back to the fifth rule: hold locks for the shortest duration possible. When we talked about this rule before, we said that holding a lock for too long can lead to synchronization. Now we see that in extreme cases, we get starvation when we hold a lock for way too long.

Starvation is also often caused by some threads monopolizing other resources—often the CPU. If you have high-priority threads that do not block, they might prevent lower-priority threads from running. For example, this program creates two threads: the first thread writes minus signs to the console in an infinite loop, and the second write x characters. I've bumped the second thread's priority to `AboveNormal` and made the whole program use just the first CPU core (because otherwise, we'd have to create enough threads to saturate all cores and risk making your computer unresponsive when you run this program). This is called *processor affinity*.

Listing 7.15   Starvation due to thread priority

```
using System.Diagnostics;

Process.GetCurrentProcess().ProcessorAffinity = new IntPtr(1);      ◄──────┐
                                                                    Runs only on the
var thread1 = new Thread(() =>                                      first CPU core
{
    while (true)
    {
        Console.Write("-");
    }
});
thread1.Start();

var thread2 = new Thread(() =>
{
    while (true)
    {
        Console.Write("x");
    }
});
thread2.Priority = ThreadPriority.AboveNormal;   ◄──────┘ Increases thread priority
thread2.Start();
```

If we run this program on Windows, we will get a screen full of x characters with a single minus thrown in every once in a while. This happens because of an anti-starvation mechanism Microsoft added to the Windows thread scheduler. On Linux, we will see roughly the same number of x characters and minuses because by default, Linux does not allow changing the thread priority.

Running this program on those two operating systems shows the two sides of the problem with changing the threads' or processes' priority and affinity:

- The Windows example showed us that even a tiny bump in a single thread's priority can significantly limit the processing power that other threads can use.

- The Linux example showed us that priority and affinity sometimes don't work like we expect them to.

And this gives us the final rule for easy multithreading: don't change priority or processor affinity.

Now that we have covered the most common multithreading mistakes and know how to avoid them, it's time to talk about different strategies for writing multithreaded code.

Summary

- The compiler and CPU may reorder or even eliminate memory access operation (as long as the result of your code doesn't change in a single-threaded environment). You can't count on other threads seeing the state that is consistent with the code you wrote unless you use locks. So always use a lock when accessing shared data.

- Always acquire the locks in the same order; that is called *lock hierarchy*.

- Never call code that is not under your control while holding a lock.

- Composing several thread-safe operations together rarely results in a thread-safe operation.

- Hold locks for entire operations.

- Hold locks for the shortest possible duration.

- The last two bullet points contradict each other. If you hold locks for too long, you might get synchronization. If your locks are not long enough, you get race conditions. Try to find something in the middle. If you can't do it, opt for longer locks because race conditions are typically worse than synchronization.

- Synchronization is sometimes desirable. There are operations you want to perform sequentially, even when most of the system can work in parallel.

- Don't change the thread's and processes' priority or processor affinity.

Part 2

Advanced uses of async/await and multithreading

Now that you know all about async/await and multithreading, it's time to dive deeper and understand that there's much more to multithreading and asynchronous programming than the await keyword and Task.Run.

Part 2 discusses different ways to process data in the background (chapter 8) and then explains how to cancel background processing (chapter 9). Next, you will learn how to build complex asynchronous components (chapter 10) and how to customize async/await's threading behavior (chapter 11). We'll have a short discussion about the complexity of exceptions in asynchronous programming (chapter 12) and talk about thread-safe collections (chapter 13). In the final chapter, we'll talk about how to write our own asynchronous collection-like components (chapter 14).

By the end of part 2 (and the book), you should have everything you need to understand and develop multithreaded applications. You will know how all the parts work and how to combine them.

Processing a sequence of items in the background

This chapter covers

- Processing items in parallel
- Performance characteristics of different ways to run code in parallel
- Processing items sequentially in the background
- Background processing of important jobs

There are three primary reasons for using multithreading in everyday applications. The first, and the most common, is when an application server needs to manage requests from multiple clients simultaneously. Typically, this is handled by the framework we use, such as ASP.NET, and it is beyond our control. The other two reasons for using multithreading are to finish processing sooner by performing parts of the processing in parallel and to push some tasks to be run later in the background. Both of these can significantly improve your program performance (or, at least, responsiveness and perceived performance). Let's begin by discussing the first reason: completing our processing faster.

8.1   *Processing items in parallel*

To demonstrate parallel processing, we will write the world's simplest mail merge software. Mail merge is a process that takes a mail template and creates an individual customized message for each recipient by replacing tokens in the template with information about the recipient.

Listing 8.1   World's simplest mail merge

```
void MailMerge(
    string from,
    string subject,
    string text,
    (string email,string name)[] recipients)
{
    var sender = new SmtpClient("smtp.example.com");
    foreach(var current in recipients)                        ◄─── Loops over all
    {                                                               recipients
        try
        {
            var message = new MailMessage();
            message.From = new MailAddress(from);
            message.Subject = subject;                         Replaces token
            message.To.Add(new MailAddress(current.email));    with value
            message.Body = text.Replace("{name}", current.name);  ◄─┘
            sender.Send(message);                              ◄──── Sends message
        }
        catch
        {
            LogFailure(current.email);
        }
    }
}
```

This method accepts the sender's e-mail address, the mail subject line, the e-mail template text, and a list of recipients' names and addresses. It then replaces the token {name} for each recipient with the recipient's name and sends the message. If there's an error, we just log it and continue (in real code, sending an e-mail can fail for many reasons, many of them being transient, so we'll usually have some retry logic).

Note that, due to constant abuse by spammers, e-mail service providers are very strict about enforcing their terms of use. If you need to send e-mail from your program, make sure you comply with your provider's terms and consider using a transactional e-mail–sending service instead of your regular e-mail service provider. I highly recommend you never write code that sends e-mail in a loop unless you've cleared it with your e-mail service provider.

If we use this method in a web application, we will quickly run into an issue: sending an e-mail is slow and can take up to several seconds per message. The typical timeout for a web request is 30 seconds. That means we will start timing out and not returning the results to the user at somewhere between 10 and 40 messages, and this is a really small number of messages for anything that requires automated mail merge.

8.1.1 *Processing items in parallel with the Thread class*

We don't have time to wait for all the messages to be sent sequentially, so the obvious solution is to just send all the messages in parallel. That way, we only have to wait for as long as it takes to send the longest message. To parallelize this, we can use any of the options we talked about in chapter 4, for example, the Thread class.

Listing 8.2 Mail merge with a thread per message

```
void MailMerge(
   string from,
   string subject,
   string text,
   (string email,string name)[] recipients)
{
   var processingThreads = new Thread[recipients.Length];
   for(int i=0;i< recipients.Length;++i)
   {
      processingThreads[i] = new Thread(()=>          ◄─── Sends each message
      {                                                    in its own thread
         try
         {
            var sender = new SmtpClient("smtp.example.com");
            var message = new MailMessage();
            message.From = new MailAddress(from);
            message.Subject = subject;
            message.To.Add(new MailAddress(recipients[i].email));
            message.Body = text.Replace("{name}", recipients[i].name);
            sender.Send(message);
         }
         catch
         {
            LogFailure(current.email);
         }
      });
      processingThreads[i].Start();
   }
   foreach(var current in processingThreads)      ◄─── Waits for all threads
   {                                                    to complete
      current.Join();
   }
}
```

In this code, we create a thread for every message we want to send, run all those threads in parallel, and then wait for all those threads to finish.

This can work just fine, but it does have a few weaknesses—most obviously, there is no limit to the number of threads this code can create. For example, if we have 10 simultaneous users, and each sends 100 messages (and those are not big numbers), this code is going to create 1,000 threads, and we don't know how that will affect our program's performance. But we can write a small program to estimate that effect.

Listing 8.3   Thread-per-message performance benchmark

```
for (int j = 0; j < 5; ++j)
{
    var sw = Stopwatch.StartNew();

    var threads = new Thread[1000];
    for (int i = 0; i < 1000; i++)
    {
        threads[i] = new Thread(() => Thread.Sleep(1000));
        threads[i].Start();
    }
    foreach (var current in threads)
        current.Join();
    sw.Stop();
    Console.WriteLine(sw.ElapsedMilliseconds);
}
```

This program creates 1,000 threads, where each thread just sleeps for 1 second. We repeat this five times just to make sure we didn't get an incorrect number because of something that isn't related to our code running simultaneously.

When running in release configuration and without a debugger, my laptop outputs between 1.1 and 1.2 seconds for each iteration. This shows us that with a modern computer, the overhead of 1,000 threads is acceptable for our program.

If we increase the number of threads to 10,000, the output will be just over 2 seconds, and if we go to 100,000 threads, it will be between 15 and 20 seconds, and that is in a program that does nothing. In a real server, things are likely to be worse because the server needs to actually do useful work and not just play around with threads, so please don't create a huge number of threads and assume the overhead will be negligible.

Note that if you run the program under a debugger, you will get significantly worst results because the debugger monitors thread creation and destruction. When I ran the program under a debugger, it took 14 seconds instead of just 1.2—be careful with your performance tests!

8.1.2   *Processing items in parallel with the thread pool*

Creating an arbitrarily large number of threads inside our server process seems bad. Fortunately for us, the thread pool was designed exactly for this situation. Let's move our message processing to the thread pool. We could use `ThreadPool.QueueUser-WorkItem` to run our code in the thread pool, but then we will have to write our own mechanism for detecting when all the threads finish sending the message. Writing this code isn't that difficult, but it's even easier to not write it, and Microsoft has been nice enough to include this feature in `Task.Run`.

Listing 8.4   Mail merge with each message processed in the thread pool

```
void MailMerge(
    string from,
    string subject,
```

```
        string text,
        (string email,string name)[] recipients)
{
    var processingTasks = new Task[recipients.Length];
    for(int i=0;i< recipients.Length;++i)
    {
        processingTasks[i] = Task.Run(()=>          ◄────── Uses Task.Run to run
        {                                                    in the thread pool
            try
            {
                var sender = new SmtpClient("smtp.example.com");
                var message = new MailMessage();
                message.From = new MailAddress(from);
                message.Subject = subject;
                message.To.Add(new MailAddress(recipients[i].email));
                message.Body = text.Replace("{name}", recipients[i].name);
                sender.Send(message);
            }
            catch
            {
                LogFailure(current.email);
            }
        });
    }
    Task.WaitAll(processingTasks);              ◄────── Waits for all threads
}                                                       to finish
```

This is almost the same code as that in listing 8.2. We just replaced new Thread with Task.Run, removed the call to Thread.Start, and changed the Join loop at the end to a single call to Task.WaitAll.

This will solve the problem of potentially creating a huge number of threads. The thread pool will limit the number of threads to a sane number the system can handle, and there's no longer any thread creation and destruction overhead. However, we do introduce the possibility of oversaturating the thread pool. If we try to send the same 1,000 messages from the previous example, we will tie up the thread pool until all those messages are sent, and in the meantime, anything else that uses the thread pool (like ASP.NET, for example) will have to wait. That means our server might stop processing web requests if we try to send too many messages.

Let's modify our performance test program and see how switching to the thread pool improves our performance.

Listing 8.5 Thread pool performance benchmark

```
for (int j = 0; j < 5; ++j)
{
    var sw = Stopwatch.StartNew();

    var tasks = new Task[1000];
    for (int i = 0; i < 1000; i++)
    {
        tasks[i] = Task.Run(() => Thread.Sleep(1000));
```

```
    }
    Task.WaitAll(tasks);
    sw.Stop();
    Console.WriteLine(sw.ElapsedMilliseconds);
}
```

Here we just took our code from listing 8.3 and made the same changes to switch from dedicated threads to the thread pool.

When I ran this performance test, I got 69 seconds for the first iteration, 37 for the second, 27 for the third, 23 for the fourth, and 20 seconds for the fifth and final iteration. What does this tell us? First, obviously, we completely overwhelmed the thread pool, and this version took 60 times longer to run compared to the previous one. But there's something weird in the results: each iteration is faster than the previous one. The reason for this is that the thread pool is always automatically optimizing the number of threads, and it will continue to become faster with every iteration. This means that while this is unacceptably slow for a program that does something that rarely requires a lot of threads, in a system that continuously uses a large number of threads, this will run very well.

If we are writing a program that we know will require a large number of thread pool threads, we can just tell the system about it and not wait for the automatic optimizations. If we tell the thread pool, we will require 1,000 worker threads by using the following two lines of code:

```
ThreadPool.GetMinThreads(out _, out var completionPortThreads);
ThreadPool.SetMinThreads(1000, completionPortThreads);
```

The first iteration will be just as fast as using the `Thread` class, and subsequent iterations will be faster, averaging 1,025 milliseconds on my computer.

8.1.3 *Asynchronously processing items in parallel*

In the previous example, we overwhelmed the thread pool because we added too many long-running work items, and there were not enough available threads to process them. In our case, the threads are long running because we used blocking operations. If those work items were doing calculations, the thread pool wouldn't have been slower than any other options because we would have been limited by the number of CPU cores. But our program is spending most of its time just waiting for the server and doing nothing. All those thread pool threads are just blocked and doing nothing. We already said that this is the exact situation where asynchronous techniques shine, so let's make our mail merge asynchronous.

> **Listing 8.6   Asynchronous mail merge using `Task.Run`**

```
void MailMerge(
    string from,
    string subject,
    string text,
```

```
    (string email,string name)[] recipients)
{
    var processingTasks = new Task[recipients.Length];
    for(int i=0;i< recipients.Length;++i)
    {
        processingTasks[i] = Task.Run(async ()=>          ◄─────┐ Added async
        {
            try
            {
                var sender = new SmtpClient("smtp.example.com");
                var message = new MailMessage();
                message.From = new MailAddress(from);
                message.Subject = subject;
                message.To.Add(new MailAddress(recipients[i].email));
                message.Body = text.Replace("{name}", recipients[i].name);
                await sender.SendMailAsync(message);          ◄─────┐
            }                                                       │ Added await
            catch
            {
                LogFailure(current.email);
            }
        });
    }
    Task.WaitAll(processingTasks);
}
```

We only had to make two tiny changes to the code from listing 6.4. We added the
async keyword and switched from using Send to SendMailAsync awaiting the result
(the async version of Send is called SendMailAsync and not SendAsync because that
name was already taken by an older method that predates async/await).

And, of course, we are also going to update our performance test to be asynchronous. This only requires changing ()=>Thread.Sleep(1000) to async ()=> await Task
.Delay(1000).

Listing 8.7 Asynchronous performance benchmark

```
for (int j = 0; j < 5; ++j)
{
    var sw = Stopwatch.StartNew();

    var tasks = new Task[1000];
    for (int i = 0; i < 1000; i++)
    {
        tasks[i] = Task.Run(async () => await Task.Delay(1000));
    }
    Task.WaitAll(tasks);
    sw.Stop();
    Console.WriteLine(sw.ElapsedMilliseconds);
}
```

How is this going to affect performance? Running this code, I got results between
1,001 and 1,017 *milliseconds*, which means that here, the thread pool has virtually no

overhead. It's important to remember that in the mail merge program, the code will spend most of its time waiting, but in our performance test, it spends *all* of its time waiting, so those results do not perfectly translate to the real program (I already said you need to be careful with your performance tests).

8.1.4   *The Parallel class*

In all the samples so far, we wrote a loop that created threads or added items to the thread pool. We then collected the `Thread` or `Task` objects so we could wait until they were all completed. This is tedious and exactly the kind of boilerplate code we don't like to write. Luckily, the .NET library has the `Parallel` class that can do all of this for us.

The `Parallel` class has four static methods:

- `Invoke`—Takes an array of delegates and executes all of them, potentially in parallel. This method returns after all the delegates finish running.
- `For`—Acts like a `for` loop, but iterations happen in parallel. It will return after all the iterations finish running.
- `ForEach`—Acts like a `foreach` loop, but iterations happen in parallel. It will return after all the iterations finish running.
- `ForEachAsync`—Similar to ForEach, but the loop body is an async method. It will return immediately and return a `Task` that will complete when all the iterations finish running.

In this chapter, we talk about `Parallel.ForEach` and `Parallel.ForEachAsync` because they are useful for our mail merge example. Internally, `Invoke` and `For` use the same code as ForEach. Here is what that code will look like if we use the `Parallel` class.

Listing 8.8   Mail merge with the `Parallel` class

```
void MailMerge(
    string from,
    string subject,
    string text,
    (string email,string name)[] recipients)
{
    var processingTasks = new Task[recipients.Length];
    Parallel.ForEach(recipients,
        (current,_) =>
        {
            try
            {
                var sender = new SmtpClient("smtp.example.com");
                var message = new MailMessage();
                message.From = new MailAddress(from);
                message.Subject = subject;
                message.To.Add(new MailAddress(current.email));
                message.Body = text.Replace("{name}", current.name);
                sender.Send(message);
            }
```

```
        catch
        {
            LogFailure(current.email);
        }
    }).Wait();
}
```

We can see that this code looks closer to the original nonmultithreaded code from listing 8.1. Basically, we swapped `foreach` for `Parallel.ForEach`, which made our code run in parallel. The ignored parameter is a cancellation token. We will talk about those in the next chapter.

The `Parallel` class also supports cancellation, setting a scheduler, and controlling the maximum number of items we process simultaneously. Cancellation is easy to implement ourselves, and we will talk about it in the next chapter. Using schedulers is also widely supported, and we will talk about it in chapter 11. Controlling the maximum number of items processed in parallel is not easily available elsewhere and is, surprisingly, the biggest pitfall of using the `Parallel` class. If we migrate our performance test to use `Parallel.ForEach`, we get the following.

> **Listing 8.9 `Parallel.ForEach` performance benchmark**

```
for (int j = 0; j < 5; ++j)
{
    var items = Enumerable.Range(0, 1000).ToArray();
    var sw = Stopwatch.StartNew();
    Parallel.ForEach(items,
        (item)=>Thread.Sleep(1000));
    sw.Stop();
    Console.WriteLine(sw.ElapsedMilliseconds);
}
```

In this version of the performance test, we create an array of numbers from 0 to 999 and use `Parallel.ForEach` to iterate over them, waiting 1 second for each item. I fully expected this code to have exactly the same performance characteristics as when using `Task.Run` in listing 8.5 because it's a different syntax for doing exactly the same thing. But when I ran it, I was surprised. The first iteration took 48 seconds—faster than the almost 70 seconds we got using `Task.Run`. However, all subsequent iterations took 31 seconds, which was faster than the first two iterations with `Task.Run` but slower than the third iteration and later.

What happened here is that contrary to what is explicitly written in the documentation, `Parallel.ForEach` by default limits the number of items processed in parallel, so it didn't quite overwhelm the thread pool as much as our `Task.Run` code did. However, because of that, the thread pool self-optimization didn't create so many threads in response to our unreasonable load, and that is why later iterations are slower with `Parallel.ForEach`.

We can test this theory by setting the max number of items to be processed in parallel to a high number, by replacing the `Parallel.ForEach` line with

```
Parallel.ForEach(items,
    new ParallelOptions { MaxDegreeOfParallelism = 1000 },
    (item)=>Thread.Sleep(1000));
```

If we do that and set `MaxDegreeOfParallelism` to the length of the list (thereby telling it to process everything simultaneously), we do get the exact same performance characteristics we got with `Task.Run` in listing 8.5. This is in contradiction to the official documentation that clearly states that the default behavior is to use all threads and that setting `MaxDegreeOfParallelism` can only reduce but never increase the number of threads used. This means `Parallel.ForEach` works very well for shorter collections and when the thread pool didn't have a chance to create a lot of threads already.

Note that whenever we find that the observed behavior contradicts the documented behavior, we have a problem. Obviously, we can't rely on the documented behavior because that's not how the system actually works. But it's also risky to rely on the observed behavior because any update can fix the bug and make the system work as documented. We need to either write code that works well with both the documented behavior and the observed behavior or take the risk that we will need to issue as emergency update if this ever gets fixed in the future.

In the previous examples that used `Task.Run`, we got an enormous speed boost when we switched from blocking operations (listings 8.4 and 8.5) to asynchronous operations (listings 8.6 and 8.7). Unfortunately, this doesn't happen when switching from `Parallel.ForEach` to its async/await compatible counterpart `Parallel.ForEachAsync`. Unlike `Parallel.ForEach`, the default `MaxDegreeOfParallelism` is, according to the documentation, the number of cores, and this is logically and theoretically the most efficient number of threads for asynchronous code. However, here is the problem: `Parallel.ForEachAsync` uses this as the number of items that are processed at the same time and not the number of threads.

For example, our code waits asynchronously for 1 second 1,000 times, and my laptop has 12 cores, so `Parallel.ForEachAsync` will start working on the first 12 items. They will all take exactly 1 second to complete, and it will then start working on the next 12, for a total run time of 84 seconds (because 1,000 divided by 12 rounded up is 84).

This behavior is problematic, and unless it's changed in a future version of .NET, I would recommend avoiding `Parallel.ForEachAsync` or, if you have to use it, choosing a good value for `MaxDegreeOfParallelism`.

For completeness, here is a version of the code with `Parallel.ForEachAsync`.

Listing 8.10   Asynchronous mail merge with the `Parallel` class

```
void MailMerge(
    string from,
    string subject,
    string text,
    (string email,string name)[] recipients)
{
    var processingTasks = new Task[recipients.Length];
```

```
Parallel.ForEachAsync(recipients,                    ◄───── Uses Parallel.ForEach
    new ParallelOptions {
        MaxDegreeOfParallelism= recipients.Length    ◄─── Don't forget
    },                                                     MaxDegreeOfParallelism.
    async (current,_) =>                        ◄────
    {                                                 Makes the loop body
        try                                           lambda async
        {
            var sender = new SmtpClient("smtp.example.com");
            var message = new MailMessage();
            message.From = new MailAddress(from);
            message.Subject = subject;
            message.To.Add(new MailAddress(current.email));
            message.Body = text.Replace("{name}", current.name);
            await sender.SendMailAsync(message);    ◄───
        }                                                 Awaits the async
        catch                                             version of Send
        {
            LogFailure(current.email);
        }                                  ┌── At the end, waits until
    }).Wait();                          ◄──┘   all threads complete
}
```

In this code, we made the following changes:

- We made the loop body lambda `async`, switched from `Send` to `SendMailAsync`, and awaited it (like the changes we made when we converted the `Task.Run` example to `async` in listing 8.6).
- We used `Task.Wait()` on the task returned from `Parallel.ForEachAsync` to wait until all the processing completes (in listing 8.6, we used `Task.WaitAll` for the same purpose).
- And finally, we set `MaxDegreeOfParallelism` to the length of the list. This is probably not the optimal value, but it's much better than the default.

8.2 Processing items sequentially in the background

In all the preceding examples, we always waited until all the messages were sent, but we didn't do anything with the result of the sending operation. We could have just moved the sending operation to a background thread and returned a reply to the user immediately without waiting for the result. Basically, if we don't wait for all the messages to be sent, we don't care how long it takes to send them.

If we just move the entire e-mail sending loop to a background thread, we solve all our performance problems. And, as a bonus, we are also nicer to our e-mail service provider because we don't try to send an unreasonable number of messages simultaneously.

8.2.1 Processing items sequentially in the background with the Thread class

Way back at the beginning of the chapter, when we started running things in parallel in listing 8.2, the first thing we used was the `Thread` class, so it only seems fitting that the first thing we use here is also the `Thread` class.

Listing 8.11   Moving the entire loop to a background thread

```
void MailMerge(
    string from,
    string subject,
    string text,
    (string email,string name) [] recipients)
{
    var processingThread = new Thread(()=>         ◄─────┘ Creates thread here
    {
        var sender = new SmtpClient("smtp.example.com");
        foreach(var current in recipients)
        {
            Try                                    ◄──────────┘ Instead of here
            {
                var message = new MailMessage();
                message.From = new MailAddress(from);
                message.Subject = subject;
                message.To.Add(new MailAddress(current.email));
                message.Body = text.Replace("{name}", current.name);
                sender.Send(message);
            }
            catch
            {
                LogFailure(current.email);
            }
        });
        processingThread.Start();
    }
}
```

This code is very similar to listing 8.2. Basically, the only difference is that we create our thread outside the loop instead of inside. We still don't have a limit on the number of threads this code can create, but it's now one per request and not one per message, so the performance implications should really be negligible.

It's important to note that if we try to exit our program normally (which never happens in ASP.NET applications but does happen in the command line and native UI apps), the program will not exit until the thread finishes sending all the messages. This can be an advantage or a disadvantage, depending on the situation. If we want the program to exit without waiting for the thread, we can set the thread's IsBackground property to true.

Spinning up a new thread to run some process in the background is useful in single-user applications, such as native UI apps, because we only need to run work in the background occasionally, and if the app does produce too many threads and overwhelms the CPU, the only person that suffers from the degraded performance is the user who made the app do it. This is not true for servers. In servers (and other multiuser scenarios), we tend to have to manage sustained load and prevent any single user from overwhelming the system. That is why in servers we need to better control the number of threads, and for this, we will usually use the work queue pattern.

8.2.2 *The work queue pattern and BlockingCollection*

If we no longer care about the time it takes to send the messages, it's better to just use one thread, or a small, fixed number of threads, that will send everything. This is called the *work queue pattern* and is implemented by creating a queue where every thread can add items to the queue, and there is a dedicated set of threads that processes all the items. Those threads just have a loop that reads the next item from the queue and handles it. To keep the code simple, we'll have just one processing thread in our example.

There are a surprisingly large number of tiny details you must get right when building this queue, but Microsoft has been nice enough to do most of the work for us with the `BlockingCollection<T>` class.

`BlockingCollection<T>` can be used in multiple ways. For example, it can be used as a thread-safe `List<T>`. But the interesting scenario is when we use `Blocking-Collection<T>` as a work queue. In this case, there are only three methods we care about:

- `Add`—Unsurprisingly, adds a new item to the end of the queue.
- `CompleteAdding`—Indicates that we will not add any more items, and the thread that is processing the items can exit after it finishes with items already in the queue.
- `GetConsumingEnumerable`—Returns an object that can be used with a `foreach` loop to iterate over all the items in the queue. If the queue is empty, `foreach` will block until another item is added to the queue or `CompleteAdding` is called. When `CompleteAdding` is called, the enumerable will indicate that there are no more items, and the `foreach` loop will exit.

Because this is a bit longer than the previous examples, I've written it as a class and not as a method. We'll start with the class definition, a record to store all the information we need to store in the queue and the `BlockingCollection` queue itself.

Listing 8.12 **Work queue with `BlockingCollection`**

```
public class MailMerger
{
    private record MailInfo(
        string from,
        string subject,
        string text,
        string email);

    BlockingCollection<MailInfo> _queue = new();
```

Now we need to create a thread to process the queue (the code to run in that thread is in the `BackgroundThread`):

```
public void Start()
{
```

```
    var thread = new Thread(BackgroundProc);
    thread.Start();
}
```

We will also add a way to close the background thread, so we should add a method that calls `CompleteAdding`; that will cause the background thread to exit once everything in the queue is already handled:

```
public void Stop()
{
    _queue.CompleteAdding();
}
```

Now we add a method that acts like the `MailMerge` from the previous code listings. In this example, this method only adds to the queue and doesn't actually send the mail. We run the mail merge loop here and add the individually prepared messages to the queue. Preparing the messages before inserting them into or after reading them from the queue doesn't make any difference here, but it is important for persistent queues (we will talk about that in just a few paragraphs):

```
public void MailMerge(
    string from,
    string subject,
    string text,
    (string email, string name)[] recipients)
{
    foreach(var current in recipients)
    {
        _queue.Add(new MailInfo(
            from,
            subject,
            text.Replace("{name}", current.name),
            current.email));
    }
}
```

And finally, the part you've all been waiting for—the code that runs in the background thread and sends this message. This method is somewhat anticlimactic. It just uses `foreach` on the return value of the `BlockingCollections.GetConsumingEnumerable` and sends the message:

```
private void BackgroundProc()
{
    var sender = new SmtpClient("smtp.example.com");
    foreach (var current in _queue.GetConsumingEnumerable())
    {
        try
        {
            var message = new MailMessage();
            message.From = new MailAddress(current.from);
```

```
        message.Subject = current.subject;
        message.To.Add(new MailAddress(current.email));
        message.Body = current.text.Replace("{name}", current.name);
        sender.Send(message);
      }
      catch
      {
        LogFailure(current.email);
      }
    }
  }
}
```

This is a complete work queue implementation of our mail merge feature. We used the `Thread` class because this is a very long-running thread—probably it will run for the entire run time of the program—and using the thread pool will just use up one of the thread pool threads without giving us the benefit of being able to reuse that thread for something else after we finish with it (because we will never finish with it). We saw back in chapter 5 that the `Thread` class doesn't work well with asynchronous code, but `BlockingCollection` is not asynchronous and does not have an asynchronous version that does not block. You will see how we can build one in chapter 10.

`BlockingCollection` is stored only in memory, meaning that if the process crashes or exists in any other way (including if the computer is rebooted or someone pulls the power cord), all unprocessed items that are still in the queue will be lost. This makes it suitable only for "best effort" work (the system will try to do the work, but it can fail unexpectedly for any reason). If you need a more reliable work queue implementation, you need to use persistent queues.

8.2.3 Processing important items with persistent queues

In all the previous samples, if the process crashes (and in some of them, even if the process exists normally), all the messages that are still pending would be lost. In many cases, this is unacceptable. For those situations, we will use persistent queues (also called durable queues).

Persistent queues are simply queues stored on disk and not in memory, so they are not lost if the program crashes. You can write your own queue by just storing the items in a database table, or you can use a separate queues server. If you are running in a cloud environment, your cloud provider probably has a cheap and easy-to-use queueing service you can use (AWS has SQS, and Azure has storage queues). Another common option is the free RabbitMQ server. However, how exactly to use Azure, AWS, or RabbitMQ is outside the scope of this book.

When you use a persistent queue, reading the next item from the queue and removing it can be separate operations. This is important because it lets us select what happens when there's a failure.

The first option is to remove the item from the queue after we finish processing it. In this case, if a stray cat pulls the power cord out of the wall right after we finish processing but before we remove the item, then after the computer restarts, we won't know that we already processed this item, and we will process it again. This is called "at-least-once delivery."

The second option is to remove the item from the queue before we process it. In this case, if a good dog wags his tail because he is happy to see us and hits the power switch after we remove the item from the queue but before we process it, then after the computer restarts, the item will not be in the queue and will never be processed. This is called "at-most-once delivery."

What we really want is to guarantee each item will be processed once and only once. This is called "exactly once delivery" and, unfortunately, is usually impossible. For example, in our mail merge program, even if our queue supports exactly one delivery, if we lose connection to the mail server after we finished sending the message but before we got the confirmation from the server, we have no way of knowing whether the message was sent. And that brings us back to the same situation where we must either risk sending the message twice or risk not sending it at all.

In almost all cases, losing data is worse than processing it twice, and we will opt for at least one delivery. But if we opt for at least one delivery, and there is a message in the queue that causes our program to crash, we will be stuck in an infinite loop where the program starts, reads the first item from the queue, crashes while trying to process it, restarts, and repeats the whole process. That is why it's important to have something that monitors the processing code for failure (this can be as simple as a try-catch block around the processing code), and if processing fails repeatedly for the same message, removes this message from the queue.

Messages that always cause code to crash are called *poison messages*, and the best practice is to save them somewhere (often in another persistent queue) so we can inspect the message and find the bug that caused the crash. Queues that store those messages, as well as messages that weren't processed for other reasons, are often referred to as *dead letter queues*.

It's also important to think about failures when we design the items that we store in the queue. This is why the last example in listing 8.12 prepared the messages before adding them to the queue. That way, a failure to process an item will only affect one message and not all the messages in our mail merge operation.

Summary

- If you have work items that are processed individually, you can make the processing finish faster by processing the items in parallel.
- You can use the Thread class for parallel processing. This works well but can be resource intensive.
- You can use the thread pool using ThreadPool.QueueUserWorkItem or Task.Run. The thread pool is efficient and self-tuning. But it can take a while to get to peak performance if you throw a lot of work at it all at once. This can be mitigated by

changing the thread pool settings if you know in advance the number of threads you will need.

- The thread pool is especially efficient with asynchronous code.
- The `Parallel` class is a simpler syntax to use the thread pool, but if you use it on a large collection, you should use a performance test to get a good value for `MaxDegreeOfParallelism`.
- If you don't care how much time it takes to finish the operation but just want to free the current thread, you can process work items sequentially in the background.
- You can use the `Thread` class or the thread pool. Both options will work.
- However, a better option is to use the work queue pattern, probably with the `BlockingCollection` class.
- If you don't want to lose data when the program crashes, you should use a persistent queue. You can implement one yourself using a database or use a dedicated queue solution such as RabbitMQ, AWS SQS, or Azure Storage Queues.
- With persistent queues, you should consider whether you want an "at-least-once delivery" or an "at-most-once delivery" system. You should also handle poison messages.

9

Canceling background tasks

In the previous chapter, we talked about how to run stuff in the background. In this chapter, we are going to talk about how to make it stop. The .NET library provides a standard mechanism for signaling that a background operation should end, which is called `CancellationToken`. The `CancellationToken` class is used consistently for (almost) all cancelable operations in the .NET library itself and in most third-party libraries.

9.1 Introducing CancellationToken

For this chapter, we need an example of a long-running operation we can cancel. So let's write a short program that will count for the longest time possible—forever.

Listing 9.1 Running a background thread forever

```
var thread = new Thread(BackgroundProc);
thread.Start();
Console.ReadKey();

void BackgroundProc()
{
    int i=0;
    while(true)
    {
        Console.WriteLine(i++);
    }
}
```

This program starts a thread that counts forever. It then waits for the user to press any key, and when the user finally does so, nothing happens. The program won't end until the second thread stops, and because we didn't write any mechanism that will make it stop, this program will continue forever, or more correctly, until you use some external means to terminate the entire process (you can use Task Manager, the `taskkill` command, debugger, hitting Ctrl-C, rebooting the entire machine, etc.)

The easiest way to make the program terminate is to mark the thread as a background thread. A process terminates when the last thread *that is not marked as a background thread* terminates, so we can make the program exit when the user hits a key by simply adding this line before the call to `Thread.Start`:

```
thread.IsBackground = true;
```

While this can solve the problem in some cases, it has two major drawbacks:

- You can only use this technique to cancel an operation when you completely exit your program.
- This will stop the background thread in the middle of whatever it was doing without giving it a chance to complete an operation or save its state (however, it will not leave your program in an unstable state because the program is no longer running).

The first problem alone already makes this unsuitable for most scenarios. When we look for a way to stop a thread without closing the entire program, we can see that the `Thread` class has a method named `Abort` that seems promising. However, that method still suffers from the second problem. It's actually worse than the previous example because terminating a thread in the middle of whatever it was doing can leave the entire program in an inconsistent state if that process, for instance, was allocating memory and updating the memory manager internal data structures.

This makes `Abort` too dangerous to use, so dangerous that Microsoft made it not work anymore in .NET Core and .NET 5 and later (it now just throws a `PlatformNot-SupportedException` on all platforms).

So with no built-in way to stop a thread, we have no choice but to code something ourselves. Let's start with the simplest possible option, just a flag that tells us when to stop the thread.

Listing 9.2   Using a flag to cancel a background thread

```
var thread = new Thread(BackgroundProc);
bool isCancellationRequested = false;        ◀────── Flags variable
thread.Start();
Console.ReadKey();
isCancellationRequested = true;              ◀────── Sets flag to exit

void BackgroundProc()
{
    int i=0;
    while(true)
    {
        if(isCancellationRequested) return;  ◀────── If a flag is set, exit.
        Console.WriteLine(i++);
    }
}
```

This option works in the current version of .NET and on current hardware, but it isn't guaranteed to work. As we talked about in chapter 7, high-end CPUs can have per-core cache, and when the main thread sets the flag, it actually updates its own core's cached version. Likewise, when the background thread checks the flag, it might be reading from a different core's cached version. On your development machine, you'll typically have a smaller number of cores and a lot of programs running (such as your development environment and a web browser), so the CPU cores need to switch threads and processes often, and this problem will never surface. But if you then run your software on a high-end server with many CPU cores and a smaller number of processes, the cancellation might be delayed because setting the flag won't propagate to the background thread until both cores flush their cache.

In addition, as also discussed chapter 7, the compiler is allowed to rewrite your code to make it run faster as long as it does not change the result of the code *in a single-threaded environment*. And in a single-threaded environment, the flag can't change during the loop, so it's safe to remove the check. This problem is especially difficult to debug because it tends to happen only in release builds (debug builds are usually not optimized) and can appear only in some environments; thus, the code can run perfectly fine on your development machine and fail on the production server. It can even run on the server today but start failing when something on the server is upgraded in the future.

The solution, as we've also seen in chapter 7, is to use locks when accessing the flag. There are better and faster ways to protect access to a single `bool` variable, but I'm going to use the `lock` statement for simplicity. Don't worry. We will change it to something better in the next code listing.

Listing 9.3 Using locks to protect the cancellation flag

```
var thread = new Thread(BackgroundProc);
var cancelLock = new object();
bool isCancellationRequested = false;
thread.Start();
Console.ReadKey();
lock(cancelLock)                        ◀──┐ Locks when
{                                          │ setting the flag
    isCancellationRequested = true;
}

void BackgroundProc()
{
    int i=0;
    while(true)
    {
        lock(cancelLock)                ◀──┐ Locks when
        {                                  │ checking the flag
            if(isCancellationRequested) return;
        }
        Console.WriteLine(i++);
    }
}
```

We just took the previous example and wrapped all access to the flag with `lock` statements. Now we have a thread-safe, future-proof way to cancel the background thread. But we created a maintainability problem. It's just a matter of time until some future team member forgets to add a lock and introduces a bug that only happens in production under load. This is bad, but fortunately for us, object-oriented programming already solved this problem more than 50 years ago (object-oriented programming was first formalized in 1967): just write a class that encapsulates the flag and controls all access to it.

Listing 9.4 Wrapping the cancel flag in a class

```
public class CancelFlag
{
    private bool _isCancellationRequested;
    private object _lock = new();

    public void Cancel()
    {
        lock(_lock)
        {
            _isCancellationRequested = true;
        }
    }

    public bool IsCancellationRequested
    {
        get
        {
```

```
            lock(_lock)
            {
                return _isCancellationRequested;
            }
        }
    }
}
```

This class is about as simple as it can get: there's a `Cancel` method that lets you set the cancel flag and an `IsCancellationRequested` property that lets you check the value of the cancel flag. Inside each of those, access to the flag is protected by locks.

Now we just need to change our program to use the `CancelFlag` class:

```
var thread = new Thread(BackgroundProc);
var shouldCancel = new CancelFlag();        ◀——— Creates cancel flag
thread.Start();
Console.ReadKey();
shouldCancel.Cancel();                      ◀——— Sets cancel flag

void BackgroundProc()
{
    int i=0;
    while(true)
    {
        if(shouldCancel. IsCancellationRequested) return;   ◀——— Checks cancel flag
        Console.WriteLine(i++);
    }
}
```

We have now created a thread-safe, future-proof, and maintainable way to cancel the background thread. But—and you know there has to be a but because we're not even close to the end of the chapter—the `CancelFlag` API has a weak point. It's easy to abuse the `CancelFlag` and use it in a way that will have unexpected effects on other parts of the program. For example, if we add another background thread that sometimes needs to cancel itself, it might look something like this:

```
void SomeOtherBackgroundProcesses()
{
    int i=0;
    while(true)
    {
        if(shouldCancel. IsCancellationRequested) return;
        Console.WriteLine(i++);
        if(i==7) shouldCancel.Cancel();     ◀——— Uses the cancel flag
                                                 to cancel itself
    }
}
```

This is a method similar to `BackgroundProc` from the previous example that has an additional exit condition, and the developer noticed there is already a way to stop the thread (our cancel flag), so they used it. This works for this method, but it also has the side effect of canceling the other background thread simply because both threads are using the same flag, which is probably not what we want. We can fix this shortcoming by splitting our `CancelFlag` into two classes: one lets us set the cancel flag, while the other can only check it. We then get an API that looks like

```
class CancelFlag
{
    public bool IsCancellationRequested {get;}
}
class CancelFlagSource
{
    public void Cancel();
    public CancelFlag Flag {get;}
}
```

We separated the interface into two classes: the `CancelFlagSource` creates and controls the `CancelFlag`, and the `CancelFlag` is only used for checking if cancellation was requested. Code that may cancel the operation uses `CancelFlagSource`, while code that can be canceled only gets the `CancelFlag`. If we change the program to use our new cancel flag interface, we get the following.

Listing 9.5 Using `CancelFlag` and `CancelFlagSource`

```
var thread = new Thread(BackgroundProc);
var cancelFlagSource = new CancellationFlagSource();      ◄──┘ Creates flag source
var shouldCancel = cancelFlagSource.Flag;        ◄───
thread.Start();                                          Gets flag for
Console.ReadKey();                                       background thread
cancelFlagSource.Cancel();           ◄───

                                          │ Sets flag
void BackgroundProc()
{
    int i=0;
    while(true)
    {
        if(shouldCancel. IsCancellationRequested) return;    ◄───  Checks whether
        Console.WriteLine(i++);                                    flag was set
    }
}
```

There is one important thing missing in this example: we didn't implement the `CancelFlagSource` and `CancelFlag` classes. But that's okay because Microsoft has done all the work and implemented the `CancellationToken` and `CancellationTokenSource` classes that do everything we talked about and more. Here's how our program looks when we use `CancellationToken`.

Listing 9.6 Using `CancellationToken`

```
var thread = new Thread(BackgroundProc);                        Creates
var cancelTokenSource = new CancellationTokenSource();   ◄──┘  CancellationTokenSource
```

```
var shouldCancel = cancelTokenSource.Token;          ◄─┐ Gets token for
thread.Start();                                         │ background thread
Console.ReadKey();
cancelTokenSource.Cancel();          ◄─┐ Cancels token

void BackgroundProc()
{
    int i=0;
    while(true)
    {
        if(shouldCancel. IsCancellationRequested) return;   ◄─┐ Checks whether
        Console.WriteLine(i++);                                │ token was canceled
    }
}
```

This is exactly the same code as in listing 9.5. I just replaced `CancelFlag` with `CancellationToken`.

It's important to remember that at its core, `CancellationToken` is just a `bool` variable (wrapped in a thread-safe, future-proof, abuse-resistant class); there's nothing magic about it, and it doesn't know by itself how to cancel anything. If our previous program did something time consuming in the loop instead of `Console.WriteLine` (for example, a calculation that takes 1 full minute), the thread cancellation will be delayed until that long calculation completes.

> **Listing 9.7 Delayed cancellation with a long operation**

```
var thread = new Thread(BackgroundProc);
var cancelTokenSource = new CancellationTokenSource();
var shouldCancel = cancelTokenSource.Token;
thread.Start();
Console.ReadKey();
cancelTokenSource.Cancel();

void BackgroundProc()
{
    int i=0;
    while(true)
    {
        if(shouldCancel.IsCancellationRequested) return;
        ACalculationThatTakesOneMinute();
        Console.WriteLine(i++);
    }
}

void ACalculationThatTakesOneMinute()
{
    var result = 0;
    var start = DateTime.UtcNow;
    while((DateTime.UtcNow - start).TotalMinutes < 1)      ◄─┐ For 1 full minute
    {
        result++;                      ◄─┐ Calculates stuff
    }
}
```

In this code, the background thread main loop, which does the cancellation checking, calls another long-running method. That means that we wait until this method returns before the next cancellation check, and because the time between cancellation checks is 1 minute in this example, it would take between 0 and 1 minute (or 30 seconds on average) from the time we cancel the background thread until it finally terminates.

If you do anything time-consuming inside the loop, you either have to accept that canceling may take a while or change the long-running code to check the `Cancellation-Token` periodically. For example, we can modify our previous example to check for cancellation inside `ACalculationThatTakesOneMinute`.

Listing 9.8 Using `CancellationToken` with a long operation

```
var thread = new Thread(BackgroundProc);
var cancelTokenSource = new CancellationTokenSource();
var shouldCancel = cancelTokenSource.Token;
thread.Start();
Console.ReadKey();
cancelTokenSource.Cancel();

void BackgroundProc()
{
    int i=0;
    while(true)
    {
        if(!ACalculationThatTakesOneMinute(cancelTokenSource.Token))
            return;
        Console.WriteLine(i++);
    }
}

bool ACalculationThatTakesOneMinute(CancellationToken shouldCancel)
{
    var start = DateTime.UtcNow;
    var result = 0;
    while((DateTime.UtcNow - start).TotalMinutes < 1)
    {
        if(shouldCancel.IsCancellationRequested)       ◀──────┐  Inner cancellation
            return false;                                     │  check
        result++;
    }
    return true;
}
```

In this code, we moved the cancellation check into the `ACalculationThatTakesOne-Minute` method and changed it to return `bool` where `true` means the method has completed successfully, and `false` means it has been canceled. This is required because most of the time in a real program, it's useful to know whether the calculation has completed, and we can use the result or not.

9.2   *Canceling using an exception*

In our previous examples, we moved the cancellation check into the ACalculation-ThatTakesOneMinute method. This means calling the method changed from the nice and straightforward

```
ACalculationThatTakesOneMinute();
```

to the more convoluted

```
if(!ACalculationThatTakesOneMinute()) return;
```

This doesn't only clutter our code with ifs, but it also creates a maintenance risk because someone in the future might change the code and forget to add the if. It also uses up the method return value, so if our method needs to return a value, we must use tuples or out parameters.

We can solve all those problems by using an exception. We can solve those problems if we replace our cancellation check that returns false on cancellation from

```
if(shouldCancel.IsCancellationRequested)
    return false;
```

with a very similar code that throws an exception

```
if(shouldCancel.IsCancellationRequested)
    throw new OperationCanceledException();
```

This is so common that Microsoft has provided a method that does just that, and the cancellation check becomes just

```
shouldCancel.ThrowIfCancellationRequested();
```

In all the examples so far, the background operations we wanted to cancel were some kind of calculations, a piece of code that is doing some work, and we can embed the cancellation check inside that work. But what if we want to cancel an operation that we can't insert cancellation checks into?

9.3   *Getting a callback when the caller cancels our operation*

Let's say we have a library that has its own cancellation system not based on CancellationToken. For example, it can have an interface that looks like

```
class MyCalculation
{
    void Start();
    void Cancel();
    event Action Complete;
}
```

With this interface, in normal operation, we call `Start` and wait for the `Complete` event. If we want to cancel an ongoing operation, we call the `Cancel` method. We sometimes find interfaces like those in code that calls remote servers, code that uses some non-.NET libraries, or more rarely, in third-party libraries written by someone who just for whatever reason doesn't like `CancellationToken`.

We can add another background thread that just repeatedly checks the status of `CancellationToken` and calls `MyCalculation.Cancel` when `IsCancellation-Requested` becomes `true`, but this is obviously wasteful. That is why `CancellationToken` can call a callback when it is canceled. That way, using the example `MyCalculation` class is easy:

```
void RunMyCalculation(CancellationToken cancel)
{
    var calc = new MyCaclulation();
    cancel.Register(()=>calc.Cancel());          ◀——— Registers a callback
    calc.Complete += CalcComplete();
    calc.Start();
}
```

The `CancellationToken.Register` method is used to register the callback we want the `CancellationToken` to call when it is canceled. Calling `Register` multiple times will cause all callbacks to run when the `CancellationToken` is canceled. Calling `Register` when the `CancellationToken` is already canceled will run the callback immediately. `Register` returns an object that can be used to unregister the callback.

Note that the callback you pass to `Register` will run in the thread calling `Cancel` and not in the background thread you are trying to cancel. Make sure everything you do in the callback is thread safe and avoid doing things that can interfere with the calling thread.

9.4 Implementing timeouts

A very common scenario for cancellation is the timeout, where we want to cancel an operation if it hasn't completed in a certain time. For example, if we tried to open a network connection, and we didn't get a reply, we can't tell if we didn't get an answer because the network packet hasn't reached us yet or because the computer we are trying to connect to doesn't exist. So we wait for a certain time, and if we don't get a reply by then, we assume that the reply will never arrive and cancel the operation.

It would have been easy to write code that starts a timer and calls the `Cancellation-TokenSource.Cancel` when the timer elapses, but because this is such a common scenario, `CancellationTokenSource` already has this feature built in with the `CancelAfter` method. The `CancelAfter` method has two overrides, one that accepts the number of milliseconds to wait

```
var cancelSource = new CancellationTokenSource();
cancelSource.CancelAfter(30000);
```

and the nicer, more modern override that accepts a `TimeSpan`:

```
var cancelSource = new CancellationTokenSource();
cancelSource.CancelAfter(TimeSpan.FromSeconds(30));
```

Both of those code snippets create a `CancellationToken` (accessible as `cancelSource.Token`) that will cancel automatically after 30 seconds.

Calling `CancelAfter` when the `CancellationToken` is already canceled does nothing. Calling `CancelAfter` a second time, before the `CancellationToken` is canceled, will reset the timer. Calling `CancelAfter(-1)` before the `CancellationToken` is canceled will cancel the timeout.

9.5   *Combining cancellation methods*

Sometimes you want to be able to cancel an operation for two completely different reasons. For example, let's say you have code that can be canceled by the user, and you want to add a timeout. For this example, we'll write code that performs an HTTP GET request to a server and returns the result as a string.

> **Listing 9.9   HTTP call that can be canceled by the user**

```
public async Task<string>
    GetTextFromServer(CancellationToken canceledByUser)
{
    using(var http = new HttpClient())
    {
        return await http.GetStringAsync("http://example.com",
            canceledByUser);
    }
}
```

This method accepts a `CancellationToken` called `canceledByUser`, unsurprisingly indicating that the operation was canceled by the user. We now want to add a timeout, but we can't because we need a `CancellationTokenSource`, and we only have a `CancellationToken`.

The `CancellationTokenSource.CreateLinkedTokenSource` static method can create a `CancellationTokenSource` from one or more `CancellationToken` objects. We can then use the new `CancellationTokenSource` to create a `CancellationToken` we control and add the timeout to it.

> **Listing 9.10   HTTP call that can be canceled by the user or a timeout**

```
public async Task<string>
    GetTextFromServer(CancellationToken canceledByUser)       Creates a
{                                                    CancellationTokenSource
    var combined = CancellationTokenSource.CreateLinkedTokenSource(   we control
        canceledByUser);                               ◄
    combined.CancelAfter(TimeSpan.FromSeconds(10));     ◄┐  Adds timeout
    using(var http = new HttpClient())
```

```
    {
        return await http.GetStringAsync("http://example.com",
            combined.Token);
    }
}
```
                                                          ◄─────────┐
                                                                    │ **Uses new token**

You can pass any number of `CancellationToken` objects to `CreateLinkedToken-Source`; the token controlled by the new `CancellationTokenSource` will be canceled automatically if any of them are canceled. You can then use the new `Cancellation-TokenSource` to add a timeout or manually cancel its token. Anything you do with the new `CancellationTokenSource` will not affect the tokens used to create it.

9.6   *Special cancellation tokens*

We spent this entire chapter talking about how to use a `CancellationToken` to cancel an operation; however, sometimes, while you don't need to be able to cancel an operation, the API you are using still requires a `CancellationToken`. In those cases, you can just pass `CancellationToken.None`. This will give you a `CancellationToken` that can never be canceled. Creating a `CancellationToken` with new `CancellationToken(false)` will give you the same results but is less readable.

In contrast, new `CancellationToken(true)` will create a `CancellationToken` that is already canceled. This doesn't make much sense in normal code but can be useful in unit tests.

Summary

- `CancellationToken` is the standard way to cancel operations in .NET.
- The `CancellationTokenSource` class is used to create and control `Cancellation-Token` objects.
- `CancellationTokenSource.Cancel` is used to cancel an operation, and `CancellationToken.IsCancellationRequired` is used to check whether it has been canceled.
- `CancellationToken` is just a flag. It doesn't know how to cancel anything by itself.
- You can use `CancellationToken.Register` to run a callback when it canceled.
- You can use `CancellationTokenSource.CancelAfter` to implement timeouts.
- `CancellationTokenSource.CreateLinkedTokenSource` lets you create a `CancellationTokenSource` you control from one or more existing `CancellationToken` objects.
- When you need to pass a `CancellationToken` that you never want to cancel, you can use `CancellationToken.None`.

Await your own events

This chapter covers

- Creating `Task` objects that you can control
- `TaskCompletionSource` and `TaskCompletionSource<T>`
- Completing a `Task` successfully and with an error, and canceling a `Task`
- Adapting old and nonstandard asynchronous APIs to use tasks
- Using `TaskCompletionSource` to implement asynchronous initialization
- Using `TaskCompletionSource` to implement asynchronous data structures

Until now, we've talked about using `async`/`await` to consume asynchronous APIs. In this chapter, we'll talk about writing your own asynchronous APIs. Common reasons for doing so include adapting a non-`Task`–based asynchronous API so that it can be used with `await`, using `await` to asynchronously wait for events that happen in your application, or creating an `async`/`await`-compatible thread-safe data structure, just to give a few examples. (Spoiler: We will write code for those examples later in this chapter.)

Way back in chapter 3, to understand how the `async` and `await` keywords work, we took a method that used `async`/`await` and transformed it into an equivalent method that produces exactly the same asynchronous operation but doesn't use `async` and `await`. Back then, we didn't know how to create `Task` objects, but we did know that `await` can be implemented by a callback (specifically, `Task.ContinueWith`). So instead of a `Task`, we used callbacks to report the operation results. To make this change, we modified the method signature from

```
Task<int> GetBitmapWidth(string path)
```

to

```
void GetBitmapWidth(string path,
    Action<int> setResult,
    Action<Exception> setException)
```

`ContinueWith`, the .NET built in callback mechanism, uses a single callback that must check the `Task` for information regarding the success and failure of the asynchronous operation. However, we choose to use separate `setResult` and `setException` callbacks for the success and failure cases because it's simpler. As a byproduct, by successfully simulating a `Task` with those two calls, we showed that those `setResult` and `setException` calls are (if we have a way to connect them to a `Task`) sufficient to control it.

Surprise! The .NET library has a class named `TaskCompletionSource<T>`. It can create `Task<T>` objects and has methods named `SetResult` and `SetException`. Let's see how you can use it.

10.1 *Introducing TaskCompletionSource*

The .NET library has the `TaskCompletionSource` class to create and control `Task` objects and the `TaskCompletionSource<T>` class to create and control `Task<T>` objects. `TaskCompletionSource` and `TaskCompletionSource<T>` are exactly the same, except that for `TaskCompletionSource` (without the `<T>`), the `SetResult` and `TrySetResult` methods do not accept any parameter and just complete the `Task` without setting a result (because unlike `Task<T>`, `Task` does not have a `Result` property). For the rest of this chapter, I'm going to write `TaskCompletionSource` instead of `TaskCompletionSource` or `TaskCompletionSource<T>`, but everything I write applies to both.

`TaskCompletionSource` has a property named `Task` that lets us get the `Task` created by it. Each `TaskCompletionSource` controls one `Task`, and reading the `Task` property multiple times will return the same `Task` object.

Initially, the `Task` status is `WaitingForActivation`, and the `Task`'s `IsCompleted`, `IsCompletedSuccessfully`, `IsCanceled`, and `IsFaulted` properties are all `false`. Using `await` on the new `Task` will asynchronously wait, and calling `Wait` or reading the

`Result` property will block until you use the `TaskCompletionSource` to complete the `Task`.

To demonstrate the various ways we can complete the `Task`, we'll use the following example code.

Listing 10.1 A template for `TaskCompletionSource` demo

```
public class TaskCompletionSourceDemo
{
    private Task<int> BackgroundWork()          ◄────── No async keyword
    {
        var tcs = new TaskCompletionSource<int>();
        Task.Run(() =>                          ◄────── Runs in another thread
        {
                                                ◄────── Task completion
        });                                            should happen here.
        return tcs.Task;                        ◄──────
    }                                                   Returns Task<int>,
    public async Task RunDemo()                         not int
    {
        var result = await BackgroundWork();    ◄────── Waits for Task to complete
        Console.WriteLine(result);
    }
}
```

Note that the `BackgroundWork` method is not marked as `async`. Because of this, the compiler doesn't transform it, we can't use `await` inside of it, and the compiler doesn't wrap the result in a `Task`, which means we are responsible for creating and returning the `Task<int>` ourselves. The `RunDemo` method (that is marked as `async`) just uses `await` to get the result produced by the `BackgroundWork` method.

`TaskCompletionSource` has three sets of methods we can use to complete the `Task`:

1 `SetResult` and `TrySetResult` will complete the `Task`, change its state to `RanTo-Completion`, and in case of a `Task<T>`, store the result value in the `Task<T>` object (accessible with `Task.Result` or `await`). After calling `SetResult` or `TrySet-Result`, both `IsCompleted` and `IsCompletedSuccessfully` will be true.

Listing 10.2 `TaskCompletionSource.TrySetResult` demo

```
public class TaskCompletionSourceDemo
{
    private Task<int> BackgroundWork()
    {
        var tcs = new TaskCompletionSource<int>();
        Task.Run(() =>
        {
            tcs.TrySetResult(7)                 ◄────── Completes Task
        });                                            successfully
        return tcs.Task;
    }
```

```
public async Task RunDemo()
{
    var result = await BackgroundWork();      ◄─────┘ Continues running
    Console.WriteLine(result);                ◄──────┐
}                                                    │ Prints 7
}
```

This example shows how to complete a `Task` successfully. Calling `TrySetResult` (or `SetResult`) causes the `await` to continue running.

2 `SetException` and `TrySetException` will complete the `Task`, change its state to `Faulted`, and store the exception or list of exceptions in the `Task`. The exception or list of exceptions will be wrapped in an `AggregateException` object and stored in the `Task.Exception` property. Using `await` on the task, reading the `Result` property, or calling `Wait()` will cause the `AggregateException` to be thrown. After calling `SetException` or `TrySetException`, `IsCompleted` and `IsFaulted` will be `true`.

Listing 10.3 `TaskCompletionSource.TrySetException` **demo**

```
public class TaskCompletionSourceDemo
{
    private Task<int> BackgroundWork()
    {
        var tcs = new TaskCompletionSource<int>();
        Task.Run(()=>
        {
            tcs.TrySetException(new Exception("oops"))   ◄─────┘ Completes Task
        });                                                      with error
        return tcs.Task;
    }

    public async Task RunDemo()
    {                                                    ┌ Throws
        var result = await BackgroundWork();      ◄──────┘ AggregateException
        Console.WriteLine(result);
    }
}
```

In this example, we used `TrySetException` to complete the `Task` and change it to a faulted state. The `await` operator will throw the exception.

3 `SetCanceled` and `TrySetCanceled` will complete the `Task`, change its state to `Canceled`, and optionally, store a cancellation token in the `Task`. Using `await` on the task, reading the `Result` property, or calling `Wait()` will throw a `TaskCanceledException`. If you pass a cancellation token to `TrySetCanceled`, it will be available in the `TaskCanceledException.CancellationToken` property. After calling `SetCanceled` or `TrySetCanceled`, the `IsCompleted` and `IsCanceled` properties will be `true`. Note that although `await` will throw an exception, the `Task`'s `IsFaulted` property will be `false`, and the `Exception` property will be `null`.

Listing 10.4   `TaskCompletionSource.TrySetCanceled` **demo**

```
public class TaskCompletionSourceDemo
{
    private Task<int> BackgroundWork()
    {
        var tcs = new TaskCompletionSource<int>();
        Task.Run(()=>
        {
            tcs.TrySetCanceled()
        });
        return tcs.Task;
    }

    public async Task RunDemo()
    {
        var result = await BackgroundWork();
        Console.WriteLine(result);
    }
}
```

Completes Task by
canceling it

Throws
TaskCanceledException

In this example, we used `TrySetCanceled` to cancel the `Task`, and `await` will throw a `TaskCanceledException` exception. There is no way to use `TaskCompletion-Source` to set the `Task`'s status to any of the other options (`WaitingToRun`, `Running`, or `WaitingForChildrenToComplete`).

The difference between the two variations of each method is that the older `SetXXX` will throw an exception if the `Task` is already complete, while the newer `TrySetXXX` will not (if the `Task` is already complete, the `Task` will not change, and any parameters passed to the method will be ignored). The `TrySetXXX` variation was added because the older methods can create a race condition in any situation where you might try to complete a task from two different threads (for example, one thread doing the work and another handling cancellation). It is best practice to use the newer `Try` versions of all the methods unless you specifically rely on them to throw an exception if the `Task` is already complete. The `Try` variant will return `true` if it completes the `Task` or `false` if the `Task` was already completed.

For example, in the following code snippet, simulating a situation when a different thread cancels the `Task` right before a calculation is complete, the call to `SetResult` will throw an exception:

```
var tcs = new TaskCompletionSource<int>();
tcs.SetCanceled();
tcs.SetResult(7);
```

Cancels the task

Throws an exception

While in this code snippet, the call to `TrySetResult` will be ignored without an exception (you can still know `TrySetResult` failed because it will return `false`):

```
var tcs = new TaskCompletionSource<int>();
tcs.TrySetCanceled();
tcs.TrySetResult(7);
```

Cancels the task

Ignored, returns false

10.2 *Choosing where continuations run*

The code that runs after the asynchronous operation (the code after the `await` or the callback passed to `ContinueWith`) is called a continuation. Calling any of the `Task-CompletionSource`'s methods that complete the `Task` will cause the continuation to run (obviously, that's the whole point), and `TaskCompletionSource` lets us decide whether the continuation can run immediately in the thread that called the `Task-CompletionSource` method.

If we allow the continuation to run immediately, it can run before `TrySetResult` (or any of the other methods) return. This means that `TrySetResult` can take an arbitrarily long time to run and that our code is in a state that can run arbitrary code that isn't under our control safely. For example, the following code has a potential deadlock bug:

```
lock(_valueLock)
{
    _taskSource.TrySetResult(_value);
}
```

In this code, we want to use a value protected by a lock as the result of a task, so we acquire the lock and call `TrySetResult` with the value. This might cause code that is not under our control (the `Task` continuation) to run while we are holding the lock, and if this code waits for something else that needs the same lock in another thread, we will have a deadlock.

One solution to this problem is to move the `TrySetResult` call outside of the `lock` block:

```
int copyOfValue;
lock(_valueLock)
{
    copyOfValue = _value;
}
_taskSource.TrySetResult(copyOfValue);
```

We can't use the _value variables outside of the `lock` block, but we can copy it to a local variable and pass the copy to `TrySetResult` outside the lock. This might still run code outside our control before `TrySetResult` returns, so we can't know how much time `TrySetResult` will take, but there is no longer a risk of a deadlock.

Another option is to make `TaskCompletionSource` run the code in another thread. We do this by using the `TaskCompletionSource` constructor that accepts a `TaskCreation-Options` parameter and passes the `TaskCreationOptions. RunContinuations-Asynchronously` value:

```
_taskSource = new TaskCompletionSource<int>(
    TaskCreationOptions. RunContinuationsAsynchronously);
```

We need to decide whether we want `TaskCompletionSource` to run the continuation code in another thread at the `TaskCompletionSource` construction time. We can't choose some `TrySetResult` to run the continuation in a background thread while others don't. For example, we can't make `TaskCompletionSource` use another thread only when we are holding a lock.

I used `TrySetResult` in this example, but everything here also applies to all the other methods that complete the `Task` (`SetResult`, `SetException`, `TrySetExcetion`, `SetCanceled`, and `TrySetCanceld`).

10.3   *Example: Waiting for initialization*

Let's start with a simple example: we'll write a class that requires a lengthy initialization process and performs this initialization in the background. Whenever you call a method of this class, if the initialization hasn't completed yet, that method will await until the initialization is complete.

Listing 10.5   Class with background initialization

```
public class RequiresInit
{
    private Task<int> _value;

    public RequiresInit ()
    {
        var tcs = new TaskCompletionSource<int>();
        _value = tcs.Task;                          ◀── Assigns the Task before
        Task.Run(()=>                                    leaving constructor
        {
            try
            {                                            Simulates long calculation
                Thread.Sleep(1000);            ◀──
                tcs.TrySetResult(7);          ◀── Sets the Task's result
            }
            catch(Exception ex)
            {
                tcs.TrySetException(ex);
            }
        });
    }
    public async Task<int> Add1()
    {
        var actualValue = await _value;     ◀── Waits for result if needed
        return actualValue+1;
    }
}
```

In this example, we wrote the `RequiresInit` class. This class has a lengthy initialization process and doesn't want to (or maybe can't) let the entire initialization process run in the constructor. So inside the constructor, we just kick off that initialization process in a background thread using `Task.Run` and return immediately. To access the result of the initialization process, we create a `Task<int>` using `TaskCompletionSource<int>` and assign it to the `value` field.

Obviously, the result of this lengthy initialization is probably a complex object, but for the sake of simplicity, it's an `int` in this example. Also, the initialization is just a call to `Thread.Sleep`, and the result of the initialization is always the number 7.

In the background thread, after calculating the result, we use `TrySetResult` to complete the task and assign the calculation result to it. In case of an exception during the calculation, we use `TrySetException` to propagate the exception into the task.

Later, when we want to use the initialization result, we read it using `await _value`, and if the calculation has already completed, this will return the value immediately. If the calculation hasn't completed yet, this will asynchronously wait until the result becomes available. Finally, if the calculation has failed, this will throw an exception telling us why.

Using a task like this combines getting the result, handling the signal that the result is available, and reporting initialization errors (if any) into a single operation. This not only saves us from typing but also makes the code more maintainable because future developers can't forget to wait for the value to become available or forget to check for errors.

10.4 *Example: Adapting old APIs*

Probably the most straightforward use of `TaskCompletionSource` is adapting asynchronous APIs that are incompatible with `await`. Fortunately, this is becoming quite rare because almost all the asynchronous operations in the .NET library and common third-party components have been adapted to use `Task` objects and are already compatible with `await`. Today, libraries that don't support `async/await` are mostly either wrappers for non-.NET code or written by authors who really hate `async/await`.

To demonstrate this, we'll use a pattern that was pretty common before `async /await`, an interface that lets you start an operation and get notified when it completes:

```
public interface IAsyncOperation
{
    void StartCalculation();
    event Action<int> CalculationComplete;
}
```

Adapting this using `TaskCompletionSource` is rather simple, as shown in the following listing.

Listing 10.6 Adapting non-standard asynchronous APIs

```
public Task<int> CallAsyncOperation()
{
    var tcs = new TaskCompletionSource<int>();
    _asyncOperation.CalculationComplete +=
        result => tcs.TrySetResult(result);
    _asyncOperation.StartCalculation();
    return tcs.Task;
}
```

We just created a `TaskCompletionSource`, subscribed to the asynchronous operation's nonstandard completion notification, and called `TrySetResult` when the asynchronous operation is completed.

10.5 Old-style asynchronous operations (BeginXXX, EndXXX)

The standard pattern for asynchronous operations in .NET before tasks and async/await was a pair of methods, one with the `Begin` prefix that returns an `IAsyncResult` object and one with the `End` prefix. All those methods in the .NET library and most third-party libraries already have a task-based alternative, so it's quite rare to have to deal with those. I'm only talking about this so you'll know what all of those `BeginXXX` and `EndXXX` methods are and what to do if you find yourself using an old library that wasn't adapted to using the `Task` class.

Before async/await, writing asynchronous code was difficult. The asynchronous methods were a rarely used option for only those who really needed them, so the asynchronous version was based on the non-asynchronous API version. The asynchronous version was always composed of two methods:

- The method with the `Begin` prefix accepts all the parameters of the non-async version and two additional parameters (called callback and state). This method starts the asynchronous operation. The `IAsyncResult` object returned by the `Begin` method represents the asynchronous operation and, like `Task` in the newer APIs, can be used to detect when the operation completes.

- The method with the `End` prefix takes the `IAsyncResult` object, cleans up any resources used by the asynchronous operation, and returns the result of the operation.

To demonstrate adapting this, we'll take an old-style asynchronous operation and adapt it to the new `Task`-based style. For this example, we will use the `Stream.Read` method:

```
int Read (byte[] buffer, int offset, int count);
```

And the old-style async version is composed of two methods—`Stream.BeginRead` and `Stream.EndRead`:

```
IAsyncResult BeginRead(
    byte[] buffer, int offset, int count,
    AsyncCallback? callback, object? state);
int EndRead (IAsyncResult asyncResult);
```

As you can guess, we can use the `callback` parameter and `TaskCompletionSource` just like we used in the previous example, but there's an easier way. The .NET library contains the `Task.Factory.FromAsync` method that creates a `Task` from this method pair. Here is how it is used:

```
public Task<int> MyReadAsync(
    Stream stream, byte[] buffer, int offset, int length)
```

```
{
    return Task.Factory.FromAsync(
        (callback,state)=>stream.BeginRead(
        buffer,0,buffer.Length,callback,state), stream.EndRead, null);
}
```

The `Task.Factory.FromAsync` method takes three parameters:

- *A lambda that calls the* `BeginXXX` *method*—If the `BeginXXX` method doesn't need any parameters other than callback and state, you can pass it without wrapping it in a lambda.
- *The* `EndXXX` *method*—If this method has `out` parameters, you need to wrap it in a lambda and extract the values of those parameters.
- *The* `state` *parameter*—It isn't required if you are using lambda, and it can always be `null`.

Because most APIs (including `Stream.Read`) already have a `Task`-based version, and newer APIs only have `Task`-based asynchronous versions without the `BeginXXX` and `EndXXX` methods, having to use this is quite rare. So we will not go into any more detail about it.

10.6 *Example: Asynchronous data structures*

In this example, we'll write an asynchronous queue. Our asynchronous queue, just like a normal queue, is a FIFO (first-in, first-out) collection with two operations: enqueue and dequeue. The enqueue operation adds an item to the queue, and the dequeue operation returns the first item in the queue if the queue isn't empty. What makes our `AsyncQueue` special is that if there are no items in the queue, the dequeue operation will return a `Task` that will complete when a new item is later added to the queue. That way, `await asyncQueue.Dequeue()` will return immediately with the next value if it's already in the queue or, if the queue is empty, asynchronously wait until the next value becomes available.

Our queue class is mostly two queues, one of data waiting to be processed and one of processors waiting for data. At least one of those queues must be empty at all times, because otherwise, we have missed an opportunity to match a data item with a processor.

> **Listing 10.7** `AsyncQueue`

```
public class AsyncQueue<T>
{

    private Queue<TaskCompletionSource<T>>
        _processorsWaitingForData = new();
    private Queue<T> _dataWaitingForProcessors  = new();
    private object _lock = new object();
```

When a processor becomes available, it calls `Dequeue`. If a data item is waiting, we deliver it to the processor immediately via a completed `Task` created with `Task.FromResult`.

If no data is available, we create a new TaskCompletionSource and return its Task, and we enqueue this TaskCompletionSource in the processorsWaitingForData queue:

```
public Task<T> Dequeue(CancellationToken cancellationToken)
{
    lock (_lock)
    {
        if (_dataWaitingForProcessors.Count > 0)
        {
            return Task.FromResult(_dataWaitingForProcessors.Dequeue());
        }
        var tcs = new TaskCompletionSource<T>(
            TaskCreationOptions.RunContinuationsAsynchronously);
        _processorsWaitingForData.Enqueue(tcs);
```

Because whoever uses our class is likely to expect Enqueue and Dequque operations to be fast, we create the TaskCompletionSource objects with the TaskCreationOptions .RunContinuationsAsynchronously flag. This means the code that processes the data will run in another thread and not inside our Enqueue and Dequeue methods. It also allows us to call TrySetResult and TryCancel while holding a lock.

We also let the processor pass a CancellationToken because we need a way for a processor to indicate it is no longer available. If this cancellation token becomes canceled, we cancel the processor's Task but leave the TaskCompletionSource in the queue because it's simpler that way.

As an optimization, we only register if the CancellationToken can be canceled. An example of a CancellationToken that can't be canceled is the dummy token returned by the CancellationToken.None property:

```
        if (cancellationToken.CanBeCanceled)
        {
            cancellationToken.Register(() =>
            {
                tcs.TrySetCanceled(cancellationToken);
            });
        }
        return tcs.Task;
    }
}
```

When data is added to the queue by calling Enqueue, we try to deliver it to the first available processor, dequeue the first TaskCompletionSource from _processorsWaiting-ForData queue, and call TrySetResult. If TrySetResult returns true, we successfully completed the Task and sent the data item to the processor, so we can return.

If TrySetResult returns false, it means the Task has already completed, that is, it was canceled because the TaskCompletionSource is fully under our control, and the cancellation code is the only code we wrote that completes a task without first removing its TaskCompletionSource from the queue. In this case, we just move to the next processor.

As an optimization, we only handle the cancellation case if the `Cancellation-Token` can be canceled (for example, the `CancellationToken.None` property returns a dummy token that is never canceled):

```
public void Enqueue(T value)
{
    lock (_lock)
    {
        while (_processorsWaitingForData.Count > 0)
        {
            var nextDequqer = _processorsWaitingForData.Dequeue();
            if(nextDequqer.TrySetResult(value))
            {
                return;
            }
        }
```

If the processor queue was empty or all the entries in the queue were canceled, we enqueue the data in the _dataWaitingForProcessors queue, where it will wait until someone calls Dequeue:

```
        _dataWaitingForProcessors .Enqueue(value);
    }
}

}
```

Summary

- You can use `TaskCompletionSource` to create `Task` objects and `TaskCompletion-Source<T>` to create `Task<T>` objects.

- `TaskCompletionSource<T>.TrySetResult` is used to complete a `Task<T>` successfully and set the `Task`'s `Result` property.

- `TaskCompletionSource.TrySetResult` is used to complete a `Task` successfully. It doesn't set the result because unlike `Task<T>`, `Task` doesn't have a result.

- `TaskCompletionSource<T>.TrySetException` and `TaskCompletionSource.TrySetException` are used to complete the `Task`, change its status to `faulted`, and store one or more exceptions in the `Task<T>` or `Task`.

- `TaskCompletionSource<T>.TrySetCanceled` and `TaskCompletionSource.TrySetCanceled` are used to complete the `Task` and change its state to `Canceled`.

- While using `await`, calling `Wait` or reading the `Result` property of a canceled `Task` will throw a `TaskCanceledException`. The `Task`'s `Exception` property will be `null`. You can use the `Task`'s `Status` or `IsCanceled` properties to check whether a `Task` is canceled.

- All the `TrySetXXX` methods mentioned previously will return `true` if they completed the `Task` or `false` if the `Task` is already completed.

- There's also a `SetXXX` variant that throws an exception if the `Task` is already completed. It's best practice to use the `TrySetXXX` variant because the older `SetXXX` might cause a race condition in some multithreading scenarios.

- By default, continuations (code after the `await` or in `ContinueWith` callbacks) can run immediately inside the `TrySetXXX` or `SetXXX` call, which makes it unsafe to call them while holding a lock. To make it run in another thread (and so make it safe to call them while holding a lock), pass the `TaskCreationOptions.RunContinuationsAsynchronously` flag to the `TaskCompletionSource` constructor.

- If you need to use an old-style asynchronous operation (`BeginXXX`, `EndXXX`) with tasks, use the `Task.Factory.FromAsync` method.

Controlling on which thread your asynchronous code runs

This chapter covers

- The `await` threading behavior
- Understanding `SynchronizationContext`
- When to use `ConfigureAwait`
- Using `Task.Yield`
- The basics of `TaskScheduler`

Most of the time, you don't care on which thread your code runs. If you calculate something, your calculation will produce the exact same result regardless of the thread or CPU core it runs on. But some operations do work differently, depending on the thread that runs them, the most common being

- *GUI*—In WinForms and in WPF, all UI elements can only be accessed by the same thread that created them. Typically, all UI elements are created and accessed by just one thread (called the *UI thread*), and it is usually the process' main thread.
- *ASP.NET classic*—In ASP.NET classic, which is an older version used in .NET Framework 4.8 and earlier, the `HttpContext.Current` property will

147

only return the correct value if called from the right thread. (For anyone who doesn't have experience with ASP.NET classic, access to `HttpContext.Current` is required in many common scenarios.)

- *COM*—The rules about threads and COM components are complex, and we won't cover them in this book. But accessing a COM component from the wrong thread might fail or incur a significant performance penalty, depending on the circumstances.

- *Blocking operations*—Blocking operations can lock up the thread for a potentially long time. Blocking different threads can have different effects on the system; for example, blocking the UI thread will cause the UI to freeze, blocking a lot of thread pool threads can prevent the servers from accepting connections and continuing asynchronous operations, and so forth.

- *Potentially any other piece of third-party code*—Any code you use can have restrictions regarding its use. Newer .NET code tends to be compatible with `async`/`await` and agnostic about which thread runs it. But older code and native code can have stricter rules about threads.

In previous chapters, we talked about code after an `await` and the callbacks passed to `ContinueWith` as interchangeable. However, everything in this chapter applies only to `await`. Back in chapter 3, we implemented `await` using `ContinueWith`, and I said the code generated by the compiler is more complicated. This is what I meant: all the complexity in this chapter is implemented by code generated by the compiler for the `await` operator.

11.1 *await-threading behavior*

Basically, the rules for where the code after `await` runs are

- In UI apps (WinForms and WPF), if you are using `await` in a UI thread and don't use `ConfigureAwait` (we will talk about it later in this chapter), the code after the `await` will run in the same thread.

- In ASP.NET classic (not ASP.NET Core), if you are using `await` in a thread that is processing a web request, and you don't use `ConfigureAwait`, the code after the `await` will run in the same thread.

- In all other cases, the code after the `await` will run in the thread pool.

This list is short, simple, and easy to remember, and it reveals the motivation behind this feature—supporting UI apps and the older ASP.NET. While this is the default behavior for everything included out of the box in .NET (at least up to version 9), this behavior can be modified. Later in this chapter, we will see how this is implemented and how you (and third-party code) can change this behavior.

11.1.1 *await in UI threads*

It's common in UI apps to read values from the user, do something with them, and display the result. For example, the following methods, which are called when the user clicks a button, read the text the user has entered into a text box, pass it to the async `DoSomething` method, and display the result on screen in a label.

Listing 11.1 `await` **in a UI event handler**

```
private async void button1_Click(object sender, EventArgs ea)
{
    label1.Text = await DoSomething(textBox1.Text);
}
```

This method will be called by the UI framework on the thread that created the button. In almost all cases, this will be the thread that created all the UI (and so it will be the only thread that can access the UI). Reading `textBox1.Text` is done before the `await`, and it runs on the UI thread. Writing `label1.Text` comes after the `await`, and it will fail if not run on the UI thread.

If the code running after the `await` did not run on the UI thread, this would break one of the most useful properties of `await`—that asynchronous code using `await` is written just like non-asynchronous code. If we use what we learned in chapter 3 about converting this method from an `async` method that uses `await` to a non-async method that uses `ContinueWith`, we will get the following listing.

Listing 11.2 **UI access failure with** `ContinueWith`

```
private void button1_Click(object sender, EventArgs ea)
{
    var result = DoSomething(textBox1.Text).ContinueWith(t=>     ◄──────┐
    {                                                          Changes await to
        label1.Text = t.Result;      ◄──┐ Exception            ContinueWith │
    }                                                                       │
}
```

We just took the part after the `await` and moved it into a lambda that we passed to `ContinueWith`, but this doesn't work. If you run it, you will get an exception because `ContinueWith` always runs the callback on the thread pool (and not the UI thread). So we need to make the part that sets the label text run in the UI thread explicitly. Both WinForms and WPF provide this feature. In WinForms, this is done with `Control.BeginInvoke`, and in WPF, with `Dispatcher.BeginInvoke`.

Listing 11.3 **UI access with** `ContinueWith`

```
private void button1_Click(object sender, EventArgs ea)
{
    var result = DoSomething(textBox1.Text).ContinueWith(t=>
    {
        label1.BeginInvoke((Action)(()=>        ◄──┐ Switches to UI thread
        {
            label1.Text = t.Result));
        });
    }
}
```

In this listing, we used `ContinueWith`, like in listing 11.2, but this time, we also used `Control.BeginInvoke` to ask WinForms to run the code that writes to `label1.Text` in the UI thread. Now the UI is only accessed from the UI thread, and everything works.

Listings 11.1 and 11.3 do exactly the same thing, and you can see from the difference between them that the threading behavior of `await` saves us quite a bit of complexity and messing with threads.

11.1.2   *await in non-UI threads*

Now that we have covered the UI case and we've seen why returning to the same thread after an `await` is so important in UI threads, let's see why `await` doesn't return to the same thread when it is used in non-UI threads. To demonstrate this, we'll write a program that creates a thread and does something asynchronous in that thread.

Listing 11.4   `async` operation is a thread created by the `Thread` class

```
var thread = new Thread(async () =>
    {
        Console.WriteLine($"Thread {Thread.CurrentThread.ManagedThreadId}");
        await Task.Delay(500);
        Console.WriteLine($"Thread {Thread. CurrentThread.ManagedThreadId}");
    });
thread.Start();
Thread.Sleep(1000);
```

This program creates a thread that asynchronously waits for half a second. It also writes the thread ID to the console both before and after waiting. The main thread starts the thread we created and then waits for a second because the program will terminate when the code in the main thread ends, and we want to keep the program alive until the second thread does its thing.

If we run this code, we'll see that the thread ID before and after the `await` is different. But why didn't `await` get us back to the original thread like with UI threads?

If you remember from chapter 3, `await` sets up the asynchronous operation and then returns, in this case, from the main method of the thread (the method we passed to the `Thread` constructor). This will make the thread terminate (successfully; for all it knows, the code we ran in the thread finished doing whatever we needed it to do). After waiting for half a second, when it's time to run the code after the `await`, the original thread that called `await` no longer exists.

But what happens if we manage to call `await` in a way that doesn't terminate the thread?

Listing 11.5   `async` operation without terminating the thread

```
var thread = new Thread(() =>
{
    DoSomethingAsync();
    int i=0;
```

```
        while(true) Console.Write(++i);
});
thread.IsBackground = true;
thread.Start();
Thread.Sleep(1000);

async Task DoSomethingAsync()
{
    Console.WriteLine($"Thread {Thread.CurrentThread.ManagedThreadId}");
    await Task.Delay(500);
    Console.WriteLine($"Thread {Thread. CurrentThread.ManagedThreadId}");
}
```

In this listing, we changed the code so the `await` happens in a method that is called from the thread's main code. In the thread's main method, we ignore the `Task` returned by this method and do not `await` it. Because we don't use `await`, the compiler `await` support does not kick in, and it does not introduce a `return`. That way, the thread's main method doesn't return, and the thread does not terminate. After calling the async method, the thread starts counting forever just so it has something to do, and we can see it's working. We also marked this thread as a background thread, so the app will exit after the main thread exits (after one second) and will not keep running forever.

If we run this code, we will see that the code before and after the `await` ran on different threads (as expected). We can also see that the thread we created is busy counting. Even if the system wanted to run the code after the `await` in the same thread, it has no way of doing so. The thread is running our code, and we didn't implement any way for the system to ask us to run the code after the `await` (like WinForms's `Control.Begin-Invoke` that we used in listing 11.3).

11.2 *Synchronization contexts*

The UI thread behavior isn't magic or some special case in the compiler available just for UI frameworks written by Microsoft. This behavior is implemented using a .NET feature called `SynchronizationContext`.

A `SynchronizationContext` is a generic way of running code in another thread. Let's say that you are writing code that spins up a background thread to calculate something and then uses a callback to report the result back to its caller. By default, the callback will run in the background thread you created, which is inconvenient if used in a native UI app because trying to access the UI from that thread will cause an exception.

If you know this code will always be used in, for example, a WinForms app, you could use the `Control.BeginInvoke` method like we did in listing 11.3. However, this has the obvious limitation that it only works in WinForms. For WPF, you'll need to use `Dispatcher`, and other frameworks will have other mechanisms.

If you want your code to work in any situation, you can't use `Control.BeginInvoke` directly. You could create an abstract class that represents running stuff in another thread and require whoever uses your code to implement it. The class may look like this:

```
public abstract class RunInOtherThread
{
    public abstract void Run(Action codeToRun);
}
```

Anyone writing a WPF app will implement the `Run` method using `Dispatcher.Begin-Invoke`, anyone writing a WinForms app will implement it using `Control.BeginInvoke`, and so on for any framework that has threading limitations. That way, you can both run your callbacks in the most convenient thread for your user and not take a dependency on any UI framework. As a bonus, this will also work with future frameworks you don't even know about.

`SynchronizationContext` is the .NET built-in implementation of our `RunInOther-Thread` class. It has two ways of running code in the target thread: `Send`, which will wait until the other threads finish running our code, and `Post` which doesn't wait. `await` only uses `Post`.

But we never passed a `SynchronizationContext` to `await`, so how does it know how to use the correct one? For this, a `SynchronizationContext` can be associated with a thread by calling `SynchronizationContext.SetSynchronizationContext`. After that call, any code running in this thread can read `SynchronizationContext.Current` to retrieve it. WinForms, WPF, and ASP.NET classic all implement a class derived from `SynchronizationContext` and associate it with the UI or request handling threads so that any generic code that needs to return to the correct thread (such as `await`) can use it.

Let's write a `SynchronizationContext`-derived class that runs the code after the `await` in the same thread. We'll use `BlockingCollection` and the work queue pattern we talked about back in chapter 8.

> ### Listing 11.6 Custom `SynchronizationContext` for `async/await`

```
using System.Collections.Concurrent;

public class SingleThreadSyncContext : SynchronizationContext
{
```

We begin with a `Run` method that will start our work queue. Because we want to run everything in the current thread, the `Run` method will not return until we are finished. The `Run` method will accept as a parameter a method to run because without it, no one will be able to use our `SynchronizationContext` (only code that we run after the `Set-SynchronizationContext` call will have access to the `SynchronizationContext`, so if we need to run code, that will kick off the operation there):

```
    public static void Run(Func<Task> startup)
    {
        var prev = SynchronizationContext.Current;
        try
        {
```

```
        var ctxt = new SingleThreadSyncContext();
        SynchronizationContext.SetSynchronizationContext(ctxt);
        ctxt.Loop(startup);
    }
    finally
    {
        SynchronizationContext.SetSynchronizationContext(prev);
    }
}
```

Runs work queue ← points to `ctxt.Loop(startup);`

Associates SynchronizationContext with thread ← points to `SynchronizationContext.SetSynchronizationContext(ctxt);`

Restores original SynchronizationContext ← points to `SynchronizationContext.SetSynchronizationContext(prev);`

Now we'll implement the work queue part. Just like we did in chapter 8, we create a queue of delegates representing the work to be done. Using foreach with Get-ConsumingEnumerable, we get the next item in the queue or wait if the item isn't available yet, and then we invoke the delegate we get from the queue:

```
private BlockingCollection<(SendOrPostCallback call,object? state)>
    _queue = new();

private void Loop(Func<Task> startup)
{
    startup().ContinueWith(t => _queue.CompleteAdding());
    foreach(var next in _queue.GetConsumingEnumerable())
    {
        next.call(next.state);
    }
}
```

Stops work when the first method completes ← points to `startup().ContinueWith(t => _queue.CompleteAdding());`

Work queue loop ← points to foreach loop

The last part is the Post method that will add work to the queue. When an asynchronous operation ends, await will call it to run the code after the await (via a Task-Scheduler; we'll talk about those later in this chapter):

```
public override void Post(SendOrPostCallback d, object? state)
{
    _queue.Add((d, state));
}
```

What's left are all the parts of SynchronizationContext that are not used by await. We will just throw NotImplementedException exceptions for all of those:

```
public override void Send(SendOrPostCallback d, object? state)
{
    // not needed for async/await
    throw new NotImplementedException();
}

public override SynchronizationContext CreateCopy()
{
    // not needed for async/await
    throw new NotImplementedException();
}

public override int Wait(IntPtr[] waitHandles,
```

```
            bool waitAll, int millisecondsTimeout)
    {
        // not needed for async/await
        throw new NotImplementedException();
    }
}
```

Now we just need to test our custom `SynchronizationContext`. First, we'll run a simple `async` operation without it.

```
Console.WriteLine($"before await {Thread.CurrentThread.ManagedThreadId}");
await Task.Delay(500);
Console.WriteLine($"before await {Thread.CurrentThread.ManagedThreadId}");
```

This code just prints the current thread ID, uses `await`, and then prints the current thread ID again. If we run this, we'll see that the code after the `await` runs in a different thread than the code before the `await`, just like we expected.

And now let's run the same code with our `SingleThreadSyncContext`.

```
SingleThreadSyncContext.Run(async () =>
{
    Console.WriteLine($"before {Thread.CurrentThread.ManagedThreadId }");
    await Task.Delay(500);
    Console.WriteLine($"after {Thread.CurrentThread.ManagedThreadId }");
});
```

We took the exact code from listing 11.7 and put it into a lambda passed to `Single-ThreadSyncContext.Run`. When we run this code, we'll see that the thread ID doesn't change, and the code before and after the `await` runs in the same thread (specifically, the thread that called `SingleThreadSyncContext.Run`).

WinForms and WPF both install their own `SynchronizationContext` in the UI thread, and as we've seen in our example, any third-party code can also use its own `SynchronizationContext` by calling `SetSynchronizationContext`. But if no one called `SetSynchronizationContext` in the current thread—which is almost always the case in non-UI apps (such as console apps and ASP.NET Core apps), as well as in non-UI threads in UI apps—then `SynchronizationContext.Current` will be `null`, and like we've seen in listing 11.7, the code after an `await` will run in the thread pool.

11.3   Breaking away—ConfigureAwait(false)

We've talked about why and how `await` returns to the same thread in UI apps. Now it's time to talk about how and why to block this behavior.

The `ConfigureAwait(false)` method allows us to prevent `await` from using the current `SynchronizationContext`, as well as the current `TaskScheduler` (that we'll discuss later in this chapter). First, I want to debunk the common but wrong explanation of `ConfigureAwait(false)` that "without `ConfigureAwait(false)`, you continue on the same thread, and with `ConfigureAwait(false)`, you continue on another thread." First, let's debunk the first half of this explanation.

Listing 11.9   Console app without `ConfigureAwait(false)`

```
Console.WriteLine($"1: {Thread.CurrentThread.ManagedThreadId}");
await Task.Delay(500);
Console.WriteLine($"2: {Thread.CurrentThread.ManagedThreadId}");
```

If you run this program as a console application, you will see that we used `await` without `ConfigureAwait(false)` and switched threads. The reason is that while `await` tries to stay in the same `SynchronizationContext` (not thread), we do not have one set, and so `await` continues on the thread pool.

Now for the second part: Will `ConfigureAwait(false)` always switch to a different thread?

Listing 11.10   `ConfigureAwait(false)` and completed tasks

```
Console.WriteLine($"1: {Thread.CurrentThread.ManagedThreadId}");
await DoSomething().ConfigureAwait(false);
Console.WriteLine($"2: {Thread.CurrentThread.ManagedThreadId}");

async Task DoSomething()
{
    Console.WriteLine("did something");
}
```

If you run this code, you will see that `ConfigureAwait(false)` didn't make us switch threads. The reason for this is that `DoSomething` always returns a completed task, and using `await` on a completed task always just continues running on the same thread.

Why does `DoSomething` return a completed task? Like we said in chapter 3, a simplified but mostly correct model (except for synchronization contexts) of how the compiler deals with `async` methods is that each `await` is replaced with a call to `Task.ContinueWith`. Because `DoSomething` does not use `await`, the compiler has nothing to replace. The method remains exactly the same as it would if it weren't `async`, except that it needs to return a `Task`, so it translates roughly into

```
Task DoSomething()
{
    Console.WriteLine("did something");
    return Task.CompletedTask;
}
```

Remember, marking a method as `async` does not make it run in the background—it only turns on the compiler's support for `await`.

You might think our `DoSomething` method is a rare edge case or even a bug, but methods that always return an already completed `Task` are not uncommon. Many libraries have non-asynchronous methods that return a `Task`, mostly because the author wants to be able to support asynchronous operations in the future without changing the API or because the operation was asynchronous in a previous version.

Now let's see what `ConfigureAwait(false)` really does. We'll start with this WinForms code.

```
private async void Button1_Click(object sender, EventArgs ea)
{
    Debug.WriteLine($" before: {Thread.CurrentThread.ManagedThreadId }");
    await Task.Delay(500).ConfigureAwait(false);
    Debug.WriteLine($" after: {Thread.CurrentThread.ManagedThreadId }");
}
```

This code uses `await` with `ConfgureAwait(false)` to wait for half a second and prints the thread ID both before and after the `await`. We know that without `ConfigureAwait(false)`, both should print the same thread ID, but if we run this code, we'll see two different thread IDs, exactly like we've seen in listing 11.9. The difference between listings 11.9 and 11.11 is that listing 11.9 is a console app, and as such, it doesn't have a `SynchronizationContext`, while listing 11.11 is a WinForms app, and so it has a `SynchronizationContext`. So what `ConfigureAwait(false)` does is simply ignore any `SynchronizationContext` associated with the current thread.

If we summarize everything we've talked about so far, the rules for where the code after an `await` runs are the following:

- If the task has already completed, the code continues to run in the same thread. `ConfigureAwait(false)` has no effect in this case.
- If there is a `SynchronizationContext` set for the current thread, and `ConfigureAwait(false)` is not used, the code after the await will use the `SynchronizationContext` to run.
- In all other cases, the code will run using the thread pool.

And now I'm going to write something that might seem controversial to readers who have seen `async`/`await` best practices' lists (but really isn't): don't use `ConfigureAwait(false)` every time you use `await`.

A lot of best practice lists state you should use `ConfigureAwait(false)` whenever you use `await`. They say that because misusing `async`/`await` in UI apps and ASP.NET classic apps (not ASP.NET core) can cause deadlocks, and `ConfigureAwait(false)` will prevent them. However, this is throwing out the baby with the bathwater. The official guidance from Microsoft agrees with me and says you should always use `ConfigureAwait(false)` in library code and not application code.

Quite a few best practice lists adopted the use "always use `ConfigureAwait(false)`" part but leave out the "in library code" part because it seems like just putting

`ConfigureAwait(false)` everywhere will prevent deadlocks without making the developer think about it or debug their code, which sounds nice but doesn't work so well. I will show the problem with this approach and other solutions for this deadlock. But first, let's see the problem.

> **Listing 11.12** `async/await` **deadlock**

```
private void button1_Click(object sender, EventArgs ea)
{
    var task = DoSomething();
    label1.Text = task.Result;
}

private async Task<string> DoSomething()
{
    await Task.Delay(500);
    return "done";
}
```

This code combines asynchronous calls with blocking calls. The first method, `button1_Click`, calls `DoSomething` without using `await`, and then it reads the `Task.Result` property—that makes the thread block because `DoSomething` hasn't completed yet. Meanwhile, inside `DoSomething`, `Task.Delay` completes, and the next line (`return "done"`) is ready to run. As we've seen in this chapter, the code after the `await` will run on the UI thread, but the UI thread is busy waiting in `Task.Result`.

So what we have here is that the UI thread is busy waiting for `DoSomething` to complete, but `DoSomething` can't complete until the UI thread frees up—a classic deadlock. If we just add `ConfigureAwait(false)` to the `await`, we get the following.

> **Listing 11.13 Deadlock prevented by using** `ConfigureAwait(false)`

```
private void button1_Click(object sender, EventArgs ea)
{
    var task = DoSomething();
    label1.Text = task.Result;
}

private async Task<string> DoSomething()
{
    await Task.Delay(500).ConfigureAwait(false);      ◄——— Added ConfigureAwait
    return "done";
}
```

Now, in `button1_Click`, the UI thread blocks waiting for `DoSomething` to complete just like in listing 11.12. But this time, after `Task.Delay` completes, `DoSomething` continues to run on the thread pool and not the UI thread. This means `DoSomething` will complete in the background, `Task.Result` will stop blocking and return the result, and everything will just work.

So if just dropping `ConfigureAwait(false)` mechanically everywhere prevents deadlocks, why am I so against it? First, in this case, there's an easier fix: if we don't mix asynchronous and blocking operations and just stick to using `await`, we don't have that problem.

Listing 11.14   Deadlock prevented by using `await`

```
private async void button1_Click(object sender, EventArgs ea)
{
    var result = await DoSomething();          ◄——————┐  Changed to await
    label1.Text = result;
}

private async Task<string> DoSomething()
{
    await Task.Delay(500);
    return "done";
}
```

We solved this problem by using `await` instead of reading `Task.Result`. Now `button1_Click` does not block the thread until `DoSomething` completes, and we have no deadlock. Note that using `await` isn't always possible, and we did change the way the program operates in case there's an exception in `DoSomething`. We'll cover those problems in a bit, but first, let's see what happens if we introduce `ConfigureAwait` to this version of the code.

Listing 11.15   WinForms code with `ConfigureAwait(false)` everywhere

```
private async void button1_Click(object sender, EventArgs ea)
{
    var result = await DoSomething().ConfigureAwait(false);  ◄——┐  Adds
    label1.Text = result;                              ◄——┐       ConfigureAwait
}                                                           Exception

private async Task<string> DoSomething()
{
    await Task.Delay(500).ConfigureAwait(false);
    return "done";
}
```

In this listing, we added `ConfigureAwait(false)` to the first `await`. This means the code after the `await` will run in the thread pool instead of taking up the UI thread, but this code modifies the UI (now from the wrong thread), and we get an `InvalidOperation-Exception` exception.

To make this code work with `ConfigureAwait(false)`, we need to use `Control`
`.BeginInvoke`, like we did in listing 11.3 where we didn't use `await` at all.

Listing 11.16 WinForms code that works with `ConfigureAwait(false)` everywhere

```
private async void button1_Click(object sender, EventArgs ea)
{
    var result = await DoSomething().ConfigureAwait(false);     ◄─────┐ ConfigureAwait
    label1.BeginInvoke((Action)(()=>                        ◄─────
        {
            label1.Text = result));                             Sets label text
        });                                                     on UI thread

}

private async Task<string> DoSomething()
{
    await Task.Delay(500).ConfigureAwait(false);
    return "done";
}
```

In this listing, because the code after the `await` no longer runs in the UI thread (due to our usage of `ConfigureAwait(false)`), we had to use other means to run the code that updates the UI on the UI thread, and this looks very much like code that doesn't use `await` at all, which shows us that `ConfigureAwait(false)` outright negates the benefits of `await`.

But `ConfigureAwait` isn't totally evil. If we only use `ConfigureAwait(false)` on the `await` inside `DoSomething`, everything still works.

Listing 11.17 WinForms code with `ConfigureAwait(false)` only in non-UI methods

```
private async void button1_Click(object sender, EventArgs ea)
{
    var result = await DoSomething();
    label1.Text = result;                  ◄─────┐ No ConfigureAwait—
}                                       ◄─────     return to UI context

private async Task<string> DoSomething()       No exception
{
    await Task.Delay(500).ConfigureAwait(false);
    return "done";
}
```

Here, inside `DoSomething`, we break out of the UI context, and the return line will run on the thread pool. But the `await` in `button1_Click` (that does not use `Configure-Await(false)`) will return us to the UI thread, and the line that modifies the label will work.

Also note that the `DoSomething` method in this listing is exactly the same as the one in listing 11.12, so `ConfigureAwait(false)` can be beneficial if you don't know if your caller is asynchronous, like in listing 11.16, or blocking, like in listing 11.13, as would commonly happen if you were writing a library. Note that `ConfigureAwait(false)` works here because `DoSomething` doesn't access the UI itself and thus doesn't care in what context the code after the `await` runs.

Remember that even in libraries, you often do care about the context (and thread) in which your code runs. An obvious example is a library designed to be used specifically in a UI application. A less obvious example is a library that uses callbacks to call the application that uses it. Even if the library doesn't care in which thread it runs, the code inside the application's callback might.

Before we wrap up our discussion of `ConfigureAwait(false)`, I'll mention how we can solve our deadlock without using `ConfigureAwait`. This deadlock, in its general form—UI waiting for something that is waiting for UI—has existed ever since we started making UI applications; it predates `async/await`, it predates .NET and C#, it even predates asynchronous IO in the Windows operating system. And so, unsurprisingly, there is a standard solution for this problem already built into WinForms (and WPF and all other UI frameworks I know about). This solution is to let the UI handle events (or *pump messages*, in Windows API terminology) while we are waiting for the background task to complete. In WinForms, we do this by calling the `Application .DoEvents` method.

Listing 11.18 Prevent the deadlock with `DoEvents`

```
private void button1_Click(object sender, EventArgs ea)
{
    var task = DoSomething();
    while(!task.IsCompleted)              Processes events
        Application.DoEvents();           while waiting
    label1.Text = task.Result;
}

private async Task<string> DoSomething()
{
    await Task.Delay(500)
    return "done";
}
```

This works exactly like we expected our original code in listing 11.11 would work. It doesn't deadlock, the `button1_Click` method isn't asynchronous, and as an added benefit, the UI doesn't freeze until `DoSomething` completes.

A note about DoEvents

Note that the `DoEvents` loop will take 100% CPU (of one core) while waiting. It does not affect your app (specifically your app's UI thread) because this loop will run any UI events as soon as possible, but it does take resources that could be used by another app and prevent the CPU core from switching to idle power saving mode. As such, it is not recommended to use `DoEvents`; yet, it is better than having a deadlock. It's mostly okay to use a `DoEvents` here because we know we are only waiting for half a second, and the effect on the system will be minimal, but we need to consider this every time we write `DoEvents` loops.

To summarize, my suggested rules for using `ConfigureAwait(false)` are

- If you are writing application code, avoid using `ConfigureAwait(false)`; the default behavior is there for a reason.
- If your code is only designed to run in environments that don't use `SynchronizationContext` (for example, Console apps and ASP.NET core), don't use `ConfigureAwait(false)`.
- If you are writing library code, and you don't care in which context your code runs, use `ConfigureAwait(false)` on every `await`.
- If you want to leave the current context, use `Task.Run` and not `ConfigureAwait(false)`, because `ConfigureAwait(false)` does nothing if the `Task` is already completed.

There are some unit-testing frameworks that will not work unless you always use `ConfigureAwait(false)`. I personally think this is a bug in the unit-testing framework, and I will let you decide if it's better to change the threading behavior of the app to compensate for a technical bug in your unit-test framework or to use a different unit–test framework.

After all this talk about `ConfigureAwait(false)`, you may be curious about `ConfigureAwait(true)`. `ConfigureAwait(true)` is the default behavior and has no effect on your code whatsoever (except for silencing static code analyzers that complain about not using `ConfigureAwait(false)`).

11.4 More ConfigureAwait options

.NET 8 added a new version of `ConfigureAwait` with new and exciting options that further complicate things. Those options are implemented as an overload of `ConfigureAwait` that accepts a `ConfigureAwaitOptions` parameter. Unfortunately, while useful in specialized cases, all those options have hidden complexities, and I recommend not using them in normal application code.

Just in case you encounter them in code you have to debug, these are the options, each with its biggest pitfall identified:

- `None`—Calling `ConfigureAwait(ConfigureAwaitOptions.None)` is equivalent to `ConfigureAwait(false)`, that is, it changes the behavior of `await` and makes it run continuations on the thread pool. I recommend using the old `ConfigureAwait(false)` and not the new `ConfigureAwait(ConfigureAwaitOptions.None)`. The new version is somehow even worse at actually saying what it does (considering the meaning of "none" in the English language, I would expect `None` to do nothing, but it changes the behavior), and the old one is at least more concise.
- `ContinueOnCapturedContext`—This value keeps the default `await` behavior; using it by itself does nothing. It is required because the `ConfigureAwaitOptions` options are flags, which means this can be combined together, and with `None` being the default. All the other options also include the `ConfigureAwait(false)` behavior unless you combine them with the `ContinueOnCapturedContext` option.

- `ForceYielding`—This option makes `await` always return and schedule the continuation to run later, even if it doesn't have to because the `Task` has already completed. This does not make the code you are calling run in the background—it just switches to the thread pool after the `await`. Using this option is equivalent to writing `await Task.Yield().ConfigureAwait(false);` in the next line.
- `SuppressThrowing`—This option makes `await` ignore *some* errors. It is meant for situations where you don't care if the operation you run succeeds or fails. However, it will only ignore errors that occur after the first `await` inside the method you are calling, so it doesn't guarantee that no exception will be thrown. Also, it will throw an exception at run time if you try to use it with a `Task<T>`.

In conclusion, out of the four new options, `None` and `ContinueOnCapturedContext` are already more concisely supported with the old `ConfigureAwait`. `ForceYielding` is not very useful, and `SuppressThrowing` doesn't do what its name implies. Also, just to add another pitfall, the new `ConfigureAwait` is not supported on `ValueTask` and `ValueTask<T>`, so I recommend sticking with the older `ConfigureAwait(bool)`.

11.5   *Letting other code run: Task.Yield*

Internally, both events generated by Windows (mouse moves, keyboard clicks, and so forth) and work queued by `Control.BeginInvoke` and the `SynchronizationContext` are stored in a queue called the input queue (because its primary function is to deliver input from the UI to the app).

We've seen in listing 11.18 that in WinForms, we can use `Application.DoEvents` to let the framework handle events and remain responsive. `DoEvents` simply reads all pending entries in the input queue, returning only when all the events are handled.

The generic `async`/`await` compatible version of `DoEvents` is `Task.Yield`. When you await `Task.Yield()` in a UI thread, the code after the `await` is added to the end of the input queue and runs after all the other events that are already pending. The following listing shows what happens if we build a WinForms app that counts forever.

Listing 11.19   Trying to count forever and freezing the app

```
private void button1_Click(object sender, EventArgs ea)
{
    int i=0;
    while(true)
    {
        label1.Text = (++i).ToString();
    }
}
```

With this method, when the user clicks a button, the program will loop forever, counting and setting the number into a label's `Text` property. If you run this code, the program will just freeze. The UI thread will be busy counting and will not handle input queue events such as mouse clicks. Also, you will not see the content of the label change because the UI thread will not handle requests to redraw the label. We can use the same strategy that worked so well in listing 11.18 and fix this with `DoEvents`.

Listing 11.20 Counting forever without freezing the app

```
private void button1_Click(object sender, EventArgs ea)
{
    int i=0;
    while(true)
    {
        label1.Text = (++i).ToString();
        Application.DoEvents();
    }
}
```

Now at every iteration, the method calls `DoEvents`. This will handle all the pending events (including the label's redraw events). The app will remain responsive, and the label with show the changing number. Note that our code will use 100% of a CPU core doing the counting, so unlike listing 11.18, it is not negatively affecting the system by calling `DoEvents`. We could also go the `async`/`await` route and do this with `Task.Yield`.

Listing 11.21 Counting forever without freezing the app using `await`

```
private async void button1_Click(object sender, EventArgs ea)
{
    int i=0;
    while(true)
    {
        label1.Text = (++i).ToString();
        await Task.Yield();
    }
}
```

In this version, at the end of every iteration, the method will queue itself at the end of the input queue and return. It is a very different technique than `DoEvents`, but with exactly the same results.

When deciding where to run the code after it, `await Task.Yield()` follows the same rules listed in this chapter, so you can use them to figure out in which thread the code will run in your specific situation.

11.6 *Task schedulers*

In this chapter, I repeatedly wrote that `await` uses `SynchronizationContext`. Well, I left something out: `async`/`await` has its own infrastructure for deciding on which thread to run code. This infrastructure is based on the `TaskScheduler` class. Classes derived from `TaskScheduler`, like classes derived from `SyncronizationContext`, know how to take a task created by `await` and schedule it to run on some thread sometime in the future.

The default task scheduler (accessible via the `TaskScheduler.Default` static property) always queues your code to run on the thread pool. If you call `await` in a thread with a `SynchronizationContext`, the compiler will create a scheduler that will use its `Post` method to schedule the code (the `TaskScheduler.FromCurrentSynchronization-Context` does this). You can get the current scheduler by reading `TaskScheduler.Current`.

Unlike `SynchronizationContext`, you can't set the current `TaskSchuduler`, but you can set the task scheduler when you call `Task.Run`, `ContinueWith`, or any of the other `async`/`await` compatible ways to run code. For example, this code will run a lambda half a second later on the thread pool:

```
Task.Delay(500).ContinueWith(t=>Console.WriteLine("Hello"));
```

This code uses `ContinueWith` to run after the timeout is passed to `Task.Delay`. Because we didn't pass the optional `TaskScheduler` parameter, this will use the default scheduler that will run the code on the thread pool. However, if we are running in a thread with `SynchronizationContext`, we can create a task scheduler that uses it:

```
Task.Delay(500).ContinueWith(t=>Console.WriteLine("Hello"),
    TaskScheduler.FromCurrentSynchronizationContext());
```

Here we passed the optional `TaskScheduler` parameter. Specifically, we passed a scheduler created from the current `SynchronizationContext`, so the lambda will run on this thread. If there's no current `SynchronizationContext`, or the `Synchronization-Context` can't be wrapped in a `TaskScheduler`, `FromCurrentSynchronizationContext` will throw an exception. In the current version of .NET at the time of this writing (version 8), this only happens if there is no current `SynchronizationContext` (that is, `SynchronizationContext.Current` is null).

Just like with `SyncronizationContext`, `ConfigureAwait(false)` will make `await` ignore the current `TaskScheduler` and use the default scheduler instead.

This completes the rules for which thread runs the code after an `await`, in this order:

- If the task is already complete, the code continues to run immediately in the same thread. `ConfigureAwait(false)` has no effect in this case.
- If the current thread has a `SynchronizationContext` set, and `ConfigureAwait (false)` is not used, the `SynchronizationContext` will be used.
- If the current task has a `TaskScheduler` associated with it, and `ConfigureAwait (false)` is not used, the `TaskScheduler` will be used.
- If `ConfigureAwait(false)` was called, or if the thread has no `Synchronization-Context` and no `TaskScheduler`, the default task scheduler will be used, and the code will run in the thread pool.

Summary

- The simplified rules regarding which thread runs the code after an `await` are as follows:
  - In UI apps (WinForms and WPF), if you are using `await` in a UI thread, and you don't use `ConfigureAwait(false)`, the code after the `await` will run in the same thread.
  - In ASP.NET classic (not ASP.NET Core), if you are using `await` in a thread that is processing a web request, and you don't use `ConfigureAwait(false)`, the code after the `await` will run in the same thread.
  - In all other cases, the code after the `await` will run in the thread pool.
- However, the real rules are
  - If the task is already complete, and `ConfigureAwait(ConfigureAwaitOptions.ForceYielding)` was not used, the code continues to run immediately in the same thread, `ConfigureAwait(false)` has no effect in this case.
  - If the current thread has a `SynchronizationContext` set, and `ConfigureAwait(false)` is not used, the `SynchronizationContext` will be used.
  - If the current task has a `TaskScheduler` associated with it, and `ConfigureAwait(false)` is not used, the `TaskScheduler` will be used.
  - If `ConfigureAwait(false)` was called, or the thread has no `SynchronizationContext` and no `TaskScheduler`, the default task scheduler will be used, and the code will run in the thread pool.
- If you are not using third-party frameworks or writing your own `SynchronizationContext` or `TaskScheduler`, those two sets of rules produce the same results.
- `ConfigureAwait(false)` makes `await` ignore the current `SynchronizationContext` or `TaskScheduler`. This may prevent deadlocks but can make using `await` much less convenient.
- The rules for using `ConfigureAwait(false)` are as follows:
  - If you are writing application code, avoid using `ConfigureAwait(false)`. The default behavior is there for a reason.
  - If your code needs to continue running on the same thread, for example, if you change the thread's settings or you use thread local storage, don't use `ConfigureAwait(false)`.
  - If your code is only designed to run in environments that don't use `SynchronizationContext` (for example, Console apps and ASP.NET core), don't use `ConfigureAwait(false)`.
  - If you are writing library code, and you don't care in which context your code runs, use `ConfigureAwait(false)` on every `await`.
  - If you want to leave the current context, use `Task.Run` and not `ConfigureAwait(false)` because `ConfigureAwait(false)` does nothing if the `Task` is already completed.

12

Exceptions and async/await

This chapter covers

- How exceptions work with asynchronous code
- How to fix lost exceptions
- Handling exceptions in async void methods

In this chapter, we are going to talk about exceptions. We'll discuss how they work in asynchronous code and the differences in how they work in non-asynchronous code. In transitional code, exceptions bubble up the call stack. As we've seen in chapters 3, 5, and 11, in asynchronous code, callbacks are constantly registered to be called later, often from other threads; thus, the call stack no longer describes the flow of your code. This knowledge and the knowledge about what `async/await` does to mitigate this are important when debugging problems related to exceptions in asynchronous code, that is, when debugging any situation where the asynchronous code fails in a non-straightforward way. We'll also cover some pitfalls you should be aware of regarding exceptions.

12.1 Exceptions and asynchronous code

Exceptions use the call stack. The call stack is a data structure (specifically a stack) used by the system to implement the concept of methods (or functions or procedures, depending on your programming language). When you call a method, the system pushes the memory address of the next instruction into the call stack, and when you execute a `return` statement, the system jumps to the address at the top of the stack (this explanation is a gross oversimplification because this book is not about processor architecture).

When an exception is thrown, if it's inside a `try` block with an appropriate `catch` clause, control passes to that `catch` clause. If the exception is thrown outside of a `try` block, or that `try` block has no appropriate `catch` clause, the exception bubbles up the call stack until it finds an appropriate `catch` clause. If it gets to the beginning of the call stack without finding a `catch` clause, the program crashes.

This exception bubbling happens in run time and uses the program's call stack, not the structure of the source code. For example, let's take a look at some code where the structure of the code doesn't match the runtime behavior:

```
public void MyMethod()
{
    try
    {
        Win.Click += ()=>
        {
            throw new NotImplementedException();
        };
    }
    catch
    {
        Console.WriteLine("In catch clause");
    }
}
```

In this code, while the `throw` statement is located inside the `try` block from a textual perspective, it doesn't run as part of this method. The lambda added to the `Click` event is separated by the compiler into a different method (like we've seen in chapter 2). It doesn't run inside our `try` block. The only thing that runs inside the `try` is attaching the `Click` event. When and if the code in the lambda runs, it will be called by the code that triggers the `Click` event, and the exception will bubble up into that code and not into our code.

`async` methods have the same problem because, as we've seen in chapter 3, `await` is equivalent to calling `ContinueWith`. So if we take a simple `async` method that throws an exception, we get

```
try
{
    await File.ReadAllBytesAsync("file.bin");
```

```
    throw new NotImplementedException();
}
catch
{
    Console.WriteLine("In catch clause");
}
```

This code awaits a call to ReadAllBytesAsync and then always throws an exception. If we translate await to ContinueWith, we get

```
try
{
    File.ReadAllBytes("file.bin").ContinueWith(()=>
    {
        throw new NotImplementedException();
    });
}
catch
{
    Console.WriteLine("In catch clause");
}
```

And this code has the same problem as the event handler example. The throw line is in the lambda (that is passed to ContinueWith), so it's not inside the try block. For this reason, the compiler will also duplicate the try-catch to make it look like await works seamlessly with try-catch blocks:

```
try
{
    File.ReadAllBytesAsync("file.bin").ContinueWith(()=>
    {
        try
        {
            throw new NotImplementedException();
        }
        catch
        {
            Console.WriteLine("In catch clause");
        }
    });
}
catch
{
    Console.WriteLine("In catch clause");
}
```

Here the compiler knows where the catch clause is, so it can do all those transformations to make try-catch work. But what if the try statement is not in our methods but in code that calls us? In this case, you can't know at compile time which catch clause to use, and the compiler can't just copy it into the continuation code. Let's see what happens with a simple async method that can throw an exception:

```
public async Task<int> MyMethod()
{
    throw new NotImplementedException();
}
```

This is an `async` method that just throws an exception, and it translates to

```
public Task MyMethod()
{
    throw new NotImplementedException();
}
```

The compiler didn't do anything! Remember, marking a method as `async` does not make it asynchronous; it's just a flag for the compiler to enable all the processing required for supporting `await`. If you don't use `await`, the only thing the compiler does is wrap the return value in a `Task` object. Note that the compiler didn't need to change the code to make exceptions behave like in a non-`async` method; calling this method will throw the exception just like a non-`async` method, which is what we wanted.

Now let's take a look at a method that uses `await`:

```
public async Task<int> MyMethod()
{
    await File.ReadAllBytesAsync("file.bin");
    throw new NotImplementedException();
}
```

This is a method that awaits `ReadAllBytesAsync` and then throws an exception. In this case, to support reporting the error to the calling code, the compiler will add a `try-catch` that will catch the exception and stash it in the returned task:

```
public async Task<int> MyMethod()
{
    var result = new TaskCompletionSource<int>();
    File.ReadAllBytesAsync("file.bin").ContinueWith(t=>
    {
        try
        {
            throw new NotImplementedException();
        }
        catch(Exception ex)
        {
            result.TrySetException(new AggregateException(ex));
        }
    });
}
```

Here, the compiler added a `try` block inside the continuation (the code that it passed to `ContinueWith`). Note that, like in our previous example, the compiler did not add a `try` block to the part before the first `await` and the call to `ReadAllBytesAsync` itself.

If an error occurs before the first `await`, the method will throw a regular exception. Only if the error occurs after the first `await` will the exception be caught by compiler generated code and stored in the returned `Task`. This is how most asynchronous code works; an asynchronous method can both throw a regular exception and report an error using the `Task` object (by setting the `Task`'s `Status` property to `Faulted` and storing the exception in the `Task.Exception` property).

If you use `await` when you call the method, both situations look the same. But if you are not using `await` (for example, if you are collecting multiple tasks and using `Task.WhenAny` or `Task.WhenAll`), you need to handle both exceptions thrown by the asynchronous methods and exceptions stored in the returned `Task`. Also, remember that the continuation usually runs after the method returns, so in case of an error, the `Task` returned by the asynchronous method will be in the `Created`, `WaitingForActivation`, or `Running` state when it's returned, and it will only change to the `Faulted` state later.

There's just one difference between using `await` to rethrow the exception or using the `Task.Exception` property, and that is how they use the `AggregateException`.

12.2 *await and AggregateException*

The `Task.Exception` property always stores an `AggregateException`. The `AggregateException` class, as the name suggests, is an exception class that stores multiple other exceptions inside it.

`Task` uses `AggreggateException` because a `Task` can represent the result of multiple operations running in parallel (for example, multiple asynchronous operations passed to `Task.WhenAll`). Because more than one of those background operations can fail, we need a way to store multiple exceptions.

In practice, this feature is almost never used. In fact, this feature is so rarely used that if you use `await`, and the `Task` you are awaiting fails, the await operator will always throw the first exception inside the `AggregateException` and not the `AggregateException` itself. If there is more than one exception inside, the `AggregateException` await will still throw just the first one and ignore the rest. All exceptions except for the first one, along with any information stored inside them, will be lost. Here is code showing how `await` throws the stored exception:

```
var tcs = new TaskCompletionSource();                          AggregateException
tcs.SetException(new NotSupportedException());
Console.WriteLine("In tasks: "+tcs.Task.Exception.GetType());  ◄─┘
try
{
    await tcs.Task;            ◄───┐  Will throw the
}                                  │  inner exception
catch(Exception ex)
{
    Console.WriteLine("Thrown: "+ex.GetType());    ◄─────┘  NotSupportedException
}
```

This program stores a `NotSupportedException` in a `Task` using `TaskCompletionSource` (we talked about creating your own tasks with `TaskCompletionSource` back in chapter 10). Then we check to see what exception is stored inside the `Task` and get an `AggregateException` wrapping our exception. However, we then use `await` because the `Task` in the `Failed` state `await` will throw an exception, but it will throw the inner `NotSupportedException` and not the `AggregateException`.

12.3 *The case of the lost exception*

We've seen that the compiler will generate code to catch exceptions and stash them inside the `Task`. And `await` will rethrow that exception. But what happens if, for some reason, we don't use `await`?

The answer is nothing. The compiler-generated code will catch the exception and store it in the `Task`. And that's it. If no one reads the exception from the `Task` (either by using `await` or by reading the `Task`'s `Exception` property), the exception will be ignored.

Let's take a look at another piece of code:

```
Public async Task MethodThatThrowsException()
{
    await Task.Delay(100);
    throw new NotImplementedException();
}

Public async Task MethodThatCallsOtherMethod()
{
    MethodThatTHrowsException();
}
```

Here we have two methods. The first method, `MethodThatThrowsException`, throws an exception after an `await`, so the compiler will catch the exception and stash it in the returned `Task`. The second method calls the first, but when I wrote it, I forgot the `await`, so no one is looking at the retuned `Task`. The exception was caught in the first method by the compiler-generated code but ignored by the second method because I didn't use `await`. And so the runtime thinks we handled the exception (because the compiler generated code caught it), and the code continues to run while ignoring the error.

If the method that throws the exception is in a library, and you have the "just my code" feature of the debugger enabled, you won't even see the exception in the debugger. So if some code in your program seems to stop running with no indication of why, there's a good chance someone forgot an `await` somewhere.

12.4 *Exceptions and async void methods*

In `async void` methods, the method does not return a `Task` (obviously). Because there is no `Task` to stash the exception in, the compiler doesn't know what to do with the exception thrown inside the method, so it will not generate the `try-catch` block we've seen in the previous example. As a result, any exception thrown in the code will bubble up the call stack into the `SynchronizationContext` that runs the code (we talked about how `SynchronizationContext` works in chapter 11). This will most likely crash your program. Because of that, it is best practice to handle all exceptions in `async void` methods yourself and never let an exception bubble out of it.

Summary

- Exceptions use the call stack to find the correct code to run in case of error, which is a problem for asynchronous code because continuations don't run in the same call stack as the code that calls the asynchronous method.

- If you use `async/await`, the compiler will generate code to make it look like non-async code. It does this by catching exceptions inside `async` methods and stashing them in the returned `Task`. `await` then throws the exception inside the continuation, making it look like it was thrown by the `await`.

- Every asynchronous method can throw a normal exception or signal a failure using the returned `Task`. `await` makes both of those failure modes look the same. If you don't use `await`, you need to handle both yourself.

- The exception stored inside the `Task` is an `AggregateException`, just in case the `Task` represents multiple operations. `await` ignores all but the first exception inside that `AggregateException`. If you don't use `await`, you need to deal with this yourself. In rare cases, the `Task` does represent multiple operations, and if you care about multiple failures, you can't use `await` and need to read the `Task.Exception` property yourself.

- If you ignore the `Task` returned by an asynchronous method (by forgetting to use `await`, for example), and that method throws an exception, the exception will be lost.

- As a corollary, if code fails in a way that should have been an exception, but you can't see that exception, there's a good chance you forgot an `await` somewhere.

- All the exception support provided by `async/await` is dependent on the returned `Task`. `async void` methods don't return a `Task` and so don't have this support. Never throw an exception from or let an exception bubble out of an `async void` method.

Thread-safe collections

13

This chapter covers

- The problems encountered when using regular collections in a multithreaded program
- Concurrent collections
- The `BlockingCollection` class
- Asynchronous alternatives to `Blocking-Collection`
- Immutable collections and special considerations when using them
- Frozen collections

The `System.Collections.Generic` namespace contains many useful collections; however, we can't just use them in a multithreaded application because all those collections are not thread safe. In this chapter, we'll look at the problems with the simplest way of making collections thread safe—just putting a lock around any access to the collection. We'll also talk about the thread-safe alternatives provided by the .NET library.

Specifically, we'll examine the concurrent collections added in .NET framework 4, discuss the immutable collections added in .NET Core (which is the basis for .NET 5 and later), and talk about the frozen collections added in .NET 8. You will also learn how to use each type of collection and when it's appropriate to do so. But first, let's talk about why you can't just use the regular collections.

13.1   *The problems with using regular collections*

The .NET library provides many useful collection classes in the `System.Collections` `.Generic` namespace. Those collections support multiple concurrent reads, but they can be corrupted and produce unexpected results if there are multiple concurrent writers or if different threads try to read and write simultaneously.

Also, according to the official documentation, iterating over the collection is intrinsically not thread safe, which means that if you iterate over the collection, either with a loop such as `foreach` or a Linq expression, you must prevent any writes by other threads to the collection for the entire duration of the loop. To use those collections in a multithreaded program, you must take care of synchronization yourself, typically by using locks, and doing so correctly when using collections is often nontrivial.

For example, let's consider a very common use case. We want to use a `Dictionary` `<TKey, TValue>` as a cache. When we need some data item, we first check whether it's in the cache, and if not, we create and initialize the item, probably by retrieving it from an external service or by precalculating some stuff (the reason we use a cache to begin with is that initializing the item takes a long time). We'll start with the single threaded code first and add locking later.

Listing 13.1   Simple, non–thread-safe cache

```
if(!dictionary.TryGetValue(itemId, out var item))
{
    item = CreateAndInitializeItem(itemId);
    dictionary.Add(itemId,item);
}
```

This code tries to retrieve an item from the dictionary, and if the item isn't already there, it calls `CreateAndInitializeItem` to create and initialize the item. After creating an item, the code calls `Add` to add the item to the dictionary so it's available the next time we need it.

This is a perfectly good way to implement a simple in-process cache for singlethreaded applications, but this code is very much not thread safe. Calling `TryGetValue` from multiple threads simultaneously is explicitly allowed, but calling `Add` concurrently or calling `Add` and `TryGetValue` at the same time can produce unexpected results and even corrupt the dictionary.

Let's make this thread safe. We'll start with the simplest option—placing a lock around the entire block.

> **Listing 13.2   Thread-safe cache with a single lock**

```
Item item;
lock(_dictLock)                    ◄──────┤ Adds a lock
{
    if(!dictionary.TryGetValue(itemId, out item))
    {
        item = CreateAndInitializeItem(itemId);
        dictionary.Add(itemId,item);
    }
}
```

This code is the same as listing 13.1, except it uses a lock to prevent multiple threads from running it simultaneously. This does make our code thread safe, but at the cost of locking the entire cache every time we run it. If the item is already in the dictionary, the lock will be short, and everything will be fine. However, if we need to create a new item, the entire cache will remain locked for the entire duration of the initialization, meaning that other threads that are working on completely different items will have to wait every time a new item has to be initialized. To solve this problem, we must release the lock while initializing the item.

> **Listing 13.3   Non–thread-safe cache with lock released during initialization**

```
Item item;
bool exists;
lock(_dictLock)                    ◄──────┤ Lock
{
    exists = dictionary.TryGetValue(itemId, out item);
}                                           ◄──────┐ Unlock
if(!exists)
{
    item = CreateAndInitializeItem(itemId);
    lock(_dictLock)                ◄──────┤ Lock again
    {
        dictionary.Add(itemId,item);   ◄──────┐ Add—fails if already
    }                                          │ added by another thread
}
```

This code has two lock blocks, one protecting the `TryGetValue` call and the other protecting the `Add` call. Those locks ensure that `Dictionary<T>` is never called from multiple threads at the same time, which means we will not corrupt the dictionary. Unfortunately, this does not make our code thread safe. This code is actually almost guaranteed to fail if multiple threads need to use the same item that is not already in the cache.

This a common problem, where composing two (or more) thread-safe operations often does not result in thread-safe code. The call to `TryGetValue` is now thread safe because it is protected by the lock, and the call to `Add` is thread safe for the same reason. But because we don't hold a lock for the entire runtime of the code, other threads can change the dictionary between `TryGetValue` and `Add`.

If two threads run this code simultaneously for the same item, the first thread will execute the `TryGetValue` and discover that the item isn't in the dictionary, so it will go on to create and initialize the item. The second thread will then also call `TryGetValue` (before the initialization is complete, because the reason we use a cache is that the initialization takes a long time). In addition, because the first thread didn't add the item yet, it will also see that the item is not in the cache and go on to create and initialize another copy of the item.

Now we have two different threads busy initializing two different copies of the `Item` object for the same logical item. One of those threads will finish first and add the item to the cache by calling `Add`. The other thread will also finish initializing its copy at some point and attempt to add it to the cache by calling `Add`; however, because the first thread has already added the item, `Add` will now throw an `ArgumentException`. Figure 13.1 illustrates the flow of those two threads.

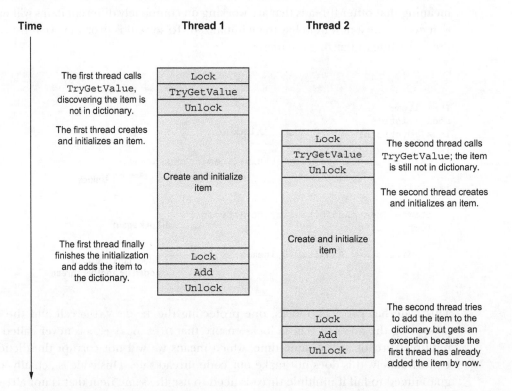

Figure 13.1 Concurrent initialization of the same item with two threads. The second thread fails because the first thread already added the item.

To make this code thread safe, we must avoid calling `Add` if another thread has already added the item while we were busy initializing it. The easiest option is to replace the call to Add with the [] operator (technically, it's the Item[] property, but I'm going to call it an operator and not a property because it's used as an operator). The [] operator adds a new item if the key does not exist and overrides the existing item if it does. This solves our exception problem but also introduces a new subtle bug.

Listing 13.4 Thread-safe cache with operator []

```
Item item;
bool exists;
lock(_dictLock)                    ◀──── Lock
{
    exists = dictionary.TryGetValue(itemId, out item);
}
if(!exists)                                      ◀────── Unlock
{
    item = CreateAndInitializeItem(itemId);
    lock(_dictLock)                    ◀───── Lock again
    {
        dictionary[itemId] = item;     ◀────── Overrides changes if already
    }                                           added by another thread
}
```

This code just replaces `dictionary.Add(itemId,item)` with `dictionary[itemId]=item`, which solves our immediate problem because operator [] will just override the previous value if it exists; however, this might introduce a bug. Now the first thread uses its own copy of the Item object, while the second and subsequent threads use the copy created by the second thread. If the Item object is immutable, and the initialization always returns an equivalent object for the same key, this can be fine; however, if the Item object is modified by the first thread, those changes will be lost.

To make sure all the threads use the same Item object, we have no choice but to recheck the dictionary after initialization and, if another thread has updated the dictionary first, use the value from the first thread.

Listing 13.5 Thread-safe cache with lock released during initialization

```
Item item;
bool exists;
lock(_dictLock)                    ◀──── Lock
{
    exists = dictionary.TryGetValue(itemId, out item);
}
if(!exists)                                      ◀────── Unlock
{
    item = CreateAndInitializeItem(itemId);
    lock(_dictLock)                    ◀───── Lock again
    {
        if(dictionary.TryGetValue(itemId,      Tests whether already
            out var itemFromOtherThread))      added by another thread
        {
            item = itemFromOtherThread;
```

```
        }
        else
        {
            dictionary.Add(itemId,item);
        }
    }
}
```

Here, we check the dictionary again instead of blindly calling `Add` or operator `[]` after the initialization. If we find the item is now in the dictionary, we drop the copy we initialized and use the one from the dictionary (because we want all threads to use the same object). We add the item only if it is still not in the dictionary.

As you can see, this code is quite complicated and difficult to follow compared to the single-threaded version in listing 13.1. Luckily, we don't have to write it because we have the concurrent collections.

13.2 *The concurrent collections*

The collections in the `System.Collections.Concurrent` are thread-safe versions of the most popular collections. The concurrent collections employ clever fine-grained locking strategies and lockless techniques to stay thread safe even when the collection is accessed by many threads simultaneously. This means all the methods and properties of the concurrent collection can be used concurrently from different threads without causing corruptions or unexpected behavior.

The concurrent collections have a different interface than the collections we all know and love from the `System.Collections.Generic` namespace because, as we've seen earlier in this chapter, just making all the normal collection's methods callable from multiple threads would not, by itself, result in thread-safe code.

This section covers the commonly used concurrent collections, starting with `ConcurrentDictionary<TKey,TValue>`, that will elegantly solve the problems we've talked about in this chapter so far.

13.2.1 *ConcurrentDictionary<TKey,TValue>*

Unsurprisingly, `ConcurrentDictionary<TKey,TValue>` is a thread-safe alternative for `Dictionary<TKey,TValue>`, but because of the problems we've seen when trying to use locks with `Dictionary<TKey,TValue>`, it has a slightly different interface geared toward solving multithreaded problems. Let's go back to the original single-threaded code of our `Dictionary<TKey,TValue>`-based cache.

Listing 13.6 Non–thread-safe cache again

```
if(!dictionary.TryGetValue(itemId, out var item))
{
    item = CreateAndInitializeItem(itemId);
    dictionary.Add(itemId,item);
}
```

This is the same code from listing 13.1. It tests whether an item is in the dictionary-based cache, and if not, it creates and initializes a new item object and adds it to the cache.

Now let's do the minimal amount of work to replace `Dictionary<TKey,TValue>` with `ConcurrentDictionary<TKey,TValue>`. The `ConcurrentDictionary<TKey,TValue>` class has a `TryGetValue` method that works the same as `Dictionary<TKey,TValue>`'s `TryGetValue`. If a value with the provided key exists in the dictionary, it returns `true` and puts the value in an `out` parameter. If a value with the key does not exist in the dictionary, it returns `false`.

But `ConcurrentDictionary<TKey,TValue>` doesn't have an `Add` method because, as we saw in listing 13.3, in multithreaded code, there's aways a chance another thread will add an item right before we call `Add` and cause it to fail with an exception. For this reason, `ConcurrentDictionary<TKey,TValue>` doesn't have an `Add` method—it is replaced with `TryAdd`.

As we've seen, no matter how small the time window between `TryGetValue` and `Add` is, there is always a chance that another thread will manage to add the item in that time-frame. To address this problem, we must treat the case where a key is already present in the dictionary, not as an exceptional error condition, but as a normal occurrence. This is what `TryAdd` does.

This difference between `Add` and `TryAdd` manifests itself in a tiny change in the method interface. While `Add` will throw an exception if the key is already in the dictionary, `TryAdd` will only return `false`.

Just replacing `Add` with `TryAdd` in the code from listing 13.6 gives this simple code that is thread safe but has a small problem. (Hint: It's the same problem from listing 13.4.)

Listing 13.7 Thread-safe cache with `ConcurrentDictionary.TryAdd`

```
if(!dictionary.TryGetValue(itemId, out var item))
{
    item = CreateAndInitializeItem(itemId);
    dictionary.TryAdd(itemId,item);
}
```

This listing replaces `Add` with `TryAdd`. And because `TryAdd` doesn't throw an exception if the key is already in the dictionary, this code works and is thread safe. It just has a variation of the problem we had in listing 13.4. If multiple threads initialize the same item at the same time, each will have its own copy of the `Item` object. If the `Item` object isn't immutable, or all those copies are not identical, this can cause a real problem.

What we really want is to combine `TryGetValue` and `TryAdd` into a single atomic operation in a way that eliminates this problem. `ConcurrentDictionary<TKey,TValue>` does this with the `GetOrAdd` method.

Listing 13.8 Thread-safe cache with `ConcurrentDictionary.GetOrAdd`

```
var item = dictionary.GetOrAdd(itemId,CreateAndInitializeItem);
```

This single line calling to `GetOrAdd` is equivalent to the 21 lines in listing 13.5. If the item is already in the dictionary, it will return the item. If not, it will call `CreateAndInitialize` to create the item. If multiple threads call `GetOrAdd` before the item completed initialization and was added to the dictionary, all of them will run `CreateAndInitialize`, but `GetOrAdd` will return the same object in all threads.

`GetOrAdd` has a version that accepts the value to add to the dictionary as the second parameter, as well as the version we used that accepts a delegate to call to initialize the value. `ConcurrentDictionary<TKey,TValue>` uses fine-grained locking so that `GetOrAdd` calls for different keys can run concurrently.

Note that if you use the version of the method that accepts a delegate, and you call `GetOrAdd` from multiple threads simultaneously, the initialization code can run more than once. The first thread to finish will get to add the value to the dictionary, and the result of the initialization code from other threads will be ignored. You should be aware whether your item requires cleanup or if you can't run the initialization code multiple times.

`ConcurrentDictionary<TKey,TVale>` also has a `TryRemove` method that will remove the value and return `true` if the value existed and was removed. However, it will return `false` if the value doesn't exist in the dictionary. Having a `TryRemove` instead of a `Remove` method solves the same kind of race condition we've seen when we've talked about `Add` and `TryAdd`.

And finally, `ConcurrentDictionary<TKey,TVale>` also has a `TryUpdate` method. This method solves a problem where one thread might overwrite data written by another thread. As an example of this problem, let's write a method that increments a value in the dictionary.

Listing 13.9 Non–thread-safe increment

```
private ConcurrentDictionary<string, int> _dictionary = new();

public void Increment(string key)
{
    int prevValue = _dictionary[key];
    _dictionary[key] = prevValue+1;
}
```

This method reads the value associated with a key, adds one to the value, and writes the new value into the dictionary.

This code also has a race condition bug. Let's say the current value for a given key is 1, and we call `Increment` simultaneously from two different threads. The expected result is that the value will be 3 (we started with 1 and incremented it twice), but if we're unlucky with our timing, we might get the following sequence:

1 Thread 1 reads the value and gets 1.
2 Thread 2 reads the value. Because the first thread hasn't written the new value yet, it also gets 1.

3 Thread 1 increments and saves the value; the value in the dictionary is now 2.

4 Thread 2 increments and saves the value; the value in the dictionary is still 2.

To solve this problem, we must either add a lock around the entire operation or at least have a way to detect this problem so we can correct it. This is what `TryUpdate` does.

Listing 13.10   Thread-safe increment with `ConcurrentDictionary.TryUpdate`

```
private ConcurrentDictionary<string, int> _dictionary = new();

public void Increment(string key)
{
    while(true)
    {
        int prevValue = _dictionary[key];
        if(_dictionary.TryUpdate(key, prevValue+1, prevValue))
            break;
    }
}
```

Now the method enters a loop, and it reads the current value into the `prevValue` variable. It then calls `TryUpdate` with both the new value (`prevValue+1`) and the old value (`prevValue`). If the current value in the dictionary is still `prevValue`, `TryUpdate` will update the value and return `true`. This will make our code break out of the loop. But if someone else changed the value in the dictionary, `TryUpdate` will leave the dictionary unchanged and will return `false`, which will make our code repeat the loop and retry incrementing the value until it succeeds.

`ConcurrentDictionary<TKey,TValue>` doesn't have asynchronous interfaces, but it only blocks for a very short time, and it works very well with asynchronous code.

13.2.2   BlockingCollection<T>

`BlockingCollection<T>` adds blocking producer–consumer operations on top of another collection. Basically, it adds the ability to wait until an item becomes available. The options for the collection backing a `BlockingCollection<T>` are `Concurrent-Queue<T>`, `ConcurrentStack<T>`, and `ConcurrentBag<T>`. (We'll talk about them more in the next section.)

The default option, and most used by an enormous margin, is `ConcurrentQueue<T>`. A `BlockingCollection<T>` backed by a `ConcurrentQueue<T>` keeps the item order—like in a queue, the first item in is the first item out. We've already seen back in chapter 8 how it can be used as the basis for a very simple and effective work queue.

The second used option is `ConcurrentStack<T>`. A `BlockingCollection<T>` backed by a `ConcurrentStack<T>` acts like a stack—the last item to be added is the first item out. This is useful if you have a multithreaded algorithm that requires a thread-safe stack, which makes the consumer wait until another thread adds items to the stack if the stack is empty.

The last option, `ConcurrentBag<T>`, is rarely used. `ConcurrentBag<T>` is a specialized collection that is optimized for the case where the same thread both reads and writes from/to the collection (more about this later in this chapter).

Apart from adding the ability to wait until an item is available, `Blocking-Collection<T>` also lets you specify the maximum size of the collection; this is useful in preventing the producer from getting too far ahead of the consumer. This feature is called *bounded capacity*.

The most common usage for `BlockingCollection<T>` is as a work queue (like our work queue example in chapter 8, where we wrote a work queue implementation with a single background thread). Let's extend the code from chapter 8 and write a `Blocking-Collection<T>`-based queue with multiple consumer threads.

Listing 13.11 `BlockingCollection` with 10 processing threads

```
BlockingCollection<int> blockingCollection = new BlockingCollection<int>();
Thread[] workers =  new Thread[10];
for(int i=0; i<workers.Length; i++)            ◄──┐ Creates 10 worker
{                                                  │ threads
    workers[i] = new Thread(threadNumber =>
    {
        var rng = new Random((int)threadNumber);
        int count = 0;
        foreach (var currentValue in
                blockingCollection.GetConsumingEnumerable())
        {
            Console.WriteLine($"thread {threadNumber} value {currentValue}");
            Thread.Sleep(rng.Next(500));
            count++;
        }
        Console.WriteLine($"thread {threadNumber}, total {count} items");
    });
    workers[i].Start(i);
}                                         ┌─ Adds 100 items
for(int i=0;i<100;i++)              ◄─────┘  to process
{
    blockingCollection.Add(i);
}                                        ┌─ Signals no more items
blockingCollection.CompleteAdding();  ◄──┘
foreach (var curentThread in workers)  ◄───────── Waits for all threads to finish
    curentThread.Join();
```

This code creates a `BlockingCollection<int>` to hold the data we need to process in the background. It then starts 10 background threads to do this processing, and each thread uses `foreach` and `GetConsumingEnumerable` to get the items to process. To simulate the processing, we just wait a small random amount of time and print the number. We insert the numbers 0 to 99 into the queue as a stand-in for the data we want to process.

When we run this code, we see that it works—all the data is processed, each data item is processed exactly once, and data items are mostly processed in order. The items are processed mostly in order because while the `BlockingCollection<T>` provides the items in order, timing problems will sometimes cause one thread to overtake a previous thread, making it look like the two items swapped position.

The bounded capacity feature mentioned earlier is mainly implemented by the `Add` method. The `Add` method adds an item to the collection. If the collection is at maximum capacity, it will block until some other thread removes an item. The `TryAdd` method is similar but adds a timeout (that can be zero). If the collection is at maximum capacity, it will block until another thread removes an item or until the timeout elapses. If the timeout elapses, `TryAdd` will fail and return `false`. If the timeout is zero, `TryAdd` will always return immediately.

The `Take` method returns the next item in the collection and removes it in a single thread-safe operation. The next item will be the oldest item in the collection if it's backed by a `ConcurrentQueue<T>`, the newest if it's backed by a `ConcurrentStack<T>`, or any of the items if the backing collection is a `ConcurrentBag<T>`. If the collection is empty, `Take` will block until another thread adds an item using `Add` or `TryAdd`. `TryTake` (like `TryAdd`) is the same as `Take` with an added timeout. If the collection is empty, and the timeout elapses before an item becomes available, `TryTake` will fail and return `false`. If you pass zero as the timeout, `TryTake` will always return immediately.

The most common way to read data from a `BlockingCollection<T>` is to use `foreach` with `GetConsumingEnumerable`, like we did in chapter 8, instead of calling `Take` or `TryTake` directly. `GetConsumingEnumerable` returns an `IEnumerable<T>` that, when used with `foreach`, removes the current item at every iteration of the loop and, if the collection is empty, blocks until another thread adds an item to the collection. It is basically equivalent to calling `Take` at the beginning of every loop iteration.

If we use `GetConsumingEnumerable` and `foreach`, we need a way to signal that there are no new items and we can exit the loop. This is done with `CompleteAdding`. After calling `CompleteAdding`, the `foreach` loop will continue to process all remaining items in the collection and then exit. Calling `Add` or `TryAdd` after `CompleteAdding` will throw an `InvalidOperationException`.

`BlockingCollection<T>` also has the static `AddToAny`, `TryAddToAny`, `TakeFromAny`, and `TryTakeFromAny` methods. They work like their non-static counterparts except that they accept an array of `BlockingCollection<T>` objects and use one of them based on the number of items in each collection. They look like a good way to build a system with multiple consumer threads where every thread has its own `BlockingCollection<T>`, but they're not.

`AddToAny` and `TryAddToAny` do not provide any load balancing. They're optimized to complete the `AddToAny` operation as quickly as possible, so they will always look for the fastest option to add to a collection. In most cases, they will just add the item to the first collection that is not at maximum capacity. So `AddToAny` and `TryAddToAny` will tend to add items to the same `BlockingCollection<T>`. If you use them to build a multiple processing threads system, then one thread will receive most of the work, and the rest of the threads will be idle most of the time.

`BlockingCollection<T>` is very useful if you manage your own threads, but as its name implies, it uses blocking operations and thus doesn't fit the asynchronous programming model.

13.2.3 *Async alternatives for BlockingCollection*

As of .NET version 8, the .NET standard library does not have asynchronous collections in general and does not have an asynchronous version of `BlockingCollection<T>`. However, it does have several other classes that can be repurposed as an asynchronous queue. One of those is `Channel<T>`, a thread-safe multiple-producers multiple-consumers queue, designed for communication between software components.

The `Channel<T>` class represents a communication channel; each channel has a writer that can add messages to the channel and a reader that can take messages from the channel. The channel keeps the message ordering, which makes it equivalent to a queue. Both the reader and the writer explicitly support concurrent access.

We can translate listing 13.11 to use `Channel<T>` instead of `BlockingCollection<T>` and get the following.

Listing 13.12 Async background processing with `Channel<T>`

```
var ch = Channel.CreateUnbounded<int>();
Task[] tasks = new Task[10];
for(int i=0; i<10;++i)                          ◀─── Starts 10 async tasks
{
    var threadNumber = i;
    tasks[i] = Task.Run(async () =>
    {
        var rng = new Random((int)threadNumber);
        int count = 0;
        while (true)
        {
            try                                                Awaits next
            {                                                  data item
                var currentValue = await ch.Reader.ReadAsync();  ◀
                Console.WriteLine($"task {threadNumber} value {currentValue}");
                Thread.Sleep(rng.Next(500));
                count++;
            }                                              This exception means
            catch(ChannelClosedException)          ◀───── no more data.
            {
                break;
            }
        }
        Console.WriteLine($"task {threadNumber}, total {count} items");
    });
}
for (int i = 0; i < 100; i++)          ◀───── Adds 100 items to process
{
    await ch.Writer.WriteAsync(i);         Signals no more data
}
ch.Writer.Complete();                                  Waits for all tasks
Task.WaitAll(tasks);                   ◀───────────── to complete
```

Here we create a `Channel<T>` instead of a `BlockingCollection<T>`, and instead of creating a thread, we use `Task.Run`. The code we pass to `Task.Run` will start running on a thread pool thread and then immediately use `await` to release the thread. We could skip this step with some clever use of `ContinueWith`, but it would make the code more complicated.

The biggest change from listing 13.11 is that instead of using `foreach`, we need to use `while(true)`, and we need to use an exception to detect when we should exit. We will see what we can do about this in the next chapter.

13.2.4 *ConcurrentQueue<T> and ConcurrentStack<T>*

`ConcurrentQueue<T>` is a thread-safe version of `Queue<T>`, and `ConcurrentStack<T>` is a thread-safe version of `Stack<T>`. `ConcurrentQueue<T>` is a FIFO (first in, first out) data structure, which means that when you read the next item, you always get the oldest item in the queue. `ConcurrentStack<T>` is a LIFO (last in, first out) data structure, which means the next item will always be the most recent one.

Both `ConcurrentQueue<T>` and `ConcurrentStack<T>` provide the same methods for adding items as their non–thread-safe counterparts (`Enqueue` for `ConcurrentQueue<T>` and `Push` for `ConcurrentStack<T>`), and both provide a way to get the next item (`TryDequeue` and `TryPop`, respectively). The interface is different from the non–thread-safe version for the same reasons that we've seen when we've talked about `ConcurrentDictionary<TKey,TValue>`. If we had a thread-safe version with the same interface as `Queue<T>`, we would need to write code like this:

```
var queue = new Queue<int>();
// ....
if(queue.Count > 0)          │  Another thread can
{                            ◄──┘  dequeue the last item here.
    var next = queue.Dequeue();
    // use next
}
```

This code checks whether there are items in the queue and then dequeues the next item; however, in multithread code, another thread can always dequeue the last item between the time we checked and the time we dequeued. This means that even if we had a thread-safe class with the same interface as `Queue<T>`, it would have been difficult to use it to write thread-safe code. In contrast, with the `ConcurrentQueue<T>` interface, we write code like this:

```
var queue = new ConcurrentQueue<int>();
// ....                         │  Check and dequeue
if(queue.TryDequeue(out var next))  ◄──┘  are combined.
{
    // use next
}
```

Here the check and dequeue operations are combined into a single `TryDequeue` call, which eliminates the time window between the check and the dequeue operation and solves this problem.

You can use `ConcurrentQueue<T>` and `ConcurrentStack<T>` directly if you need a thread-safe queue or stack and don't need a mechanism to signal when an item is available for processing. However, they are most useful in conjunction with `BlockingCollection<T>`.

13.2.5 ConcurrentBag<T>

Unlike `ConcurrentQueue<T>` and `ConcurrentStack<T>`, `ConcurrentBag<T>` doesn't have a parallel outside of the concurrent collections. The `ConcurrentBag<T>` data structure does not enforce item ordering. When you retrieve items from the bag, you can get them in any order. `ConcurrentBag<T>` can store duplicate items. `ConcurrentBag<T>` has an `Add` method for adding items and a `TryTake` method for retrieving and removing the items in the collection.

The implementation of `ConcurrentBag<T>` uses per-thread queues, and `TryTake` will try to provide items inserted by the same thread. This is helpful because with per-thread queues, the `ConcurrentBag<T>` doesn't have to block if two threads try to retrieve an item simultaneously. If an item added by the current thread isn't available, `TryTake` will get an item from another thread's queue (this is called *work stealing*), which requires thread synchronization and so is slower.

That is why you should only use `ConcurrentBag<T>` if the same thread (or set of threads) both add and retrieve items from the bag. For example, you should only use `ConcurrentBag<T>` as the backing collection for a `BlockingCollection<T>`-based work queue if the code that handles items in the collection also adds them. Also, you shouldn't use `ConcurrentBag<T>` in asynchronous code because typically, you don't control which thread runs it.

13.2.6 When to use the concurrent collections

`ConcurrentDictionary<TKey,TValue>` is a very good thread-safe alternative to `Dictionary<TKey,TValue>`. We've already seen examples of using it as an in-process cache. It can be used anytime we need to access a dictionary from multiple threads at the same time. Also, it can be used in both asynchronous and non-asynchronous code.

Likewise, `ConcurrentQueue<T>` and `ConcurrentStack<T>` are good thread-safe implementations of the queue and stack data structures. We can use them whenever we need concurrent access to a queue or a stack, and we don't need a built-in mechanism to signal when items are available. They are also perfectly usable in both asynchronous and non-asynchronous code.

If you do need this signal and want the consumer thread to block when there's no work available, then `BlockingCollection<T>` is a perfect fit. However, `BlockingCollection<T>`, especially `Take` and `GetConsumingEnumerable`, does not fit the asynchronous programming model.

13.2.7 When not to use the concurrent collections

If we need to use a lock to make our own code thread safe (except for just protecting access to the collection), then we use this lock to synchronize access to our code (and the collection) and don't need to use a collection that supports concurrent access. In this case, the non–thread-safe alternatives (`Dictionary<TKey,TValue>`, `Queue<T>`, and `Stack<T>`) are simpler and faster.

If you do need thread safety because you pass the collection to some (maybe external) code that doesn't need to modify the collection and can work if the collection is a little bit stale (that is, not completely up to date), you should look into using the immutable collections instead.

13.3 The immutable collections

The problems of thread safety always boil down to multiple threads modifying the data simultaneously, threads reading while other threads are modifying the data, or timing problems making threads modify data in the wrong order. All those problems are about modifying data—if you never modify data, you won't have any of those problems, and your code will be inherently thread safe.

While the concurrent collections use clever locking and lockless strategies to make it safe to modify a collection by multiple threads simultaneously, the immutable collections achieve thread safety by simply being immutable. If they can't be modified at all, they can't be modified by two threads at the same time.

The immutable collections work like the .NET `string` class. All the methods that modify the collection actually leave the collection untouched and return a brand-new collection that is a copy of the original collection with the requested modifications.

It might seem like all this copying is wasteful and can cause poor performance and excessive memory usage problems, but the immutable collections mitigate this problem by using internal data structures that can share parts of the data between collections. Therefore, creating a modified copy of a collection is cheap (or, at least, cheaper than copying the entire collection).

13.3.1 How immutable collections work

If you look at the standard collections, you will find that they are all based on arrays. The reason is that due to the way the CPU accesses memory, arrays are the most performant data storage option. `List<T>` is just a wrapper around an array. `Queue<T>` and `Stack<T>` are also arrays. `HashSet<T>` is a hash table implemented by using two arrays, and `Dictionary<TKey,TValue>` is implemented using four arrays. Everything is based on arrays. However, arrays are just contiguous blocks of memory; you can't share memory between arrays, which is why the immutable collections generally don't use them and instead opt for data structures that do support sharing parts of the memory between collections.

Why arrays are more efficient than other data structures

The CPU is much faster than the computer's memory. For example, for a 2GHz CPU, each CPU clock cycle is 0.5 nano seconds, while access to DDR5 memory takes around 16.67 nano seconds, give or take. Applying a little bit of math shows us that a CPU can perform about 33 internal operations in the time it takes it to retrieve anything from memory.

(continued)

Obviously, having the CPU on idle and waiting for data to arrive from memory most of the time would be bad, so clever CPU designers devised a solution—just add a little bit of memory into the CPU chip. This memory runs nearly as fast as the CPU processing cores (the reason we can't make all the computer's memory this fast is cost). We call this memory the *CPU cache memory*. We also have a hardware component inside the CPU chip that is called the *cache controller*. One of the things the cache controller does is try to preload data from the main memory into the CPU cache before we need it.

Arrays are contiguous blocks of memory. All the items in the array are stored in memory one after the other; when we iterate an array, we scan this memory sequentially. If you scan memory sequentially, it's easy for the cache controller to guess the next value you are going to retrieve from memory—it's the value immediately after your previous memory access.

Other data structures, such as linked lists and trees, are not contiguous in memory. To get the memory address of the next item in a linked list, you must read the current item's node and extract the "next" field from it. Linked lists and trees do not have a standard node layout, and the cache controller doesn't know how to parse nodes of whatever data structure from whichever library your program may be using.

That is why when you scan an array, the next value will most likely will be waiting for you in the cache ready for immediate access; however, when you access another data structure, the CPU will spend a significant amount of time waiting for data to be transferred from the computer's main memory.

And a quick note for the readers that know about CPU design and are screaming at the book about cache lines and clock cycles per operation: you are obviously right, but this is not a book about hardware design, and the explanation here is correct enough to explain the performance characteristics of arrays.

To understand the tricks used by immutable collections, we will implement an immutable stack. But before we do so, we need a regular array-based stack to compare it to.

We will implement the simplest thread-safe stack possible. Our stack will only have two methods: a `Push` method that adds an item to the top of the stack and a `TryPop` method that retrieves the item at the top of the stack or returns `false` if the stack is empty. We will also limit our array-based stack to just 10 items because I want to focus on how the immutable stack works and not on how to resize the array-based stack. We will achieve thread safety by using a lock to protect all access to the stack.

Listing 13.13 **Simple stack implementation**

```
public class MyStack<T>
{
    private T?[] _data = new T[10];
    private int _top = -1;
    private object _lock = new();
```

```
public void Push(T item)
{
    lock(_lock)
    {
        if(_top == _data.Length-1) throw new Exception("Stack full");
        _top++;
        _data[_top] = item;
    }
}
public bool TryPop(out T? item)
{
    if(_top==-1)
    {
        item = default(T);
        return false;
    }
    item = _data[_top];
    _data[_top] = default(T);
    _top--;
    return true;
}
}
```

Now let's see what happens when we run the following test code.

Listing 13.14 Test code for simple stack

```
var stack = new MyStack<int>();
stack.Push(1);
stack.Push(2);
stack.TryPop(out var item);
```

This code creates a stack and then pushes two values (one and two); it will then pop the last value out.

Let's see what happens inside the stack when we run the test code. When we create the stack, _top is set to −1 in our constructor (virtually pointing to the nonexistent item before the start of the array), and _data is initialized by the runtime to all zeros (figure 13.2).

Figure 13.2 Simple stack initial state

After the Push(1) call, we increment _top to zero, making it point at the current top of the stack and store 1 into the new top (which is _data[0]; figure 13.3).

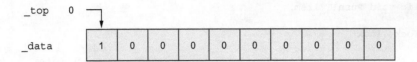

Figure 13.3   Simple stack after first push

The Push(2) call will increment _top again to 1, indicating that _data[1] is now top of the stack, and store 2 into the new top (figure 13.4).

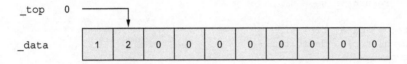

Figure 13.4   Simple stack after second push

The TryPop call will return the item at the current top of the stack (_data[1]) using the item out parameter. It will also zero out the current top and decrement _top to zero indicating the new top is _data[0], effectively returning the stack to the same state as before the last push (figure 13.5).

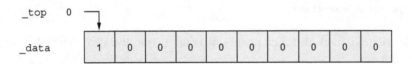

Figure 13.5   Simple stack after pop

Now that you understand how a standard stack works, let's implement an immutable stack. With an immutable stack, we no longer change the stack. Instead, each call will return a new stack. We will have a Push method, a Pop method, and an IsEmpty property. In the regular implementation, we had to combine Pop and IsEmpty into a single TryPop method because we have no way to prevent another thread from modifying the stack between the IsEmpty check and the Pop call. With the immutable stack, no one can modify the stack at all, so no one can modify the stack between the IsEmpty check and the Pop call. As the stack is immutable, Push and Pop will not modify the stack but will return a new stack with an item added or removed.

If we keep using an array, we'll have to copy the entire array on every Push and Pop, and obviously, we don't want that. Luckily, we can implement a stack using a singly linked list.

Listing 13.15 Immutable stack implementation

```
public class MyImmutableStack<T>
{
    private record class StackItem(T Value, StackItem Next);
    private readonly StackItem? _top;
    public MyImmutableStack() {}
    private MyImmutableStack(StackItem? top)
    {
        _top = top;
    }
    public MyImmutableStack<T> Push(T item)
    {
        return new MyImmutableStack<T>(new StackItem(item,_top);
    }
    public MyImmutableStack<T> Pop(out T? item)
    {
        if(_top == null)
            throw new InvalidOperationException("Stack is empty");
        item = _top.Value;
        return new MyImmutableStack<T>(_top.Next);
    }
    public bool IsEmpty => _top == null;
}
```

Now we'll run the equivalent code to listing 13.14 on this new immutable stack.

Listing 13.16 Test code for immutable stack

```
var stack1 = new MyImmutableStack<int> ();
var stack2 = stack1.Push(1);
var stack3 = stack2.Push(2);
var Stack4 = stack3.Pop(out var item);
```

This code creates a new empty stack and assigns it to the stack1 variable. Next, it calls Push, which creates another stack with the new item and assigns it to the stack2 variable. It then calls Push again, which also creates a new stack with an additional item and stores it as stack3. Finally, it calls Pop, which creates yet another stack, but this time with the top item removed, and puts it in the stack4 variable.

Let's see what happens inside the immutable stack when we run the test code. The MyImmutableStack parameterless constructor will create a new stack that has no Stack-Item (_top will be null) (figure 13.6).

stack1 ⟶ null

Figure 13.6 Immutable stack initial state

The Push(1) call will also create a new stack, which will have a single stack item with Value set to 1 and Next set to the previous _top (null) (figure 13.7).

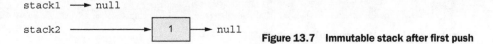

Figure 13.7   Immutable stack after first push

The Push(2) call will create a new stack and a new StackItem. The new StackItem will have Value set to 2 and Next pointing to stack2's _top, which is the existing StackItem storing the value 1. Note that now two stacks are sharing this first StackItem (figure 13.8).

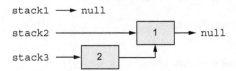

Figure 13.8   Immutable stack after second push

Finally, the Pop call will, unsurprisingly, create a new stack. The new stack will point to _top.Next, that is, to the old StackItem with the value 1 that will now be shared between the three stacks (figure 13.9).

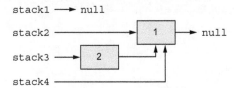

Figure 13.9   Immutable stack after pop

Usually, we will reuse the same variable and not create a new variable for each version of the stack (we'll have just one variable instead of stack1, stack2, stack3, and stack4); however, this does not change anything (except that, with the separate variable names, the figures area is easier to understand). Even if we reuse the variables, all the old stacks will still hang around in memory until the next time the garbage collector runs and frees them.

Now you can see how every operation on the immutable stack creates a new stack with a negligible amount of work and without copying any of the items already in the stack. This is at the cost of using a little bit more memory (each item now has the Next reference and all the overhead of an object) and having the items spread around in memory instead of being stored sequentially in an array (which, because of CPU cache design, slows down the access to them).

I've chosen to demonstrate how the immutable stack works because this is the simplest of the immutable collections; however, they all use the same basic tactic—place the data inside node objects and design your operation so that every "modified" copy can share most of the previous collection's nodes. As we've seen, a stack can be implemented with just one linked list. A queue needs two linked lists, and most of the other immutable collections use some kind of binary tree. The implementation details of all the immutable collections are outside the scope of this book.

13.3.2 *How to use the immutable collections*

Some data changes so rarely that storing it in a data structure that cannot change doesn't pose problems. For example, the list of countries in the world does change sometimes, but it's rare enough that we can accept having to restart our service to refresh this list. However, the data that's really critical for our software, that data that we manage, tends to change all the time.

Let's say we are building an e-commerce site that sells books. Obviously, the survival of the company depends on selling a lot of books, so we really want to be able to sell more than one book simultaneously. For this reason, we've decided to use the immutable collection to store our inventory due to the inherent thread safety. Let's write some code to manage our inventory.

Listing 13.17 Non–thread-safe stack management with `ImmutableDictionary`

```
public class InventoryManager
{
    private ImmutableDictionary<string,int> _bookIdToQuantity;

    public bool TryToBuyBook(string bookId)
    {
        if(!_bookIdToQuantity.TryGetValue(bookId, out var copiesInStock))     ◄─── Gets previous quantity
            return false;
        if(copiesInStock == 0)
            return false;
        _bookIdToQuantity =
            _bookIdToQuantity.SetItem(bookId, copiesInStock-1);     ◄─── Sets new quantity
        return true;
    }
}
```

We wrote the `InventoryManager` class with a single method called `TryToBuyBook`. This method first retrieves the number of copies we have in stock from an `Immutable-Dictionary<string,int>` that's referenced by the `_bookIdToQuantity` variable. If the book doesn't exist in the shop, or there are no copies in stock, the method returns `false` to indicate the customer can't buy the book. If everything is okay, the method updates the stock by using the dictionary's `SetItem` to create a new dictionary with the updated number of copies and stores the new dictionary in the same variable. It then returns `true`.

If you think about what happens when this code runs on multiple threads simultaneously, it's easy to see the problem: the dictionary can't change, it's immutable, and it's impossible for another thread to modify the dictionary. However, if that dictionary is referenced by a normal mutable variable, another thread can change the variable swapping the dictionary with another one, and that change is not protected by the immutable data structure. See figure 13.10.

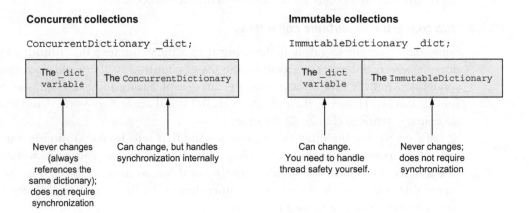

Concurrent collections

```
ConcurrentDictionary _dict;
```

The _dict variable	The ConcurrentDictionary

Never changes (always references the same dictionary); does not require synchronization

Can change, but handles synchronization internally

Immutable collections

```
ImmutableDictionary _dict;
```

The _dict variable	The ImmutableDictionary

Can change. You need to handle thread safety yourself.

Never changes; does not require synchronization

Figure 13.10   Synchronization needs of immutable collections versus concurrent collections

The simplest solution is to place a lock around the entire method. This solves our data corruption problem, but it completely nullifies any benefits we get from the immutable collection's thread safety. If we place a lock around any access to the dictionary, we might as well use the simpler non–thread-safe `Dictionary<TKey,TValue>`.

The complicated solution is to use `ImmutableInterlocked`.

13.3.3   *ImmutableInterlocked*

The `ImmutableInterlocked` class gives us lock-free operations for modifying a variable referencing an immutable collection. It contains methods that implement the same operation we've seen in the concurrent collection, but this time for the immutable collection.

For example, for `ImmutableDictionary<TKey,TValue>`, `ImmutableInterlocked` gives us `AddOrUpdate`, `GetOrAdd`, `TryAdd`, `TryRemove`, and `TryUpdate`, which are similar to the `ConcurrentDictionary<TKey,TValue>` methods with the same name.

If you remember from listing 13.10, `ConcurrentDictionary<TKey,TValue>.TryUpdate` ensures that the value we are trying to update hasn't been changed by someone else. Then, if the value hasn't been changed, it will replace that value in the dictionary. `ImmutableInterlocked.TryUpdate` does the same for immutable dictionaries; it will make sure that the value we are trying to update hasn't been changed by someone else. Then, if the value hasn't changed, it will replace the entire dictionary with a new dictionary with one different value.

Just like `ConcurrentDictionary<TKey,TValue>.TryUpdate`, it will return false without changing anything if the value was changed by another thread, and we need to deal with it, typically by reading the new value and redoing our processing until we succeed.

Listing 13.18 Thread-safe stock management with `ImmutableInterlocked`

```
private ImmutalbeDictionery<string,int> _bookIdToQuantity = new();
public bool TryToBuyBook(string bookId)
{
    while(true)
    {
        if(!_bookIdToQuantity.TryGetValue(bookId,
            out var copiesInStock))          ◄──┘  Gets previous quantity
        Return false;
        if(copiesInStock == 0)
            return false;
        if(ImmutableInterlocked.TryUpdate(         Sets new quantity only
            ref _bookIdToQuantity, bookId,         if it didn't change
            copiesInStock-1, copiesInStock))
            return true;                    ◄──
    }                        ◄──┘         On success, returns
}                             If changed, repeats loop
}
```

This is the safe version of listing 13.17. It reads the number of copies in stock and tries to decrease it by 1, and if the number of copies has already changed since we've read it, this code will read the value again, validate that it has a copy to sell again, and try to decrease the value in the _bookIdToQuantity dictionary. It will continue doing this either until it succeeds or until transactions running on other threads cause the number of copies in stock to go down to zero.

`ImmutableInterlocked` also provides `Push` and `TryPop` methods for use with `ImmutableStack<T>`, and `Enqueue` and `TryDequeue` for `ImmutableQueue<T>`. Note that using `ImmutableInterlocked` is an all-or-nothing deal—it's only safe if all your modifications use `ImmutableInterlocked`. Also note that you cannot use `ImmutableInterlocked` to update multiple collections in a thread-safe way. If, for example, you need to add the same key to two dictionaries, there is no way to do it with `ImmutableInterlocked` without having a time window where another thread can view the change in the first dictionary before you updated the second. This also goes for multiple changes in the same dictionary—you can't use `ImmutableInterlocked` to change two values at once.

13.3.4 *ImmutableDictionary<TKey,TValue>*

`ImmutableDictionary<TKey,TValue>` is, predictably, the immutable version of `Dictionary<TKey,TValue>. ImmutableDictionary<TKey,TValue>`, just like `Dictionary<TKey,TValue>`, lets us check whether a key exists by using `ContainsKey`, retrieve a value by using the `[]` operator, and do both in a single call by using `TryGetValue`.

It also has most of the methods used in `Dictionary<TKey,TValue>` to modify the dictionary (`Add`, `Remove`, and so on), but in `ImmutableDictionary<TKey,TValue>`, they leave the dictionary untouched and return a new dictionary with the modifications. To change a specific value inside the dictionary, you use the `UpdateValue` method instead of the `[]` operator because there's no good way for the `[]` operator to return a new dictionary.

The `ImmutableDictionary<TKey,TValue>` does not itself have any of the special operations found in `ConcurrentDictionary<TKey,TValue>`, such as `GetOrAdd`, because since the `ImmutableDictionary<TKey,TValue>` is immutable, it can't change between the `Get` and the `Add`.

If you need to add, remove, or update multiple values simultaneously, `Immutable-Dictionary<TKey,TValue>` provides the `AddRange`, `RemoveRange`, and `UpdateItems` methods. These methods are important for writing high-performance code because they create just one new `ImmutableDictionary<TKey,TValue>` for the entire method call instead of one new dictionary for each and every value changed.

If you need to make multiple modifications of different types (for example, adding a value and removing another), or your algorithm doesn't let you easily group changes (for example, if you can't replace several `Add` calls with one `AddRange` call), you can use a builder object. A builder object is created using the dictionary's `ToBuilder` method. The builder is not immutable, and you can use it to make multiple modifications without creating a new dictionary. When you've finished with the modifications, you call the builder's `ToImmutable` method that created one new `ImmutableDictionary<TKey,` `TValue>` with all the modifications.

The builder is not immutable and not thread safe. It is a fast and efficient way to create new `ImmutableDictionary<TKey,TValue>` objects, but it does not do anything to help with multithreading.

As we've seen earlier in this chapter, the variable holding the up-to-date version of the dictionary is just a simple variable and has the same threading behavior as any other variable (not thread-safe without locking if there are any write operations). As we've also seen earlier in this chapter, if you want a fast, lock-free way to synchronize access to that variable, you can use `ImmutableInterlocked`. It provides the `AddOrUpdate`, `GetOrAdd`, `TryAdd`, `TryRemove`, and `TryUpdate` methods, which work the same way as the `ConcurrentDictionary<TKey,TValue>` methods with the same name (except that, being immutable, the dictionary never changes, and those operation swap the dictionary with a new dictionary that has the requested modifications).

If you use `ImmutableInterlocked` with `ImmutableDictionary<TKey,TValue>`, it's likely you are doing it to get basically the same behavior that you get with `Concurrent-Dictionary<TKey,TValue>`. If this is the case, you will probably be better off just using `ConcurrentDictionary<TKey,TValue>` instead.

Remember that you can either use `ImmutableDictionary<TKey,TValue>`'s methods (and the builder) to create modified copies, or you can use `ImmutableInterlocked`. Using both is not thread safe.

13.3.5 *ImmutableHashSet<T> and ImmutableSortedSet<T>*

Naturally, `ImmutableHashSet<T>` and `ImmutableSortedSet<T>` are the immutable versions of `HashSet<T>` and `SortedSet<T>`. They both represent a set from set theory—they contain zero or more items with no duplicates and can also perform set theory operations (`Except`, `Intersect`, `IsSubsetOf`, `IsSupersetOf`, and so forth).

When you enumerate an `ImmutableHashSet<T>` (for example, by using `foreach`), the items' order is completely arbitrary and is not under your control, but operations on the set, especially lookup, are very fast. In contrast, if you enumerate an `Immutable-SortedSet<T>`, you get the item in sorted order (you can control the sort order by passing an `IComparer<T>` to the static `ImmutableSortedSet.Create<T>` method), but operation on the set will be slower. Because of the performance difference, it's recommended to prefer `ImmutableHashSet<T>` and only use `ImmutableSortedSet<T>` if you care about the items' order during enumeration.

As with all the immutable collections, all the methods that would normally change the collection return a new collection with the modifications instead. Also, like we've seen with `ImmutableDictionary<TKey,TValue>`, both `ImmutableHashSet<T>` and `ImmutableSortedSet<T>` have a `ToBuilder` method that returns an object you can use to efficiently perform many modifications and then create only one new immutable set for all the modifications. Remember, the builder object is not thread safe.

In addition, as with all of the immutable collections, if you have a variable referencing the up-to-date version of the collection, you need to synchronize access to the variable yourself (most likely, using locks). Unlike `ImmutableDictionary<TKey,TValue>`, you can't use `ImmutableInterlocked` with the immutable set classes.

13.3.6 *ImmutableList<T>*

`ImmutableList<T>` is, unsurprisingly, the immutable version of `List<T>` and, also unsurprisingly, works the same way as the previous immutable collections. All the methods that don't modify the list work exactly like in `List<T>`. All the methods that do modify the list return a new `ImmutableList<T>` instead. To set an item at a specific location, use the `SetItem` method instead of the `[]` operator because the operator has no good way to return a new `ImmutableList<T>` object.

Like all the previous immutable collections, `ImmutableList<T>` has a `ToBuilder` method that returns a mutable object you can use to perform multiple modifications without creating an excessive number of `ImmutableList<T>` objects. As always, the builder object is not thread safe.

If you have a variable holding an `ImmutableList<T>` object that is accessed by different threads, you need to synchronize access to this variable. `ImmutableInterlocked` does not support `ImmutableList<T>`.

13.3.7 *ImmutableQueue<T> and ImmutableStack<T>*

`ImmutableQueue<T>` and `ImmutableStack<T>` are, obviously, the immutable versions of `Queue<T>` and `Stack<T>`. Because queue and stack are almost always used as temporary storage, with items added and removed all the time, in almost all cases, `Concurrent-Queue<T>` and `ConcurrentStack<T>` are a better choice, with the notable exception of functional programming.

If you do use the immutable queue and stack, then the `ImmutableQueue<T>.IsEmpty` and `ImmutableStack<T>.IsEmpty` properties will tell you the collection is empty, and `ImmutableQueue<T>.Enqueue` and `ImmutableStack<T>.Push` will create a new queue or stack with the added item. `ImmutableQueue<T>.Peek` and `ImmutableStack<T>.Peek` will both return the next item without removing it from the collection, and `Immutable-Queue<T>.Dequeue` and `ImmutableStack<T>.Pop` will return a new stack with an item removed and (optionally) will place the removed item in an out parameter.

The `Peek`, `Dequeue`, and `Pop` methods will throw an exception if the queue or stack is empty. There's no way for another thread to modify the collection between checking the `IsEmpty` property and calling `Peek`, `Dequeue`, or `Pop`—the collection is immutable, it can't be modified at all, and thus it can't be modified by another thread.

If your queue or thread is referenced by a variable that is writable by other threads, you need to synchronize access to this variable and, at the minimum, copy the reference to a local variable before reading `IsEmpty` so another thread can't replace the queue or stack between you reading `IsEmpty` and calling `Peek`, `Dequeue`, or `Pop`.

`ImmutableInterlocked` supports both `ImmutableQueue<T>` and `ImmutableStack<T>` with operations similar to those available in `ConcurrentQueue<T>` and `Concurrent-Stack<T>`. However, if you need them, it's almost guaranteed you'll be better off just using `ConcurrentQueue<T>` or `ConcurrentStack<T>` instead.

13.3.8 *ImmutableArray<T>*

When I started talking about the immutable collections, I said all the non–thread-safe collections use arrays because they are fast, but immutable collections don't use arrays because this would have required them to copy all the data every time a collection is modified (that is, a new collection is created with the modification). `Immutable-Array<T>` is an exception that, like the name suggests, does use an array.

Because `ImmutableArray<T>` is not exempt from the disadvantages of arrays, this means that the immutable array does have to copy all the data every time it creates a modified collection, and this makes `ImmutableArray<T>` the slowest immutable collection to write to. However, because it uses an array, it is also the fastest immutable collection to read from. This makes `ImmutableArray<T>` more similar to frozen collections (described later in this chapter) compared to other immutable collections.

`ImmutableArray<T>` is a very good choice if you need to pass a read-only array to some code that isn't under your control. Being an array, it's fast to scan and even supports read-only memory and span objects.

Conversely, `ImmutableArray<T>` is typically not a good choice for your internal data structure because modifications are slow and require a lot of memory. This can still be acceptable if modifications are very rare or the array is small, but you need to be very careful about it.

You can use `ImmutableArray.Create<T>` to create a new immutable array from a normal array or from up to four individual data items. You can use `ImmutableArray .ToImmutable<T>` to create an immutable array from any collection, and you can use `ImmutableArray.CreateRange` to create an immutable array from a subset of another collection.

As always, if the variable referencing the immutable array is accessible from multiple threads, you need to synchronize access yourself. `ImmutableInterlocked` supports `ImmutableArray<T>` with the `InterlockedCompereExchange`, `InterlockedExchange`, and `InterlockedInitilize` methods, but you generally shouldn't use them. They are complicated and error prone compared to a `lock` statement, and unless you are in a very performance-critical code path, the trade-offs are just not worth it.

Generally, `ImmutableArray<T>` should be used like the frozen collections (which we'll discuss in just a few paragraphs). `ImmutableArray<T>` is inefficient to create (both in speed and memory usage) but very efficient to use. It should be used when we need a sequential collection (like `List<T>` or an array) that is read only and inherently thread safe. However, because recreating it is expensive, it should only be used when we do not intend to change it (that is, create a new modified copy) at all.

13.3.9 *When to use the immutable collections*

Immutable collections are very common in functional programming. If you write code in functional style or use functional algorithms, the immutable collections are perfect for you.

Immutable collections are also convenient if you need to preserve previous states of the system, for example, as a way to provide undo functionality. Note that immutable collections are irrelevant if you need to preserve the state of the system for auditing or regulatory purposes because then you need to preserve the state of the system on disk, and the immutable collections are only in-memory.

Immutable collections are also very helpful if you need to pass the collection to code that is not under your control. That way, you don't have to defensively duplicate the data and send a copy to the outside code.

But whenever you use the immutable collections, you must remember that while the immutable collections themselves are completely thread safe, "changing the collection" involves creating a new collection, and the collection is usually assigned to the same variable as the previous collection. This variable is now modified with every change, and access to it needs to be synchronized like any other variable that is concurrently accessed from multiple threads. This often requires holding a lock when updating the collection or using `ImmutableInterlocked`, and in those cases, the code is likely to be simpler and faster if you use the concurrent collections instead.

Finally, in cases where the data really never changes, you should consider using the frozen collections.

13.4 *The frozen collections*

We've seen that the immutable collections never change in the sense that if you want to change them, you need to create a copy of the collection with the required modification, and we've also seen that as a trade-off, the immutable collection uses less-efficient data structures to make the creation of modified copies faster. But what if we don't want to make this trade-off? What if the data really never changes? What if we don't want to sacrifice read performance to support write operations we don't need? This is why we have the frozen collections.

Frozen collections are read-only collections optimized for reading. Creating them is slower than creating regular, concurrent, or immutable collections, but reading from them is as fast as possible.

Frozen collections are meant only for reading. They can't be modified at all, and they don't even have methods to create modified copies like the immutable collections.

Currently, there are only two types of frozen collections—`FrozenDictionary` `<TKey,TValue>` and `FrozenSet<T>`—which are read-only versions of `Dictionary` `<TKey,TValue>` and `HashSet<T>`, respectively. If you want a frozen version of `List<T>`, you can use `ImmutableArray<T>` (we talked about it earlier in this chapter). There are no frozen queues and stacks because those don't make sense.

To create a `FrozenSet<T>`, you can take any collection and call the `ToFrozenSet` extension method.

13.19   Initializing a `FrozenSet`

```
var data = new List<int> {1,2,3,4};
var set = data.ToFrozenSet();
```

This code creates a `List<int>` with some numbers and then calls `ToFrozenSet` on it to create a `FrozenSet<int>` with the same content.

To create a `FrozenDictionary<TKey,TValue>`, you can take any collection and call the `ToFrozenDictionary` extension method. The easiest way to create a `Frozen-Dictionary<TKey,TValue>` is by using a `Dictionary<TKey,TValue>`.

13.20   Initializing a `FrozenDictionary` from a `Dictionary`

```
var numberNames = new Dictionary<int,string>
{
    {1, "one"},
    {2, "two"}
};
var frozenDict = numberNames.ToFrozenDictionary();
```

This code creates a `Dictionary<int,string>` that maps numbers to the English name of the numbers (only for one and two, just to keep the code short) and then uses `ToFrozenDictionary` to create a `FrozenDictionary<int,string>` with the same content. There's also an overload of `ToFrozenDictionary` that accepts delegates to extract the key and value so it can be used on any collection.

13.21 Initializing a `FrozenDictionary` **from a** `List`

```
var data = new List<int> {1,2,3,4};
var frozenDict = data.ToFrozenDictionary(x=>x,x=>x.ToString());
```

This code creates a `List<int>` with some numbers and then uses `ToFrozenDictionary` to create a `FrozenDictionary<int,string>`, which maps the numbers in the list to their string representation. Note that if the source data contains duplicates (in the case of `ToFrozenSet`) or duplicate keys (in the case of `ToFrozenDictionary`), the latest entry will be used, which is different than the behavior of `Dictionary<TKey,TValue>` and `HashSet<T>` that throws an exception in case of duplicate keys.

13.4.1 *When to use the frozen collections*

The frozen collection should only be used when data (almost) never changes. The frozen collections optimize for reads at the cost of making the collection creation much slower. If the data is frequently accessed but never modified, this can improve performance. In contrast, if the data changes frequently, the time it takes to create the frozen collection after each change can easily be much more than the time saved due to the faster lookups.

Summary

- It is possible to read from the regular collections in the `System.Collections.Generic` namespace from multiple threads simultaneously.
- Writing from multiple threads simultaneously or writing from one thread while reading from others is not allowed and might cause the collections to return incorrect results and even corrupt them.
- The concurrent collections in the `System.Collections.Concurrent` namespace are fully thread safe and support both reading and writing from multiple threads at the same time.
- There are concurrent versions of `Dictionary<TKey,TValue>`, `Queue<T>`, and `Stack<T>` called `ConcurrentDictionary<TKey,TValue>`, `ConcurrentQueue<T>`, and `ConcurrentStack<T>`. Their interface is different from the regular collections—it combines operations that are commonly used together into a single operation to avoid race conditions.
- There is also a `ConcurrentBag<T>` collection that is useful when you don't care about the items' order; it is designed to be used when the same threads both read and write from/to the collection.
- The `BlockingCollection<T>` class adds support for producer–consumer scenarios and for limiting the collection's size. `BlockingCollection<T>` works as a queue by default but can also be used as a stack.
- The `ConcurrentDictionary<TKey,TValue>`, `ConcurrentQueue<T>`, `ConcurrentStack<T>`, and `ConcurrentBag<T>` collections can be used with asynchronous code.

- Like the name suggests, the `BlockingCollection<T>` class is blocking, and it should be used carefully (or not at all) with asynchronous code.

- There is no asynchronous version of `BlockingCollection<T>`, but we can use `Channel<T>` to make an asynchronous version of its most common use case (more about this in the next chapter).

- The immutable collections in the `System.Collections.Immutable` namespace are collections that can't be changed (every change leaves the collection untouched and creates a new collection). They are thread safe because, since they can't be modified at all, by definition, they can't be modified by another thread while you are accessing them.

- However, if the variable that references the collections is accessed by multiple threads, you need to synchronize access yourself. The `ImmutableInterlocked` class can help with that (for dictionary, queue, and stack).

- If you need to make multiple modifications to an immutable collection, you can call `ToBuilder` to get a builder object that collects the modifications without creating new collections. After you make all the modifications to the builder, you call its `ToImmutable` method to create just one new collection with all the changes. The builder object is not thread safe.

- There are `ImmutableDictionary<TKey,TValue>`, `ImmutableHashSet<T>`, `ImmutableSortedSet<T>`, `ImmutableQueue<T>`, `ImmutableStack<T>`, and `ImmutableList<T>` classes that are immutable versions of classes with the same name but without the `Immutable` prefix.

- Those collections are slower to read than the regular or concurrent collections, but making copies of them is fast, which is important because every time you need to modify the collection, you create a copy of it.

- The `ImmutableArray<T>` collection is an immutable array. It is faster to access than the other immutable collections but slower to modify (that is, create a modified copy). It also supports read-only `Span<T>` and `Memory<T>`.

- The frozen collections are optimized for reading. Creating them is slow, but reading from them is fast. They cannot be modified.

- Like the immutable collections, the frozen collections are inherently thread safe.

- There are only two frozen collections: `FrozenDictionary<TKey,TValue>` and `FrozenSet<T>`.

- Typically, to create a frozen collection, you first use a regular collection and then `ToFrozenSet` or `ToFrozenDictionary` to create a frozen collection from the data they contain.

14

Generating collections asynchronously/await foreach and IAsyncEnumerable

This chapter covers:

- How `await foreach` works
- Using `yield return` in `async` methods
- Iterating over asynchronous data using `IAsyncEnumerable<T>` and `await foreach`

Sometimes, we may want to use `foreach` to iterate over a sequence of items we generate on the fly or retrieve from an external source without first adding the entire set of items to a collection. For example, we've seen in chapters 8 and 13 how `BlockingCollection<T>`'s support for `foreach` makes it easy to use for building a work queue. C# makes this easy with the `yield return` keyword, as discussed in chapter 2. However, both the versions of `yield return` we covered in chapter 2 and `BlockingCollection<T>` don't support asynchronous programming.

In this chapter, we'll cover the asynchronous version of `foreach` (called `await foreach`) and the `yield return` enhancement from C# 8, which allows us to use it for asynchronous code. And finally, we'll employ all of those to write an asynchronous version of `BlockingCollection<T>` and a fully asynchronous work queue.

14.1   *Iterating over an asynchronous collection*

To understand how the asynchronous await foreach works, we need to first take a look at the good old non-asynchronous foreach. The foreach keyword is syntactic sugar. It's just a nicer way to write code relative to using more basic language features. Specifically, foreach is just a nicer way to write a while loop. You can think of the compiler's implementation of foreach as a simple text replacement. The compiler takes code like

```
foreach(var x in collection)
{
    Console.WriteLine(x);
}
```

and transforms it into

```
using(var enumerator = collection.GetEnumerator())
{
    while(enumerator.MoveNext())
    {
        var x = enumerator.Current;
        Console.WriteLine(x);
    }
}
```

As you can see, foreach translates into a call to GetEnumerator that retrieves an IEnumerator<T> and a while loop that uses MoveNext to get the next item for each iteration of the loop. More generally, you can say the compiler takes code in the form of

```
foreach([loop-variable-type] [loop-variable] in [collection])
{
    [loop-body]
}
```

and translates it to

```
using(var enumerator = [collection].GetEnumerator())
{
    while(enumerator.MoveNext())
    {
        [loop-variable-type] [loop-variable] = enumerator.Current;
        [loop-body];
    }
}
```

Obviously, I'm skipping a lot of details here; there are a lot of special cases and optimizations that the compiler can use to improve this code, but functionally, the foreach loop is equivalent to this while loop.

This works very well for non-asynchronous code, but to use a collection where items are retrieved asynchronously, that is, a collection where getting the next item is an asynchronous operation, we're going to have to make some changes to the way `foreach` works. Specifically, we're going to need to add an `await` inside the `while` loop condition (third line in the previous code snippet), and to make that `await` possible, we need `MoveNext` to return a `Task<bool>` instead of a `bool`.

And that's what the `await foreach` keyword and the `IAsyncEnumerable<T>` interface are. The `IAsyncEnumerable<T>` interface is similar to `IEnumerable<T>`. It has just one method called `GetAsyncEnumerator` (like `IEnumerable<T>.GetEnumerator`) that returns an object implementing the `IAsyncEnumerator<T>` interface (like `IEnumerator<T>`). That method itself is not asynchronous and should return quickly. Any lengthy asynchronous initialization should happen the first time the enumerator's `MoveNextAsync` method is called. The `IAsyncEnumerator<T>` interface has a method named `MoveNextAsync` that acts like the `IEnumerator<T>.MoveNext` method, except it returns a `ValueTask<bool>` instead of a `bool`.

Here is the comparison between the `IEnumerable<T>` and `IAsyncEnumerable<T>` (table 14.1) and `IEnumerator` and `IAsyncEnumerator` (table 14.2).

Table 14.1 `IEnumerable` **vs.** `IAsyncEnumerable`

IEnumerable<T>	IAsyncEnumerable<T>
`IEnumerator<T> GetEnumerator()`	`IAsyncEnumerator<T>` ➥ `GetAsyncEnumerator()`

Table 14.2 `IEnumerator` **vs.** `IAsyncEnumerator`

IEnumerator<T>	IAsyncEnumerator<T>
`T Current {get;}`	`T Current {get;}`
`bool MoveNext()`	`ValueTask<bool> MoveNextAsync()`
`void Dispose()`	`ValueTask DisposeAsync()`

As you can see from the tables, the asynchronous and non-asynchronous interfaces are almost exactly the same, just with support for `async`/`await`. The tables do not contain `IEnumerable<T>`'s support for the older nongeneric `IEnumerable` interface because it's practically never used. Also, I've ignored `IAsyncEnumerator<T>.GetAsync-Enumerator`'s cancellation token parameter because we'll talk about it in detail later in this chapter.

The last piece of the puzzle is the awkwardly named `await foreach` loop, which is just like `foreach`, except it uses `IAsyncEnumerable<T>` instead of `IEnumerable<T>` and adds the required `await` to make everything work. So this loop

```
await foreach(var x in collection)
{
    Console.WriteLine(x);
}
```

translates into

```
await using(var enumerator = collection.GetAsyncEnumerator())
{
    while(await enumerator.MoveNext())          ◄────┐ Adds an await here
    {
        var x = enumerator.Current;
        Console.WriteLine(x);
    }
}
```

14.2   Generating an asynchronous collection

Now we know how to use an asynchronous collection, but asynchronous collections don't actually exist, at least not out of the box. All the collections included in the .NET library are data structures that hold items in memory, and with the items ready in memory, there is no need to retrieve them (asynchronously or otherwise).

When we talk about support for asynchronous collections, what we really want is the ability to use an `await foreach` loop to process a sequence of data items that are asynchronously generated or retrieved: we want an asynchronous version of the `yield return` keyword we've talked about in chapter 2. In chapter 2, we also used the following code to dynamically generate values 1 and 2.

Listing 14.1   `yield return` example from chapter 2

```
private IEnumerable<int> YieldDemo()
{
    yield return 1;
    yield return 2;
}

public void UseYieldDemo()
{
    foreach(var current in YieldDemo())
    {
        Console.WriteLine($"Got {current}");
    }
}
```

Now let's add an asynchronous call to the method generating the values. We'll use `Task.Delay` for simplicity.

Listing 14.2   Async `yield return` example

```
private async IAsyncEnumerable<int> AsyncYieldDemo()     ◄──────┐
{                                                    Changes IEnumerable<int> to
    yield return 1;                                  async IAsyncEnumerable<int>
    await Task.Delay(1000);          ◄────┐
    yield return 2;                        We can use await.
}
```

```
public async Task UseAsyncYieldDemo()
{
    await foreach(var current in AsyncYieldDemo())
    {
        Console.WriteLine($"Got {current}");
    }
}
```

Changes foreach to await foreach

We had to change the generator method to return IAsyncEnumerable<int> instead of IEnumerable<int> and mark it as async—and that's it. We can now use await inside of it and the await foreach keyword we talked about earlier to iterate over the generated sequence.

As we've seen in chapter 2, for the non-async yield return, when we compile this, the compiler will transform the AsyncYieldDemo method into classes that implement IAsyncEnumerable<int> and IAsyncEnumerator<int>. If we use the same transformations from chapter 2, we get the following listing.

Listing 14.3 Code generated by the compiler from listing 14.2

```
public class AsyncYieldDemo_Enumerable : IAsyncEnumerable<int>
{
    public IAsyncEnumerator<int> GetAsyncEnumerator(CancellationToken _)
    {
        return new YieldDemo_Enumerator();
    }
}

public class YieldDemo_Enumerator : IAsyncEnumerator<int>
{
    public int Current { get; private set; }

    private async Task Step0()
    {
        Current = 1;
    }
    private async Task Step1()
    {
        await Task.Delay(1000);
        Current = 2;
    }

    private int _step = 0;
    public async ValueTask<bool> MoveNextAsync()
    {
        switch(_step)
        {
            case 0:
                await Step0();
                ++_step;
                break;
            case 1:
                await Step1();
```

```
                ++_step;
                break;
            case 2:
                return false;
        }
        return true;
    }
    public ValueTask DisposeAsync() => ValueTask.CompletedTask;
}

public IAsyncEnumerable<int> AsyncYieldDemo()
{
    return new AsyncYieldDemo_Enumerable();
}
```

This is exactly the same transformation we've seen in chapter 2 (except for the added async, await, and the occasional Task where needed; changes are in bold). You can go back to listing 2.5 for a complete breakdown of this code. The short version is

- The compiler breaks the method into chunks whenever it finds a yield return. Each yield return ends a chunk.
- The yield return keyword is changed to Current =.
- The compiler generates the MoveNextAsync method that calls the first chunk the first time it's called, the second chunk the second time it's called, and so forth.

We've used await extensively in this code, but as we've seen in chapter 3, await (like yield return) is implemented by the compiler rewriting your code into a class. Let's see how the compiler generates code for the async methods in listing 14.3. We'll start with the Step0 method:

```
private Task Step0()
{
    Current = 1;
    return Task.CompletedTask;
}
```

That was easy because Step0 doesn't do anything asynchronous, the compiler doesn't need to change it, and we just drop the async keyword and return Task.Completed-Task explicitly. Now let's look at Step1:

```
private TaskCompletionSource _step1tcs = new();
private Task Step1()
{
    Task.Delay(1000).ContinueWith(Step1Part2);
    return _step1tcs.Task;
}
private void Step1Part2(Task task)
{
    Current = 2;
    _step1tcs.SetResult();
}
```

Unlike Step0, Step1 really performs an asynchronous operation, namely Task.Delay, so as we've seen in chapter 3, everything after the await is moved into a different method that is passed to ContinueWith. The Step1 method needs to return a Task, so we used the TaskCompletionSource class we talked about in chapter 10 to create this Task. To keep the code simple, I've ignored all error handling. The compiler translates the MoveNextAsync method in the same way.

14.3 *Canceling an asynchronous collection*

Asynchronous operations often support cancellation, and we obviously want to be able to support cancellation in operations called from await foreach loops. To support cancellation, the GetAsyncEnumerator method accepts a cancellation token as an optional parameter, but this by itself doesn't solve our problem because

- The code calling GetAsyncEnumerator is generated by the compiler when we use await foreach, and we have no obvious way to pass a cancellation token.
- The GetAsyncEnumerator code is also generated by the compiler, and we have no obvious way to access the method's parameter.

The first problem is solved by the WithCancellation extension method. This method can be called on any IAsyncEnumerable<T>, and it returns a new object that also implements the IAsyncEnumerable<T> interface. This new object's GetAsyncEnumerator method simply calls the original object's GetAsyncEnumerator with a cancellation token you provide. To use WithCancellation, you just call it and use the returned object. The simplest way to use it is directly in the await foreach clause:

```
await foreach(var item in collection.WithCancellation(token))
```

The WithCancellation method is pretty simple. If you want to implement it yourself, all you need to do is write a class as shown in the following listing.

Listing 14.4 WithCancellation implementation

```
public class WithCancellation<T> : IAsyncEnumerable<T>
{
    private IAsyncEnumerable<T> _originalEnumerable;      Fields for original enumerable
    private CancellationToken _cancellationToken;         and cancellation token

    public WithCancellation(
        IAsyncEnumerable<T> originalEnumerable,
        CancellationToken cancellationToken)
    {
        _originalEnumerable = originalEnumerable;         Constructs to store original
        _cancellationToken = cancellationToken;           enumerable and cancellation token
    }

    public IAsyncEnumerator<T> GetAsyncEnumerator(
        CancellationToken dontcare)
    {
```

```
        return _originalEnumerable.                    Calls original enumerable
            GetAsyncEnumerator(_cancellationToken);    with cancellation token
    }
}
```

Most of this code just stores an `async` enumerable and a cancellation token, so it can, in the `GetAsyncEnumerator` method, call the original enumerable's `GetAsyncEnumerator` method and pass the cancellation token as a parameter.

This solves the first problem. It lets us pass a cancellation token to `GetAsyncEnumerator` when it's used by `await foreach`. However, it leaves us with the second problem—receiving the token in the method generating the values.

Luckily, the C# compiler can do this; it will pass the cancellation token as a parameter to the method generating the sequence if we just tell it which parameter to use. To indicate which parameter to use, we need to decorate it with the `[Enumerator-Cancellation]` attribute. We now know how to modify the code from listing 14.2 to use a cancellation token.

Listing 14.5   Async `yield return` example with cancellation

```
private async IAsyncEnumerable<int> AsyncYieldDemo(
    [EnumeratorCancellation] CancellationToken cancellationToken = default)
{
    yield return 1;                                    Parameter to receive
    await Task.Delay(1000, cancellationToken);         cancellation token
    yield return 2;
}

public async Task UseAsyncYieldDemo()
{
    var cancel = new CancellationTokenSource();
    var collection = AsyncYieldDemo();
    await foreach(var current in
        collection.WithCancellation(cancel.Token))     Uses WithCancellation to
    {                                                  pass cancellation token
        Console.WriteLine($"Got {current}");
    }
}
```

In this listing, we added a `CancellationToken` parameter to the `AsyncYieldDemo` and decorated it with the `[EnumeratorCancellation]` attribute to allow `AsyncYieldDemo` to be canceled. We then used `WithCancellation` to pass the cancellation token to `AsyncYieldDemo`.

Obviously, because we call `AsyncYieldDemo` and iterate over it in the same method, we can just pass the cancellation token to `AsyncYieldDemo` directly, but this isn't always possible. The code that creates the `IAsyncEnumerable<T>` and the code that iterates over it might be in different components. We might not have access to source code that creates the `IAsyncEnumerable<T>` at all, or the code can be in different methods, and using `WithCancellation` is just simpler than passing the cancellation token all the way to the code that created the enumerable.

While this sample supports cancellation, it will never cancel the operation. Now let's see what happens when we do cancel. We'll start with cancellation before the loop even starts.

> **Listing 14.6 Canceling the iteration before the loop starts**

```
private async IAsyncEnumerable<int> AsyncYieldDemo(
    [EnumeratorCancellation] CancellationToken cancellationToken=default)
{
    yield return 1;
    await Task.Delay(1000, cancellationToken);
    yield return 2;
}

public async Task UseYieldDemo()
{
    var cancel = new CancellationTokenSource();        Cancels the loop
    cancel.Cancel();                              ◄────  before starting
    await foreach(var current in
        AsyncYieldDemo().WithCancellation(cancel.Token))
    {
        Console.WriteLine($"Got {current}");
    }
}
```

In this example, we call the cancellation token source's `Cancel` method before the loop starts. If we run this, we'll see that the program will print "Got 1" and only then crash with a `TaskCanceledException`. Why did it run the first iteration of the loop if the cancellation token was already canceled before we started?

We need to remember that, as discussed in chapter 9, a `CancellationToken` is just a thread-safe flag we can use to check whether an operation needs to be canceled. In this listing, we don't check for cancellation in the loop at all. In the `AsyncYieldDemo` method, we also generate the first value without checking for cancellation; the first time anyone checks for cancellation is inside the `Task.Delay` call.

14.4 *Other options*

In addition to the `WithCancellation` method, there's also a `ToBlockingEnumerable` method that wraps the `IAsyncEnumerable<T>` in a non-asynchronous `IEnumerable<T>` you can use in a normal `foreach` loop in non-asynchronous code. The `ToBlocking-Enumerable` method lets you consume an asynchronous API from non-asynchronous code. This is equivalent to calling `Wait()` on each task returned by `MoveNextAsync`.

The `ToBlockingEnumerable` method, like other ways of calling `Wait()`, negates the benefits of using asynchronous operation and can cause deadlocks in some situations. It should be used only when you must use an asynchronous collection from non-asynchronous code and have no other choice.

And finally, there's the `ConfigureAwait` extension method. Calling `ConfigureAwait` on the `IAsyncEnumerable<T>` object is equivalent to calling `ConfigureAwait` on all tasks returned by `MoveNextAsync`.

The `ConfigureAwait` method lets you decide if the code after the `await` will run in the same context as the code before the `await`. This typically only matters in local UI applications (see chapter 11 for more details).

14.5   *IAsyncEnumerable<T> and LINQ*

LINQ is a C# feature that lets us use SQL-like operators (such as `Select` and `Where`) to transform any sequence of items (usually used with the .NET collections). LINQ uses the `IEnumerable<T>` interface to interact with the sequence you are transforming.

At the time of this writing, the latest version of .NET (version 9) does not support LINQ with `IAsyncEnumrable<T>`. However, the .NET Reactive Extensions (RX) team has published the `System.Linq.Async` library (available via NuGet), which adds support for all the LINQ operators to `IAsyncEnumerable<T>` (and as such, to all asynchronous collections and sequences as well).

If .NET adds built-in support for asynchronous LINQ in the future, it's likely they will use the `System.Linq.Async` library from the RX team (`IAsyncEnumerable<T>` itself was originally written by the RX team) or, at least, make the built-in LINQ support compatible with `System.Linq.Async`.

14.6   *Example: Iterating over asynchronously retrieved data*

Let's say we need to process a binary-stream-containing numbers. We'll write two methods. One reads the stream and extracts the numbers (using `yield return`) and one processes the numbers. This stream can be a file, but it can also be a network connection. For simplicity, we'll start with a non-asynchronous version.

Listing 14.7   Reading a stream of numbers non-asynchronously

```
public class NumbersProcessor
{
    private IEnumerable<int> GetNumbers(Stream stream)
    {
        var buffer = new byte[4];
        while(stream.Read(buffer, 0, 4) == 4)          ◄──┘ Gets the next 4 bytes
        {                                                    from the stream
            var number = BitConverter.ToInt32(buffer);  ◄──┘ Converts them to an int
            yield return number;                        ◄──
        }                                                    Returns the int
    }

    public void ProcessStream(Stream stream)
    {
        foreach(var number in GetNumbers(stream))        ◄──┘ For each number in stream
        {
            Console.WriteLine(number);              ◄──┘ Processes the number
        }
    }
}
```

The first method, `GetNumbers`, reads the stream and produces a sequence of numbers. It stops as soon as it can't retrieve a whole number. The second method, `ProcessStream`, uses the first method and then does something with the numbers (because this is sample code, we're going to just print them to the console).

As we've said earlier in this book, operations such as reading from a file or a communication channel are often best done asynchronously. So let's take everything we've discussed in this chapter and make the code asynchronous.

Listing 14.8   Reading a stream of numbers asynchronously

```
public class Async NumbersProcessor
{
    private async IAsyncEnumerable<int>          IEnumerable<int> to async
        GetNumbers(Stream stream)                IAsyncEnumerable<int>
    {
        var buffer = new byte[4];
        while(await stream.ReadAsync(buffer, 0, 4) == 4)    stream.Read to await
        {                                                    stream.ReadAsync
            var number = BitConverter.ToInt32(buffer);
            yield return number;
        }
    }

    public async Task ProcessStream(Stream stream)      void to async Task
    {
        await foreach(var number in GetNumbers(stream))    foreach to await
        {                                                   foreach
            Console.WriteLine(number);
        }
    }
}
```

The asynchronous code is the same as the non-asynchronous code, except that we added the words `async` and `await` in some places. To read the stream asynchronously, we need to call `Stream.ReadAsync` instead of `Stream.Read`, which is an important change. We want to await the `ReadAsync` call, so we add an `await` before `ReadAsync`. To be able to use `await`, we have to make the method `async`, and `async` methods can't return `IEnumerable<int>`, so we mark the method as `async` and change the return type to `IAsyncEnumerable<int>`.

Now we've finished modifying the `GetNumbers` method and move on to `Process-Stream`. To process the `IAsyncEnumrable<int>` returned by `GetNumbers`, we need to replace the `foreach` with an `await foreach`. We can only use `await foreach` in an `async` method, so we mark the method as `async` and change the return type from `void` to `Task` (we talked about the problems with `async void` methods near the end of chapter 3).

14.7   *Example: BlockingCollection<T>-like asynchronous queue*

In the previous chapter, in listing 13.11, we used `BlockingCollection<T>` to implement a work queue with 10 worker threads. `BlockingCollection<T>` has the

GetConsumingEnumerable method that lets the code using it use foreach, which results in clean and readable code. However, BlockingCollection<T> does not support asynchronous operations.

In listing 13.12, we used Channel<T> to write an asynchronous version of the same program, but the Channel<T> interface isn't as nice. We had to use an infinite loop to read the items from the queue and use an exception to signal the work is done and that there will be no more items.

Now, with IAsyncEnumerable<T>, we can easily write a class that implements a BlockingCollection<T>-like GetConsumingEnumerable on top of Channel<T>. This example only implements the Add and GetConsumingEnumerable methods (which are all we need to implement our work queue).

Listing 14.9   Async version of BlockingCollection<T>.GetConsumingEnumerable

```
public class ChannelAsyncCollection<T>
{
    private Channel<T> _channel = Channel.CreateUnbounded<T>();
    public void Add(T item)
    {
        _channel.Writer.TryWrite(item);
    }

    public void CompleteAdding()
    {
        _channel.Writer.Complete();
    }
    public async IAsyncEnumerable<T> GetAsyncConsumingEnumerable()
    {
        while (true)
        {
            T next;
            try
            {
                next = await _channel.Reader.ReadAsync();
            }
            catch (ChannelClosedException)
            {
                yield break;
            }
            yield return next;
        }
    }
}
```

The Add method just calls the channel writer's TryWrite method. TryWrite shouldn't fail on unbounded channels, but in production code, we should probably check the value returned from TryWrite and throw an exception if it's false.

The GetAsyncConsumingEnumerable method is a bit more complicated; at its core, it is just a loop calling the channel reader's ReadAsync:

```
public async IAsyncEnumerable<T> GetAsyncConsumingEnumerable()
{
    while (true)
    {
        yield return await _channel.Reader.ReadAsync();
    }
}
```

But this code doesn't detect when there is no more data and we should end the loop. When there is no more data, ReadAsync will throw an exception. We need to catch this exception and end the iteration:

```
public async IAsyncEnumerable<T> GetAsyncConsumingEnumerable()
{
    while (true)
    {
        try
        {
            yield return await _channel.Reader.ReadAsync();
        }
        catch (ChannelClosedException)        ◀───  Detects when
        {                                           iteration is complete
            yield break;
        }
    }
}
```

However, this version of GetAsyncConsumingEnumerable doesn't compile because you can't use yield return inside a try block. We must move the yield return outside of the try block, and then we get the code from listing 14.7:

```
public async IAsyncEnumerable<T> GetAsyncConsumingEnumerable()
{
    while (true)
    {
        T next;
        try
        {
            next = await _channel.Reader.ReadAsync();
        }
        catch (ChannelClosedException)
        {
            yield break;
        }                                       Moves the yield return
        yield return next;               ◀───  outside of the try block
    }
}
```

Now that we have our asynchronous channel-based collection, we can use it to write a work queue. This is an asynchronous adaptation of the BlockingCollection<T>-based work queue from listing 13.11.

Listing 14.10 Async work queue with 10 threads

```
ChannelAsyncCollection <int> asyncCollection =
   new ChannelAsyncCollection <int>();
Task[] workers =  new Task[10];
for(int i=0; i<workers.Length; i++)          ◄──────── Creates 10 worker threads
{
   var threadNumber = i;
   workers[i] = Task.Run(async () =>
   {
      var rng = new Random((int)threadNumber);
      int count = 0;
      await foreach (var currentValue in
            asyncCollection.GetAsyncConsumingEnumerable())
      {
         Console.WriteLine($"thread {threadNumber} value {currentValue}");
         Thread.Sleep(rng.Next(500));
         count++;
      }
      Console.WriteLine($"thread {threadNumber}, total {count} items");
   });
}
for(int i=0;i<100;i++)          ◄──────── Adds 100 items to process
{
   asyncCollection.Add(i);
}                                            Signals no more items
asyncCollection.CompleteAdding();  ◄──────── Waits for all threads to finish
await Task.WhenAll(workers);  ◄──────
```

This code creates a `ChannelAsyncCollection<int>` to hold the data we need to process in the background. It then starts 10 background tasks to do this processing, and each thread uses `foreach` and `GetAsyncConsumingEnumerable` to get the items to process. To simulate the processing, we just wait a small random amount of time and print the number. We insert the numbers 0 to 99 into the queue as a stand-in for the data we want to process.

Summary

- The `yield return` and `yield break` keywords can be used in conjunction with async/await. You mark the method as `async` and return `IAsyncEnumerable<T>` instead of an `IEnumerable<T>`, and then you can use `await` in the iterator method.

- `IAsyncEnumerable<T>` and `IAsyncEnumerator<T>` are the asynchronous, async/await-compatible versions of `IEnumerable<T>` and `IEnumerator<T>`.

- The compiler transforms the method into a class, performing both the `yield return` transformation we talked about in chapter 2 and the `await` transformation we discussed in chapter 3.

- To iterate over the resulting `IAsyncEnumerable<T>`, use `await foreach` instead of `foreach`.

- `await foreach` is like a regular `foreach`, except it performs an `await` at each iteration.

- You can cancel an iteration by using the `WithCancellation` extension method. This method will pass a cancellation token to the `IAsyncEnumerable<T>` (or, if the `IAsyncEnumerable<T>` was created with `yield return`, it optionally passes the cancellation token to the method generating the sequence). As always with cancellation tokens, the token is just a flag. To stop the iteration, there needs to be code that checks the status of the token and stops the iteration.

- The `ConfigureAwait` extension method for `IAsyncEnumerable<T>` works like calling `Task.ConfigureAwait` at every iteration. We discussed the pros and cons of `ConfigureAwait` in chapter 11.

- The `ToBlockingEnumerable` extension method wraps the `IAsyncEnumerable<T>` in an `IEnumerable<T>` that does the equivalent of calling `Task.Wait` at every iteration. Like `Task.Wait`, it can cause performance problems and deadlocks. It should be used only for calling asynchronous APIs from non-asynchronous code and only if the API supports this use case.

- There is no built-in support for LINQ for asynchronous sequences, but the `System.Linq.Async` NuGet by the .net RX teams adds asynchronous LINQ support.

- `yield return` and `await foreach` can be used to write simple code that generates and processes sequences of asynchronous generated or retrieved data items (see listing 14.8).

- `yield return` and `await foreach` can also be used to build asynchronous work queues and other multithreaded infrastructure (see listing 14.9).

index